✰Forbes
TRAVEL GUIDE
Formerly Mobil Travel Guide

SOUTHERN
CALIFORNIA

ACKNOWLEDGMENTS

We gratefully acknowledge the help of our representatives for their efficient and perceptive inspections of the lodgings listed. Forbes Travel Guide is also grateful to the talented writers who contributed to this book.

SOUTHERN CALIFORNIA ★★★★★

2

ISBN: 9-780841-61425-3   Manufactured in the USA

10 9 8 7 6 5 4 3 2 1

TABLE OF CONTENTS

SOUTHERN CALIFORNIA
★★★★★

3

STAR ATTRACTIONS

If you've been a reader of Mobil Travel Guide, you will have heard that this historic brand partnered with another storied media name, Forbes, in 2009 to create a new entity, Forbes Travel Guide. For more than 50 years, Mobil Travel Guide assisted travelers in making smart decisions about where to stay and dine when traveling. With this new partnership, our mission has not changed: We're committed to the same rigorous inspections of hotels, restaurants and spas—the most comprehensive in the industry with more than 500 standards tested at each property we visit—to help you cut through the clutter and make easy and informed decisions on where to spend your time and travel budget. Our team of anonymous inspectors are constantly on the road, sleeping in hotels, eating in restaurants and making spa appointments, evaluating those exacting standards to determine a property's rating.

What kind of standards are we looking for when we visit a proprety? We're looking for more than just high-thread count sheets, pristine spa treatment rooms and white linen-topped tables. We look for service that's attentive, individualized and unforgettable. We note how long it takes to be greeted when you sit down at your table, or to be served when you order room service, or whether the hotel staff can confidently help you when you've forgotten that one essential item that will make or break your trip. Unlike other travel ratings entities, we visit the places we rate, testing hundreds of attributes to compile our ratings, and our ratings cannot be bought or influenced. The Forbes Five Star rating is the most prestigious achievement in hospitality—while we rate more than 8,000 properties in the U.S., Canada, Hong Kong, Macau and Beijing, for 2010, we have awarded Five Star designations to only 53 hotels, 21 restaurants and 18 spas. When you travel with Forbes, you can travel with confidence, knowing that you'll get the very best experience, no matter who you are.

We understand the importance of making the most of your time. That's why the most trusted name in travel is now Forbes Travel Guide.

STAR RATED HOTELS

Whether you're looking for the ultimate in luxury or the best value for your travel budget, we have a hotel recommendation for you. To help you pinpoint properties that meet your needs, Forbes Travel Guide classifies each lodging by type according to the following characteristics:

★★★★★These exceptional properties provide a memorable experience through virtually flawless service and the finest of amenities. Staff are intuitive, engaging and passionate, and eagerly deliver service above and beyond the guests' expectations. The hotel was designed with the guest's comfort in mind, with particular attention paid to craftsmanship and quality of product. A Five Star property is a destination unto itself.

★★★★These properties provide a distinctive setting, and a guest will find many interesting and inviting elements to enjoy throughout the property. Attention to detail is prominent throughout the property, from design concept to quality of products provided. Staff are accommodating and take pride in catering to the guest's specific needs throughout their stay.

★★★These well-appointed establishments have enhanced amenities that provide travelers with a strong sense of location, whether for style or function. They may have a distinguishing style and ambience in both the public spaces and guest rooms; or they may be more focused on functionality, providing guests with easy access to local events, meetings or tourism highlights.

★★The Two Star hotel is considered a clean, comfortable and reliable establishment that has expanded amenities, such as a full-service restaurant.

★The One Star lodging is a limited-service hotel or inn that is considered a clean, comfortable and reliable establishment.

For every property, we also provide pricing information. All prices quoted are accurate at the time of publication; however, prices cannot be guaranteed.

STAR RATED RESTAURANTS

Every restaurant in this book comes highly recommended as an outstanding dining experience.

★★★★★Forbes Five Star restaurants deliver a truly unique and distinctive dining experience. A Five Star restaurant consistently provides exceptional food, superlative service and elegant décor. An emphasis is placed on originality and personalized, attentive and discreet service. Every detail that surrounds the experience is attended to by a warm and gracious dining room team.

★★★★These are exciting restaurants with often well-known chefs that feature creative and complex foods and emphasize various culinary techniques and a focus on seasonality. A highly-trained dining room staff provides refined personal service and attention.

★★★Three Star restaurants offer skillfully-prepared food with a focus on a specific style or cuisine. The dining room staff provides warm and professional service in a comfortable atmosphere. The décor is well-coordinated with quality fixtures and decorative items, and promotes a comfortable ambience.

★★The Two Star restaurant serves fresh food in a clean setting with efficient service. Value is considered in this category, as is family friendliness.

★The One Star restaurant provides a distinctive experience through culinary specialty, local flair or individual atmosphere.

Because menu prices can fluctuate, we list a pricing range rather than specific prices. The pricing ranges are per diner, and assume that you order an appetizer or dessert, an entrée and one drink.

STAR RATED SPAS

Forbes Travel Guide's spa ratings are based on objective evaluations of more than 450 attributes. About half of these criteria assess basic expectations, such as staff courtesy, the technical proficiency and skill of the employees and whether the facility is clean and maintained properly. Several standards address issues that impact a guest's physical comfort and convenience, as well as the staff's ability to impart a sense of personalized service. Additional criteria measure the spa's ability to create a completely calming ambience.

★★★★★Stepping foot in a Five Star spa will result in an exceptional experience with no detail overlooked. These properties wow their guests with extraordinary design and facilities, and uncompromising service. Expert staff cater to your every whim and pamper you with the most advanced treatments and skin care lines available. These spas often offer exclusive treatments and may emphasize local elements.

★★★★Four Star spas provide a wonderful experience in an inviting and serene environment. A sense of personalized service is evident from the moment you check in and receive your robe and slippers. The guest's comfort is always of utmost concern to the well-trained staff.

★★★These spas offer well-appointed facilities with a full complement of staff to ensure that guests' needs are met. The spa facilities include clean and appealing treatment rooms, changing areas and a welcoming reception desk.

SOUTHERN CALIFORNIA

THE BEACHES, THE MOVIE STARS, THE ENDLESS SUNNY DAYS. THAT'S LIFE IN SOUTHERN California and it's simply fabulous. From dining and shopping in Los Angeles to the numerous attractions in San Diego to the lively beach communities, Southern California—or SoCal—is teeming with diversions. Hit the surf, explore the many wilderness areas or get away from it all in the deserts.

Few places offer such a breadth of cultural and natural landscapes. The Pacific Ocean forms the western border while the arid east is home to the Mojave and Colorado deserts. The southern border separates California from Mexico while the Tehachapi Mountains, a range rising about 70 miles north of Los Angeles, separates SoCal from the rest of the nation's most populous state.

Many of the area's towns blossomed around Spanish missions built in the late 18th century after Spain seized colonial rule of the area from its original Portuguese explorers. California changed hands twice more—flying the Mexican flag starting in 1822, after Mexico won independence from Spain. A short-lived California republic followed before Commodore John D. Sloat raised the United States flag over Monterey in July 1846. Two years later, California officially became part of the U.S. That year, 1848, marked another enormous event in California history: the discovery of gold.

The California Gold Rush set off a mass migration that transformed the sleepy, placid countryside into bustling towns. The 49ers who came for gold ultimately found greater riches in the fertile soil of the valleys. Today, almost every crop in the United States is grown in Southern California, including prunes, oranges, avocados, walnuts, grapes, olives and much more. In fact, California leads the nation in the production of 75 crop and livestock commodities. Southern California also produces electronics, aircraft, missiles and, of course, movies.

Today, California has the largest population of any state in the Union—24 million people live in SoCal (making it the second-most populated region in the country behind the Northeast corridor). Spend some time here and you'll see why.

ANAHEIM

See also Disneyland, Long Beach, Los Angeles,

Once part of a Spanish land grant, Anaheim was bought and settled by German colonists as a place to tend vineyards and make wine. The town's name reflects its dual heritage: "Ana" is derived from the nearby Santa Ana River, while "heim" is from the German word for "home." The area's best-known settlers are all very well known: Mickey, Minnie, Donald and Goofy and all the other loveable residents of Anaheim's Disneyland.

WHAT TO SEE
DISNEYLAND
1313 S. Disneyland Drive, Anaheim, 714-781-4565; disneyland.disney.go.com

If you're traveling with kids (or you just still dream of being whisked away by Prince Charming or secretly wish you could abandon your career and become a pirate), don't bypass the Happiest Place on Earth. Sure, there are Disney attractions in Orlando, Paris and even Japan. But the Anaheim location is the original Disney theme park. The park is divided into various "lands," including Fantasyland, Tomorrowland, Adventureland and Frontierland. The candy-colored Fantasyland gives you the classic Disney experience with Sleeping Beauty's Castle, the Mad Hatter's Tea Cups and the pleasant Dumbo ride that flies gently in the air. Take a spin on the ride that inspired Johnny Depp's blockbuster film trilogy, Pirates of the Caribbean. The ride has been updated to feature elements of the pirate movies. The boat is part musical show and part water ride as it shimmies along a shallow waterway while pirate robots sing those familiar chanties. After the ride, grab lunch at the Blue Bayou (714-781-3463), a Creole-style restaurant bedecked with rainbow lanterns and housed inside the Pirates ride. Then head to the Haunted House, a surprisingly spooky and surreal display of ghost-story horror that is a welcome break from Disney's signature smiles and songs. The theme park glitters after dark. The "Main Street" portion of the park is particularly wondrous when the white lights turn on, and the Castle glows in pink and blue lights.

Admission: adults $69, children 3-9 $59, children under 3 free. Monday-Thursday 10 a.m.-8 p.m., Friday-Sunday 8 a.m.-midnight. Hours vary for holidays or special events.

DISNEY'S CALIFORNIA ADVENTURE
1313 S. Harbor Blvd., Anaheim, 714-781-4565; disneyland.disney.go.com

California Adventure may be Disneyland's smaller, younger sibling, but that doesn't mean you should overlook it. Located a hop, skip and a jump from Disneyland Park, California Adventure specializes in more intense rides. You'll feel like you're rafting down an actual California river on Grizzly River Run, get a simulated bird's-eye view of the California landscape on Soarin' Over California, and get jostled around on mini-roller coaster Mulholland Madness. If you're really feeling brave, get in line for The Twilight Zone Tower of Terror, where you'll free-fall 13 stories in the fictional Hollywood Tower Hotel. The park is also the new host to the Main Street Electrical Parade, a nighttime event that showcases light bulb-encrusted Disney floats.

Admission: adults $69, children 3-9 $59, children under 3 free. Monday-Friday 10 a.m.-6 p.m., Saturday-Sunday 10 a.m.-8 p.m. Hours vary for holidays and special events.

WHERE TO STAY
★AYRES HOTEL ANEHEIM
2550 E. Katella Ave., Anaheim, 714-634-2106; www.ayreshotel.com

Rooms at this cozy and relaxing hotel feature a French country decor with Queen Anne beds, mahogany armoires and velvet curtains. Located just two miles from Disneyland, you can get to the park via Anaheim Resort Transit. 133 room. Complimentary breakfast. Pool. $151-250

★AYRES SUITES YORBA LINDA

22677 Oakcrest Circle, Yorba Linda, 714-921-8688, 800-706-4891;
www.ayreshotel.com

This suite hotel offers all the amenities you'd expect, plus a location that's convenient to many of southern California's major tourist attractions, including Disneyland, Disney's California Adventure and Angel Stadium, home of the California Angels baseball team. If you want a break from all things Mickey, head over to the Richard M. Nixon Library and Birthplace for a lesson in history. Forty miles from both Los Angeles and Long Beach, the hotel makes a great resting point for business and leisure travelers, including families.

112 suites. Complimentary breakfast. Fitness center. Pool. $151-250

★★★DISNEY'S GRAND CALIFORNIAN

1600 S. Disneyland Drive, Anaheim, 714-956-6425, 800-207-6900;
disneyland.disney.go.com

Conveniently situated between Disney's California Adventure theme park and the vibrant Downtown Disney entertainment complex, this giant alpine lodge is designed in an early-20th-century Arts and Crafts style. The Napa Rose, a gourmet restaurant with an extensive list of California wines, is a lovely place to dine after a day in the park.

751 rooms. Restaurant, bar. Business center. Fitness center. Pool. $151-250

★★DISNEY'S PARADISE PIER HOTEL

1717 S. Disneyland Drive, Anaheim, 714-956-6425999-0990; disneyland.disney.go.com

This family-friendly Disney hotel gets its name from Paradise Pier in Disney's California Adventure park, which is just across the street. When you stay here, you get exclusive park access. In addition to convenient access to all that Disneyland has to offer, the hotel has a rooftop pool and spa, a workout room for adults, a game room and Paradise Theater, where kids come to be transfixed by Disney movies. At Disney's PCH Grill, you can have breakfast with Lilo and Stitch, and in the afternoons and evenings, kids enjoy designing their own pizzas or noshing on burgers and fries.

481 rooms. Restaurant, bar. Business center. Fitness center. Pool. $151-250

★★DISNEYLAND HOTEL

1150 Magic Way, Anaheim, 714-778-6600; disneyland.disney.go.com

A Disneyland tradition since 1955, this family lodge remains as bright and fresh as the classic Disney-costumed characters, who welcome guests in the lobby. Many rooms offer spectacular views of the Magic Kingdom, the Downtown Disney shopping district and Disney's California Adventure park, and direct I-5 access makes it easy to reach.

990 rooms. Restaurant, bar. Business center. Fitness center. Pool. $151-250

★FAIRFIELD INN ANAHEIM DISNEYLAND RESORT

1460 S. Harbor Blvd., Anaheim, 714-772-6777, 800-403-3818; www.fairfieldinn.com

This hotel is a nice base from which to explore the park. Kid-friendly features include an impressive children's arcade and pull-out sofa beds in the guest rooms.

467 rooms. Pool. $151-250

★★★HILTON SUITES ANAHEIM/ORANGE

400 N. State College Blvd., Orange, 714-938-1111; www.anaheimsuites.hilton.com

Located on the border of Anaheim and Orange, this comfortable property is within walking distance of Angel Stadium and minutes from Disneyland. Rooms feature plush beds and spacious bathrooms with separate tubs and Crabtree & Evelyn products. An indoor and outdoor pool, whirlpool, sundeck and dry sauna help guests relax.

230 rooms. Complimentary breakfast. Restaurant, bar. Business center. Fitness center. Pool. Tennis. Golf. $151-250

★★★HYATT REGENCY ORANGE COUNTY

11999 Harbor Blvd., Garden Grove, 714-750-1234, 800-233-1234; www.hyatt.com

Business and leisure clientele mingle at this hotel, brushing up their golf swings on the adjacent driving range, dipping in the rooftop pool or sipping drinks beneath the soaring 17-story atrium. Suites offer convenience and comfort. Knott's Berry Farm, Crystal Cathedral and the Discovery Science Center are among the top attractions within a 10-mile radius; popular Southern California beaches are a short drive away. There's also a complimentary shuttle to the Anaheim Convention Center and Disneyland Resort.

654 rooms. Restaurant, bar. Business center. Fitness center. Tennis. Pool. $151-250

★RAMADA MAINGATE

1650 S. Harbor Blvd., Anaheim, 714-772-0440; www.ramada.com

Perfect for families and visitors to Disneyland, this comfortable hotel is close to the freeway, not to mention right across the street from the famous amusement park.

185 rooms. Complimentary breakfast. Pool. $151-250

★★★SHERATON ANAHEIM HOTEL

900 S. Disneyland Drive, Anaheim, 714-778-1700, 325-3535; www.sheraton.com

This English manor-style lodge may seem misplaced so close to Disneyland, but its grand rotunda, stone fireplace and koi pond, which runs through the lobby to the outside rose garden, makes it the perfect post-theme-park refuge.

489 rooms. Restaurant, bar. Pets accepted. $151-250

★★★SHERATON CERRITOS HOTEL

12725 Center Court Drive, Cerritos, 562-809-1500, 800-598-1753; www.sheraton.com

This hotel is among the Towne Center shops and is adjacent to the Cerritos Center for Performing Arts. Many corporate offices (Siemens, Yamaha) are nearby, making this hotel a convenient choice for business travelers. The elegant, contemporary guest rooms and suites have large windows (some with park views), dark wood furniture, comfortable chairs and ottomans, large work desks and ergonomic chairs. The onsite restaurant, Grille 91, offers a California menu in a casual, bistro-style setting.

203 rooms. Restaurant, bar. Business center. Fitness center. Pool. $151-250

WHERE TO EAT

★★★ANAHEIM WHITE HOUSE
887 S. Anaheim Blvd., Anaheim, 714-772-1381; www.anaheimwhitehouse.com

Many celebrities have visited this converted 1909 Victorian-style mansion. Twelve intimate dining rooms bring back Hollywood glamour with fabric-draped ceilings. A roaring fireplace warms the Reagan Room, while those who prefer a porch setting can reserve a table in the Nixon Room. The wine list includes more than 200 selections. Free shuttle service is offered to and from area hotels.

French, Italian. Lunch, dinner. $36-85

★★★THE CELLAR
305 N. Harbor Blvd., Fullerton, 714-525-5682; www.cellardining.com

The path to this restaurant—literally a cellar underneath Villa del Sol (the old California Hotel)—is down a set of dimly lit stairs. Once there, visitors are transported to what feels like an old European restaurant. The cave-like walls are decorated with wine casks and lanterns. The French cuisine includes roasted pheasant and filet of ostrich.

French. Dinner. Closed Sunday-Monday. $36-85

★★MR. STOX
1105 E. Katella Ave., Anaheim, 714-634-2994; www.mrstox.com

The fresh-baked gourmet breads are not to be missed at this family-run restaurant that specializes in fresh seafood, top-quality meats, and pasta dishes. Many of the herbs used in the kitchen, which turns out contemporary California fare, are grown on the premises. The wine list offers more than 25,000 bottles from 12 countries and ten U.S. states.

American. Lunch, dinner. $36-85

★★★SUMMIT HOUSE RESTAURANT
2000 E. Bastanchury Road, Fullerton, 714-671-4111; www.summithouse.net

This cozy, friendly inn is on the hilltop of Vista Park, offering one of the best views in Orange County while diners dig into filet mignon or Colorado lamb.

American. Lunch, dinner. $36-85

★★YAMABUKI
1717 S. Disneyland Drive, Anaheim, 714-956-6755; disneyland.disney.go.com

Sushi and Disney may not seem to go hand in hand, but they pair nicely at this restaurant in Disney's Paradise Pier Hotel, an appealing option for parents who are tired of kid food but still need to find a family-friendly place to

---

DON'T MISS

RICHARD NIXON LIBRARY AND BIRTHPLACE
18001 Yorba Linda Blvd., Yorba Linda, 714-993-5075; www.nixonfoundation.org

This tribute to the 37th president includes a gallery devoted to the Watergate scandal, a World Leaders section showcasing priceless gifts the Nixons received from governments around the world, the farmhouse in which Nixon was born in 1913, and the memorial burial sites of both the president and his wife.

Admission: adults $9.95, seniors $6.95, children 7-11 $3.75, children 6 and under free. Monday-Saturday 10 a.m.-5 p.m., Sunday 11a.m.-5 p.m.

eat. The restaurant features a full sushi bar, teriyaki and tempura entrées, and Japanese beers and sake.

Japanese. Lunch, dinner. $36-85

ARCADIA

See also Los Angeles, Pasadena

Arcadia is home to the Santa Anita Park Racetrack, a world-class thoroughbred racing facility.

WHAT TO SEE

IRWINDALE SPEEDWAY

500 Speedway Drive, Irwindale, 626-358-1100; www.irwindalespeedway.com

Located less than 25 minutes from downtown Los Angeles in California's San Gabriel Valley, Irwindale hosts NASCAR events from mid-March to November. The award-winning NASCAR Toyota All-Star Showdown, first run in 2003, brings together the top regional touring drivers from across the country in a one-of-a-kind, head-to-head event.

LOS ANGELES COUNTY ARBORETUM & BOTANIC GARDEN

301 N. Baldwin Ave., Arcadia, 626-821-3222; www.arboretum.org

This 127-acre public garden has been a Los Angeles-area oasis since 1948. Featured are beautiful plants from around the world and wildlife such as fish, turtles and migrating birds, which roam the arboretum's lakes and grounds. Classes, lectures, workshops and resources abound. Take advantage of everything from the Botanical Watercolor Workshop to the Plant Science Library, a reference collection for the public that contains information on garden design, flower gardening and vegetable and fruit growing.

Daily 9 a.m.-5 p.m.; extended summer hours.

SANTA ANITA PARK

285 W. Huntington Drive, Arcadia, 626-574-7223; www.santaanita.com

Located on 320 acres at the base of the San Gabriel Mountains, Santa Anita has been a favorite of Southern California horseracing fans since it opened in 1934. In his last race in 1940, the legendary Seabiscuit won the Santa Anita Handicap.

January-April; hours vary by season.

WHERE TO STAY
★★EMBASSY SUITES ARCADIA-PASADENA HOTEL
211 E. Huntington Drive, Arcadia, 626-445-8525; www.embassy-suites.com

All of the two-room suites have two televisions, work desks, and refrigerators and microwaves. The hotel also features an indoor pool and dry sauna, complimentary wireless throughout the hotel and the manager's reception each evening.

192 suites. Restaurant, bar. Fitness center. Pool. $61-150

★HAMPTON INN LOS ANGELES/ARCADIA/PASADENA
311 E. Huntington Drive, Arcadia, 626-574-5600, 800-426-7866;
www.hampton-inn.com

Spacious rooms include desks and free wireless Internet access. Wake up and grab a breakfast to-go on your way out to area attractions, or enjoy a hot breakfast at the hotel first.

130 rooms. Complimentary breakfast. Pool. $61-150

WHERE TO EAT
★★THE DERBY
233 E. Huntington Drive, Arcadia, 626-447-2430; www.thederbyarcadia.com

The Derby offers everything from shrimp scampi to oven-baked lasagna to the family-recipe sirloin stuffed with Italian breading, fresh herbs and parmesan cheese. With a side of garlic mashed potatoes or steakhouse fries, you can't lose.

Seafood, steak. Lunch (Monday-Friday), dinner. $36-85

AVALON (CATALINA ISLAND)
See also Laguna Beach, Long Beach, Newport Beach

Chewing gum magnate William Wrigley, Jr. bought controlling interest in the Santa Catalina Island Company in 1919 and established a program of conservation on the island that still applies today. The island is located 26 miles off the coast near Los Angeles, and tourism is its only industry. Scuba diving, kayaking, golf, tennis, horseback riding, swimming and hiking are popular. Avalon, Catalina's quaint harbor town, offers sport fishing and is dotted with resorts. Daily air or boat service to the island is available year-round from Long Beach and San Pedro; boat service available from Newport Beach.

WHAT TO SEE
CATALINA ISLAND MUSEUM
Casino Building, 1 Casino Way, Avalon, 310-510-2414; www.catalina.com/museum.html

See permanent exhibits on the history of the island, its natural history and its archaeology.

January-March, Friday-Wednesday 10 a.m.-4 p.m.

CATALINA TOURS AND TRIPS
150 Metropole Ave., Avalon, 310-510-2500

Santa Catalina Island Company Discovery Tours (www.scico.com) and Catalina Adventure Tours (www.catalinaadventuretours.com) offer boat and bus tours to several points of interest.

WRIGLEY MEMORIAL AND BOTANICAL GARDEN

1400 Avalon Canyon Road, Avalon, 310-510-2595; www.catalinaconservancy.org

Native trees, cacti, succulent plants and flowering shrubs on 37.85 acres surround a memorial to the man who contributed much to Catalina Island. Admission: adults $5, seniors $3, children free. Daily 8 a.m.-5 p.m.

WHERE TO STAY
★★★HOTEL METROPOLE

205 Crescent Ave., Avalon, 310-510-1884, 800-300-8528; www.hotel-metropole.com

Only steps from the beach, this charming hotel features cottage-style guest rooms with a choice of ocean, mountain or courtyard views. Each room is different but all have a beach decor; VIP suites are very luxurious with plasma TVs and Jacuzzi tubs.

48 rooms. Complimentary breakfast. $251-350

★★HOTEL VILLA PORTOFINO

111 Crescent Ave., Avalon, 310-510-0555, 888-510-0555; www.hotelvillaportofino.com

This charming hotel overlooks the water. Rooms are basic but clean and comfortable, and some have fireplaces and wrap-around balconies. The beautiful sundeck is the perfect spot for a little sunbathing. The warm and friendly staff make your stay even more relaxing.

44 rooms. Complimentary breakfast. Restaurant, bar. $151-250

★HOTEL VISTA DEL MAR

417 Crescent Ave., Avalon, 310-510-1452, 800-601-3836; www.hotel-vistadelmar.com

While it may be located on Avalon's promenade, most rooms here actually face the courtyard. Only two suites have ocean views but guests can take in all the action below from the lobby. The hotel serves breakfast as well as milk and cookies each evening in the lobby. Rooms have wet bars, refrigerators and fireplaces.

15 rooms. Complimentary breakfast. $251-350

★★★★THE INN AT MT. ADA

398 Wrigley Road, Avalon (Catalina Island), 310-510-2030, 800-608-7669;
www.innonmtada.com

This colonial-style mansion, with its sparkling white exterior and hunter-green shutters, recalls the grand summer residences more often seen on the East Coast. It is the highest point on the island, and rests amid beautiful shrubbery and landscaping. Completed in 1921, the former home of chewing gum magnate William Wrigley, Jr. hosted important social gatherings during its heyday. Nowadays, you're the guest of honor in the cozy Inn's six guest rooms and suites, which feature ocean or harbor views (some rooms have fireplaces and others have terraces or decks). Floral-patterned wallpaper, bed coverings and window treatments lend a New England ambience, while high ceilings and large windows make the rooms feel spacious.

7 rooms. No children under 14. Complimentary breakfast and lunch. $351 and up

WHERE TO EAT
★★ARMSTRONG'S FISH MARKET AND SEAFOOD RESTAURANT
306 Crescent Ave., Avalon, 310-510-0113; www.armstrongseafood.com
Located right on the bay, Armstrong's serves fresh seafood, including crab cakes, deep-fried calamari and steamed clams.
Seafood. Lunch, dinner. $16-35

BAKERSFIELD
See also Santa Barbara
An important trading center surrounded by oil wells and fields of cotton and grain, Bakersfield, founded by Colonel Thomas Baker in 1885, exploded into a wild mining community when gold was discovered in Kern River Canyon. A decade later, oil was discovered in the area and remains an important part of the city's economy. Bakersfield is also known as Nashville West—Merle Haggard and Buck Owens were born here.

WHAT TO SEE
CALIFORNIA LIVING MUSEUM
10500 Alfred Harrell Highway, Bakersfield, 661-872-2256; www.calmzoo.org
Otherwise known as CALM, the California Living Museum features native California animals (including a new porcupine), plants, fossils and artifacts.
Daily 9 a.m.-5 p.m.

KERN COUNTY MUSEUM
3801 Chester Ave., Bakersfield, 661-852-5000; www.kcmuseum.org
Stop at the Kern County Museum located just north of downtown Bakersfield to learn all about how oil is created and the different methods of its discovery. The exhibit, Black Gold: The Oil Experience, is for all ages. The museum also includes a Children's Discovery Center, where one recent exhibit toured the world of women's fashion from 1860 to 1920.
Admission: adults $10, seniors $9, students 13-17 $9, students 6-12 $8, children 3-5 $7, children under 3 free. Monday-Saturday 10 a.m.-5 p.m., Sunday noon-5 p.m.

WHERE TO STAY
★★BEST WESTERN HILL HOUSE
700 Truxtun Ave., Bakersfield, 661-327-4064; www.bestwestern.com
If you're looking for an affordable place to stay near Yosemite, the Best Western Hill House offers reasonable rates, which are made even more affordable when you add in free breakfast and Internet usage. The hotel is also near the Rabobank Area and the Bakersfield Speedway.
97 rooms. Restaurant, bar. Complimentary breakfast. Pool. Pets accepted. $61-150

★★FOUR POINTS BY SHERATON
5101 California Ave., Bakersfield, 661-325-9700, 800-500-5399; www.fourpoints.com
Located in Bakersfield's business district, the Four Points by Sheraton is surrounded by more than seven acres of pretty landscaping and includes a heated outdoor pool. Newly renovated rooms feature large work desks, LCD

televisions and coffee makers. A free shuttle service will take you around town.

197 rooms. Restaurant, bar. Complimentary breakfast. Pool. $61-150

WHERE TO EAT
★★MAMA TOSCA'S
9000 Ming Ave., Bakersfield, 661-831-1242; www.mamatoscas.com
For heaping plates of spaghetti and linguini, Mama Tosca's has been the go-to spot for locals since 1982. The family-owned restaurant has an extensive menu of Italian comfort foods. For starters, try the fried meatballs, which are topped with red sauce and cheese and then baked in the oven. The Butterfinger pie is another must.
Italian. Lunch, dinner. Closed Sunday. $16-35

★★WOOL GROWERS
620 E. 19th St., Bakersfield, 661-327-9584; www.woolgrowers.net
This family-owned Basque restaurant has been operating in Bakersfield for more than half a century and is still packed six days a week with local families who come to feast on the family-style roast beef, pork loin, lamb chops and other dishes. All dinners are served with bread, soup, pink beans, hot sauce, hors d'oeuvres, vegetable, French fries and spaghetti. Or you can simply order all these delicious sides as your meal.
French. Lunch, dinner. Closed Sunday. $16-35

BIG BEAR LAKE
See also Redlands, Riverside
Angelenos head to Big Bear in the San Bernardino Mountains in the winter to ski and enjoy the Alpine setting (the average annual snow fall is 100 inches). There are two excellent ski resorts less than five minutes from the quaint village. Big Bear is also a nice place to visit in warmer months for fishing, boating, canoeing, hiking and other outdoor activities.

WHAT TO SEE
ALPINE SLIDE AT MAGIC MOUNTAIN
800 Wildrose Lane, Big Bear Lake, 909-866-4626; www.alpineslidebigbear.com
Check out the bobsled-style Alpine Slide in winter and the double waterslide in summer. The site is a popular year-round attraction. Other activities include tubing, miniature golf and go-carts.
Alpine slide: single ride $4, five-ride book $18. Waterslide: single ride $1, 10-ride book $8. Daily.

BIG BEAR MARINA
Big Bear Marina, 500 Paine Road, Big Bear Lake, 909-866-3218;
www.bigbearmarina.com
Big Bear Marina offers a variety of boat rentals including fishing boats that can hold four to five people ($45 for two hours) and large pontoons that can accommodate up to 12 people ($140 for two hours). You can also rent wave runners ($85 per hour for a two-seater), kayaks/canoes ($20 per hour) and boats with waterskiing ($150 per hour). (Note: All rentals require a security deposit and fuel charges are extra; additional fees may apply.) If you'd rather

join an organized ride, you can board the Big Bear Queen, a small Mississippi-style paddle wheeler, for a 90-minute narrated tour of Big Bear Lake. Adults $15, children $9. April-November.

BIG BEAR MOUNTAIN RESORTS

880 Summit Blvd., Big Bear Lake, 909-866-5766; www.bearmountain.com

Big Bear Mountain Resorts is made up of Bear Mountain and Snow Summit ski areas, which together offer 438 skiable acres, 26 lifts and 55 runs. Snow Summit includes plenty of wide-open groomed runs, a family park with low-intermediate terrain and three double black-diamond runs. Big Bear has the longest advanced run (nearly a mile) and includes a park with 150 jumps. You'll also find six full-service ski and snowboard rental facilities, 14 food outlets and four full-service bars between the two areas. One lift ticket is good for both resorts; a free shuttle will take you back and forth from both resorts. When the weather warms up, you can ride the sky chair at Snow Summit for an incredible view, then hike back down or go mountain biking on the web of trails at 8,000 feet. There's also a nine-hole golf course at the base of the mountain that's open from April through November.

Admission: Ski pass: Adult $66 during peak season (January 10-March 15, Saturday-Sunday)/$53 during regular season; young adults 13-21 $56 during peak season/$43 during regular season; children 7-12 $29 during peak season/$20 regular season; Children under 7 free. Green Fees: Monday-Friday $25, weekends and holidays $30. Sky Chair (roundtrip): Adults $10, children $5.

WHERE TO STAY

★★★NORTHWOODS RESORT AND CONFERENCE CENTER

40650 Village Drive, Big Bear Lake, 909-866-3121, 800-866-3121;
www.northwoodsresort.com

This rustic mountain resort and conference center offers rooms and suites filled with handcrafted wood furniture and is located just minutes from the lake and ski resorts. Many rooms feature fireplaces, and suites have spa tubs and wet bars.

147 rooms. Restaurant, bar. Fitness center. Pool. Spa. $61-$150.

CAMBRIA

See also Morro Bay, San Simeon

Centrally located between San Francisco and Los Angeles, this laid-back coastal community is a frequent stop between L.A. and Big Sur, and is just six miles from San Simeon where Hearst Castle is located (if you're driving up to Big Sur from L.A. and plan to tour Hearst Castle, it's best to stay overnight in Cambria rather than attempt the mountainous drive after dark). Cambria's peaceful and somewhat remote setting attracted many artists back in the 1970s. Today, the downtown area is packed with charming art galleries and gift and antique shops.

WHAT TO SEE

MOONSTONE BEACH

This pretty stretch of beach with waves crashing on the rocks is perfect for a walk along the coastline. A boardwalk winds along the beach and the large rocks are a refuge for sea lions.

WHERE TO STAY
★BEST WESTERN FIRESIDE INN ON MOONSTONE BEACH

6700 Moonstone Beach Drive, Cambria, 805-927-8661, 888-910-7100; www.bestwesternfiresideinn.com

This Best Western enjoys an idyllic location overlooking Moonstone Beach. Rooms are spacious and comfortable, and many have fireplaces, Jacuzzi tubs and patios. The amenities are a step above your typical budget chain hotel room (and you pay for it).

46 rooms. Complimentary breakfast. Pool. $251-350

WHERE TO EAT
★★ROBIN'S

4095 Burton Drive, Cambria, 805-927-5007; www.robinsrestaurant.com

Located in an old home in the historic east village, Robin's focuses on fresh, made-from-scratch meals with an eclectic menu. Start off with the salmon bisque and a hunk of sourdough garlic bread or the meze platter with taboulleh, roasted red pepper hummus, tzaziki, Greek olives, feta and whole wheat chips. Dinners range from pork osso bucco to lobster enchiladas to a number of curries. The Angus burger with vine ripe tomatoes, grilled sweet onions, white cheddar, house pickles and garlic herb fries is a crowd-pleaser at lunch.

International. Lunch, dinner. $16-35

CLAREMONT

See also Pasadena, Riverside

Known as "the city of trees and PhDs," this lovely community east of Los Angeles is home to the Claremont Colleges, a consortium of seven respected higher learning institutions laid out right next to each other on a leafy boulevard. The village, which feels like something straight out of the 1950s with its small storefronts and historic homes, is a charming spot to spend an afternoon.

WHAT TO SEE
CLAREMONT COLLEGES

150 E. Eight St., Claremont, 909-621-8000; www.claremont.edu

This distinguished group of institutions is composed of Pomona College, Claremont Graduate School, Scripps College, Claremont McKenna College, Harvey Mudd College, Pitzer College and Keck Graduate Institute. Self-guided tours are available through Claremont Heritage (909-621-0848; www.claremontheritage.org).

RANCHO SANTA ANA BOTANIC GARDEN

1500 N. College Ave., Claremont, 909-625-8767; www.rsabg.org

Founded in 1927, the botanic garden's 86 acres are home to more than 6,000 kinds of native California plants. Meandering paths take you past manzanetas in winter, wildflowers in spring and native fruit in summer. Stop by the gift shop on your way out to pick up books, seeds and more.

Admission: $4 suggested donation/$8 per family. Daily 8:00 a.m.–5 p.m.

DANA POINT

See also Laguna Beach

Named in honor of the noted author Richard Henry Dana of Two Years Before the Mast fame, this quiet, unhurried town located about halfway between Los Angeles and San Diego has nearly seven miles of prominent ocean-facing bluffs and an exquisite man-made marina. The harbor has more than 50 specialty shops and restaurants and is a popular spot for boaters from around the world. It's also the main funnel to the 62-acre Doheny State Park, a popular beach for surfing, snorkeling and camping.

WHAT TO SEE
DOHENY STATE BEACH

Del Obispo/Dana Harbor Drive (just south of Dana Point Marina), 914-496-6171; www.dohenystate.beach

Surfers come for the waves—Doheny State Beach is regarded as one of Southern California's premier surfing beaches—but it's fun in the sun for everyone at this bustling, picture-perfect beach. Doheny is also known a great camping site (with some spots right on the beach), and there are volleyball courts, a pier for fishing, tide pools, food stands and picnic areas.

Call ahead to reserve a camping spot, which can fill up months in advance.

WHERE TO STAY
★★★LAGUNA CLIFFS RESORT & SPA BY MARRIOTT
25135 Park Lantern, Dana Point, 949-661-5000, 800-533-9748; www.lagunacliffs.com
Located on cliffs above the bay, this hotel sits on 42 acres and has great views of the Pacific Ocean. Rooms have a beachy décor and pop with color. There's also a nice pool with chaise lounges to relax and soak up the California sunshine, and the property is within walking distance of the harbor's restaurants and shops. A new 14,000-square-foot spa offers several invigorating orange-based treatments.
376 rooms. Restaurant, bar. Business center. Fitness center. Pool. Spa. Pets accepted. Tennis. $251-350

★★★★★ST. REGIS RESORT, MONARCH BEACH
1 Monarch Beach Resort, Dana Point, 949-234-3200, 800-722-1543; www.stregismb.com
Even seasoned travelers will swoon over the luscious, secluded setting and the Tuscan-inspired design of this resort, which is tucked away on 200 acres high above the Pacific Ocean. Elegant marble floors, plush carpets and massive sofas grace the public areas. The spacious guest rooms have dramatic contemporary décor with wood shutters, marble bathrooms, private balconies, goose down comforters and 300-thread count sheets. The resort has an 18-hole championship golf course, swank poolside cabanas, award-winning spa, beach club (with surfing lessons) and nature trails. Restaurants include Michael Mina's acclaimed StoneHill Tavern.
400 rooms. Restaurant, bar. Business center. Fitness center. Pool. Spa. Pets accepted. Tennis. Golf. $351 and up

★★★★THE RITZ-CARLTON, LAGUNA NIGUEL
1 Ritz-Carlton Drive, Dana Point, 949-240-2000, 800-241-3333; www.ritzcarlton.com
Situated atop a 150-foot bluff overlooking the ocean, this Mediterranean style villa is an elegant retreat. Guest rooms have been decorated in a palette of cream and soft blue to reflect the beach setting and have ocean, pool or garden views. The resort has three restaurants, including the unique wine tasting room, ENO, which offers an extensive menu of wines, cheeses and chocolates from around the globe. Surfing lessons are available at the beach, and the spa is fabulous with its contemporary California-glam décor and full menu of luxurious treatments. Golfers come to play several spectacular courses nearby.
393 rooms. Restaurant, bar. Business center. Fitness center. Pool. Spa. Pets accepted. Tennis. $351 and up

WHERE TO EAT
★★★RESTAURANT 162'
1 Ritz Carlton Drive, Dana Point, 949-240-2000; www.ritzcarlton.com
Named for its location 162 feet above sea level, this restaurant provides a spectacular view from its dazzling blue and cream-colored dining room. The cuisine focuses on fresh fish, with dishes such as Alaskan king crab with red Thai curry risotto. A seafood buffet is popular on Friday nights. Lunch items include a chef's inspiration pizza and grilled sirloin, turkey or barley burger.
Seafood. Breakfast, lunch, dinner. $36-85

★★SAVANNAH STEAK & CHOP HOUSE
32441 Golden Lantern St., Laguna Niguel, 949-493-7107; www.culinaryadventures.com

Savannah Steak and Chop House, part of a group of popular restaurants in Orange County, is the type of place that allows you to kick back in one of the red leather half-moon booths with a chilled martini and a grilled steak. Contrary to what the menu claims, you won't find many Southern influences here, but with the nice selection of house-smoked meats and steaks (which come with three different choices of sauce for dipping, including a blue cheese butter), you're not likely to even notice. You'll find live jazz in the lounge on most nights, and the outdoor patio with fire pit is a nice place to dine year-round.

Contemporary American. Dinner. $36-85

★★★★STONEHILL TAVERN
1 Monarch Beach Resort, Dana Point, 949-234-3318; www.michaelmina.net/stonehill

Famed San Francisco chef-turned-restaurateur Michael Mina's urban bistro, located in the St. Regis, is a sleek, intimate spot designed by Tony Chi with comfortable couches, glass-enclosed booths and a large terrace. The menu includes Mina's signature appetizer trios—three different preparations of one ingredient, such as tuna, lobster or duck, as well as twists on American classics (think fried chicken with mascarpone polenta and a root beer float for dessert). An impressive wine program focuses on boutique California producers, but also includes a diverse selection from Austria and Burgundy.

American. Dinner. Closed Monday-Tuesday. $86 and up

SPAS

★★★★THE RITZ-CARLTON SPA, LAGUNA NIGUEL
1 Ritz-Carlton Drive, Dana Point, 949-240-2000, 800-241-3333; www.ritzcarlton.com

Eleven treatment rooms, a full-service beauty salon, a circular manicure and pedicure station and a modern Fitness center are available to guests at the Ritz-Carlton Spa. Choose from holistic treatments grounded in ancient practices as well as the latest skin treatments, massages and exfoliations. Collagen infusion facials and California citrus body polishes stand out among the spa's signature treatments. There are also seasonal treatments such as a summer chocolate sugar scrub pedicure. Treatments are rooted in the sea's purifying elements: rich minerals, sea salt or nutrient-rich algae and water.

★★★★★SPA GAUCIN
1 Monarch Beach Resort, Dana Point, 949-234-3200, 800-722-1543;
www.stregismonarchbeach.com

Spa Gaucin at the St. Regis is the picture of elegance with dark woods, Asian-style accents and three-story waterfalls. The warm cream interior accentuates specially commissioned artwork throughout the space and the 25 treatment rooms offer state-of-the-art amenities (including gas fireplaces to cozy up to). The spa menu includes everything from Mediterranean massage to total vitamin facials to the Chardonnay sugar scrub. Try the Solace Mineral Trio, a hydrating treatment utilizing grapeseed body exfoliation and a volcanic clay wrap, or the Dermal Quench facial to ward off road-lag. There's also an extensive offering of beauty treatments from microdermabrasion to pedicures.

DEATH VALLEY NATIONAL PARK

See also Huntington Beach, Irvine, Laguna Beach, Newport Beach

Scorching heat, frigid cold, the driest atmosphere you can imagine. The 49ers would have never dreamed that this would someday be a tourist destination. But that's exactly what this inhospitable, 5,200 square miles of rugged desert, peaks and depressions officially became when President Herbert Hoover designated it a national monument in 1933. Located approximately 300 miles northeast of Los Angeles, Death Valley was so named for a party of gold hunters who took a shortcut through here and many of them perished. The discovery and subsequent mining of borax, hauled out by the famous 20-mule teams, kept tourists away until the mid-1920s.

The park is one vast geological museum. Millions of years ago, this was part of the Pacific Ocean. Violent uplifts of the earth occurred, creating mountain ranges and draining water to the west. Today, 200 square miles of the valley are at or below sea level. The lowest point on the continent (282 feet below sea level) can be found here. Telescope Peak, at 11,049 feet, towers directly above it. The average rainfall is less than two inches a year. The climate is pleasant from October to May, but it's very hot in summer—a maximum temperature of 134° F has been recorded.

Venturing off paved roads in this area in the summer can be dangerous. Carefully obey all National Park Service signs and regulations and make sure that your vehicle has plenty of gas and oil. Carry water when you explore this park, especially in hot weather.

WHAT TO SEE
20-MULE-TEAM CANYON
Lone Pine, 760-786-2331; www.nps.gov/deva
Named for the 20 mule teams that carried loads of borax out of the desert, this canyon is viewed from an unpaved, twisting road that leads you past some of the best scenery in the park.

ARTIST'S PALETTE
Death Valley National Park, 760-786-2331; www.nps.gov/deva
This is one of the most spectacular sights in Death Valley National Park. Artist's Drive, a nine-mile loop, leads you (on a narrow, topsy-turvy road) past a kaleidoscope of colors from all the volcanic deposits.

DANTE'S VIEW
Death Valley National Park, 760-786-2331; www.nps.gov/deva
The view from this lookout located at 5,000 feet is mind-boggling. That small black dot way down below? That would be Badwater Basin, which is 282 miles below sea level, the lowest spot in the Western Hemisphere.

DEVIL'S GOLF COURSE
Death Valley National Park, 760-786-2331; www.nps.gov/deva
It was said that only the devil could play golf on this terrain, thanks to the vast beds of rugged salt crystals that make up the surface.

GOLDEN CANYON

Death Valley National Park, 760-786-2331; www.nps.gov/deva

A one-mile trail provides access to the canyon, which displays a range of colors from deep red to rich gold.

RHYOLITE GHOST TOWN

Death Valley National Park, 760-786-2331; www.nps.gov/deva

Once the largest mining town in Death Valley in the early 1900s, by 1911, it was a ghost town. One structure still left standing from that era is the "bottle house," constructed of beer and liquor bottles.

SCOTTY'S CASTLE

Death Valley National Park, 760-786-2331; www.nps.gov/deva

This desert mansion from the early 1920s was designed as both a work of art and a winter home for Chicago millionaire Albert Johnson, and is one of the most popular tourist attractions in the park. The furnishings are typical of the period and many were specially designed and handcrafted for this house. Costumed interpreters lead living history tours.

Daily 9:00 a.m.-6 p.m.

TELESCOPE PEAK

Death Valley National Park, 760-786-2331; www.nps.gov/deva

You'll have to hoof it to reach the highest peak in the Panamint Range—it's a 3,000-foot-climb to the 11,049-foot summit and a 14-mile round trip.

UBEHEBE CRATER

Death Valley National Park, 760-786-2331; www.nps.gov/deva

A volcanic steam explosion left this colorful crater.

ZABRISKIE POINT

Death Valley National Park, 760-786-2331; www.nps.gov/deva

Catch one of the most scenic views here, especially at sunrise or sunset, when the multicolor hills are bathed in natural light.

WHERE TO STAY
★★STOVEPIPE WELLS VILLAGE

Highway 190, Death Valley, 760-786-2345; www.stovepipewells.com

This one-story lodge offers modest hotel rooms with air-conditioning and private bathrooms. You won't find a telephone and only the deluxe rooms have televisions. But there are desert views and plenty of quiet (apart from the crickets). The main building houses a restaurant, bar and gift shop. There is also an RV park with hook-ups.

83 rooms. Restaurant, bar. Pool. Pets accepted. $61-150

WHERE TO EAT
★THE 19TH HOLE

Highway 190, Furnace Creek, 760-786-2345; www.furnacecreekresort.com

For burgers, subs and other American favorites, the 19th Hole at the Furnace Creek Inn and Ranch Resort is a nice spot offering views of Panamint Mountains and the golf course. But perhaps the best part about this place is that you can drive your golf cart up a ramp and order a drink.

American. Breakfast, lunch. Closed June-September. $15 and under

FALLBROOK

See also Temecula

Fallbrook is the self-proclaimed avocado capital of the world. Twenty-eight square miles are devoted to growing and packing the fruit. One day each April is set aside to celebrate the crop with a festival that includes crafts, games, contests, entertainment and a tour of the Del Rey Avocado Company. The best reason for coming is to taste the world-class guacamole, avocado sandwiches, grilled avocado halves with lemon and other samples.

SPECIAL EVENT
FALLBROOK AVOCADO FESTIVAL
233 E. Mission Road, Fallbrook, 760-728-5845; www.fallbrookca.org
Check the Web site to find out which date in April this delicious festival falls on. Culinary demonstrations take place all day and there are lots of activities—though you may be too busy eating.
April.

WHERE TO STAY
★★★PALA MESA RESORT
2001 Old Highway 395, Fallbrook, 760-728-5881, 800-722-4700; www.palamesa.com
If sleeping right on the golf links is your idea of a perfect getaway, book a room at the Pala Mesa. Set on more than 200 acres surrounded by citrus and avocado groves, this golf resort offers spacious guest rooms with balconies and patios, and more important, access to the 18-hole, par 72, championship course.

133 rooms. Restaurant, bar. Tennis. Golf. Pool. Pets accepted. $151-250

FRESNO

See also Bakersfield

In the geographic center of the state and the heart of the San Joaquin Valley, Fresno is undergoing tremendous growth. The county claims the greatest agricultural production of any in the United States, handling more than $3 billion annually. The world's largest dried fruit packing plant, Sun-Maid, is here.

WHAT TO SEE
CALIFORNIA STATE UNIVERSITY, FRESNO
5241 N. Maple Ave., Fresno, 559-278-4240; www.csufresno.edu
The grounds include a farm, an arboretum and California wildlife habitat exhibits. Tours are available.

DISCOVERY CENTER
1937 N. Winery Ave., Fresno, 559-251-5533; www.thediscoverycenter.net
Kids get an opportunity to discover nature and science through hands-on learning. Exhibits include a cactus garden and space shuttle.

Monday-Friday 9 a.m.-5 p.m., Saturday 10 a.m.-4.p.m.

FORESTIERE UNDERGROUND GARDENS

5021 W. Shaw Ave., Fresno, 559-271-0734; www.undergroundgardens.info
This former home of Sicilian immigrant Baldassare Forestiere has 10 acres of underground tunnels filled with citrus plants, grape vines, rose bushes and other flora.
May-September, Wednesday-Sunday.

FRESNO ART MUSEUM

2233 N. First St., Fresno, 559-441-4221; www.fresnoartmuseum.org
The only modern art museum between Los Angeles and San Francisco, the Fresno Art Museum showcases works from an international group of contemporary artists and houses an impressive collection of Mexican art dating from the pre-Columbian era to present day.
Admission: $5. Tuesday-Wednesday, Friday-Sunday 11 a.m.-5 p.m., Thursday 11 a.m.-8 p.m.

FRESNO CHAFFEE ZOO

894 W. Belmont Ave., Fresno, 559-498-5910; www.fresnochaffeezoo.com
This 18-acre zoo has more than 650 animals representing 200 species and includes a reptile house, an elephant exhibit and a Sunda forest. There's also a tropical rain forest exhibit containing plants and animals found primarily in South American regions.
Admission: adults $14, children $12. February-October, daily 9 a.m.-4 p.m.; November-January, daily 10 a.m.-3 p.m.

FRESNO METROPOLITAN MUSEUM

1555 Van Ness Ave., Fresno, 559 441-1444; www.fresnomet.org
Learn all about the heritage and culture of the San Joaquin Valley at this interesting museum. The Native American Collection showcases the work of Native American groups from the Central Valley. Other permanent exhibits include a collection of jigsaw puzzles and the photos of Ansel Adams.
Admission: adults $9, students and seniors $7, children 3-12 $5, children under 3 free. Wednesday-Sunday 10 a.m.-5 p.m.

KEARNEY MANSION MUSEUM

7160 W. Kearney Blvd., Fresno, 559-441-0862; www.valleyhistory.org
This restored historic mansion has many of its original furnishings, European wallpapers and Art Nouveau light fixtures. There is alsso a narrated 45-minute tour.
Friday-Sunday 1:00 p.m., 2:00 p.m. and 3 p.m.

MILLERTON LAKE STATE RECREATION AREA

5290 Millerton Road, Fresno, 559-822-2332; www.parks.ca.gov
You'll have your choice of activities in this recreation area: swimming, waterskiing, fishing, boat launching, hiking and riding trails, picnicking and camping are some of the offerings.

ROEDING PARK

890 W. Belmont Ave., Fresno, 559-621-2900; www.fresno.gov

Walk through a variety of trees and shrubs, ranging from high mountain to tropical species, on 157 acres. The park also offers boating, tennis, a camellia garden and picnic areas.
Daily.

SIERRA NATIONAL FOREST

1600 Tollhouse Road, Clovis, 559-297-0706; www.fs.fed.us/r5/sierra

These nearly 1.3 million acres range from rolling foothills to rugged, snow-capped mountains. Check out two groves of giant sequoias, hundreds of natural lakes, 11 major reservoirs and unique geological formations. The topography can be rough and precipitous in higher elevations, with deep canyons and many beautiful meadows along streams and lakes. Jump into some action with rafting, boating, sailing, fishing, hunting, downhill and cross-country skiing and camping.

SIERRA SUMMIT SKI AREA

59265 Highway 168, Huntington Lake, 559-233-2500; www.sierrasummit.com

The longest of the 25 ski runs here is 2¼ miles and the vertical drop is 1,600 feet. There are three triple and two double chairlifts as well as four surface lifts. Take advantage of half-day rates on weekends and holidays.
Admission: adults $48, children 13-17 $38, children 6-12 $16, children under 6 free. Mid-November-mid-April, daily.

WILD WATER ADVENTURES

11413 E. Shaw Ave., Clovis, 559-299-9453, 800-564-9453; www.wildwater.net

This water park has one of the West Coast's largest wave pools, plus water-slides for teens and a water play area for children.
Admission: adults $25.99, under 48 inches $18.99, seniors $10.99, children under 3 free. Days and times vary.

SPECIAL EVENTS
BIG FRESNO FAIR

1121 S. Chance Ave., Fresno, 559-650-3247; www.fresnofair.com

At this fair, you'll find a carnival, horse racing, livestock exhibits, and arts and crafts. October.

CLOVIS RODEO

Clovis Arena, 559-299-5203; www.clovisrodeo.com

The four-day festival features a parade, a kids' rodeo and competition categories that include bull riding, team roping, barrel racing and bareback riding.
Late April.

FRESNO COUNTY BLOSSOM TRAIL

2629 S. Clovis Ave., Fresno, 559-262-4271; www.gofresnocounty.com

Take this 62-mile driving tour of fruit orchards, citrus groves and vineyards during peak season.
February-mid-March.

HIGHLAND GATHERING AND GAMES

Roeding Park, 890 W. Belmont Ave., Fresno, 559-265-6507; www.scottishsociety.org
Gather to watch Scottish athletics, dancing contests and a bagpipe competition.
Mid-September.

SWEDISH FESTIVAL

1475 Draper St., Kingsburg, 559-897-1111; www.cityofkingsburg-ca.gov
After a traditional Swedish pancake breakfast, stick around for a parade,
entertainment, arts and crafts, a carnival, folk dancing and more food.
Third weekend in May.

WHERE TO STAY
★★FOUR POINTS BY SHERATON

3737 N. Blackstone Ave., Fresno, 559-226-2200, 888-627-7141; www.fourpoints.com
This clean and comfortable Four Points by Sheraton offers spacious rooms,
a well-equipped Fitness center and nice outdoor pool with private cabanas.
It's also conveniently located in the downtown area within a short drive to
most sites.
204 rooms. Restaurant, bar. Business center. Fitness center. Pool. $151-250

★PICCADILLY INN-UNIVERSITY

4961 N. Cedar Ave., Fresno, 559-224-4200, 800-468-3587; www.piccadillyinn.com
This Old English Tudor-style hotel is adjacent to California State University,
Fresno, only eight miles from downtown Fresno and a short drive to Yosemite. Amenities include a fitness center, heated spa and 24-hour coffee bar.
190 rooms. Complimentary breakfast. Fitness center. Pool. $151-250

★★RADISSON HOTEL & CONFERENCE CENTER FRESNO

2233 Ventura St., Fresno, 559-268-1000, 800-201-1718; www.radisson.com
All guest rooms here feature Radisson's trademark beds with air chambers
that allow you to adjust the firmness. Rooms also have free Internet and large
work desks. Parking is also free.
321 rooms. Restaurant, bar. Business center. Fitness center. Pool. $61-150

WHERE TO EAT
★★RIPE TOMATO

5064 N. Palm Ave., Fresno, 559-225-1850
Long considered one of Fresno's best restaurants, the Ripe Tomato serves
authentic French fare in a charming (though somewhat dated) setting.
French. Lunch, dinner. Closed Sunday-Monday. $36-85

HUNTINGTON BEACH

See also Newport Beach
This quirky city features more than eight miles of beaches, all of them great
for swimming and many favorable to surfers. Locals call Huntington Cliffs
"Dog Beach" because pooches are welcome. It's also the site of Huntington
Pier, a structure that has seen damage from heavy surf, earthquake and fire.
This version, the locals say, is built to last. Take a hike out to the very end

and have a meal at Ruby's Restaurant.

Named after Henry E. Huntington, a fabled entrepreneur from California's freewheeling past, Huntington Beach was a vital rail terminus, an oil boom town and a posh resort. The Newland House evokes the feel and architecture of the first decade of the 20th century in California. The City Gym and Pool on Palm Avenue date to the early 1930s and have survived numerous earthquakes.

WHERE TO STAY
★COMFORT SUITES
16301 Beach Blvd., Huntington Beach, 714-841-1812; www.comfortsuites.com
An affordable choice near the Huntington Beach Pier, Disneyland, Knott's Berry Farm and other attractions, rooms here include refrigerators and microwave. A Jack in the Box restaurant is conveniently located on the premises.
106 rooms. Complimentary breakfast. Fitness center. Pool. $61-150

★★★HILTON WATERFRONT BEACH RESORT
21100 Pacific Coast Highway, Huntington Beach, 714-845-8000, 800-822-7873;
www.waterfrontbeachresort.hilton.com
This hotel was recently updated with touches such as flat-screen TVs, sleek furniture and vanities with more space for storing your things. Beach views and an indoor waterfall add to the appeal.
290 rooms. Restaurant, bar. Business center. Fitness center. Pool. Pets accepted. Tennis. $151-250

INDIAN WELLS
See also Palm Springs
This city, which hosts the Indian Wells Masters golf tournament, is in the Palm Springs area and boasts the highest proportion of millionaires of any city in the United States.

WHERE TO STAY
★★★HYATT GRAND CHAMPIONS RESORT AND SPA
44-600 Indian Wells Lane, Indian Wells, 760-341-1000, 800-554-9288;
www.grandchampions.hyatt.com
This classic California Palm Desert resort has luxury accommodations with furnished balconies and marble baths with separate tubs and showers. Duffers will enjoy the 36 holes of the Golf Resort at Indian Wells, which surrounds the hotel. The sprawling resort also includes a 30,000-square-foot spa, seven pools, an espresso bar and a café offering light fare.
530 rooms. Restaurant, bar. Business center. Fitness center. Pool. Pets accepted. Golf. Tennis. $251-350

★★★INDIAN WELLS RESORT HOTEL
76661 Highway 111, Indian Wells, 760-345-6466, 800-248-3220;
www.indianwellsresort.com
This European boutique-style hotel surrounded by the Indian Wells Golf Course features spacious accommodations and personalized service and is close to top shopping and recreation. The pool overlooks the golf course.
155 rooms. Restaurant, bar. Complimentary breakfast. Fitness center. Pool.

Golf. Tennis. $151-250

★★★MIRAMONTE RESORT AND SPA
45-000 Indian Wells Lane, Indian Wells, 760-341-2200, 800-237-2926;
www.miramonteresort.com
Just 15 minutes from Palm Springs, this charming resort is nestled at the base of the Santa Rosa Mountains. The lovely grounds are dotted with courtyards and manicured rose gardens. Order lunch from the restaurant and someone will hop on a bike and deliver it to your room or wherever you are. Three golf courses surround the property and there's a superb spa for pampering.
215 rooms. Restaurant. Fitness center. Tennis. Pool. Business center. $251-350

★★★RENAISSANCE ESMERALDA RESORT
44-400 Indian Wells Lane, Indian Wells, 760-773-4444;
www.renaissanceesmeralda.com
This luxurious resort has a full-service spa, championship golf, tennis, plus a camp for kids with arts and crafts activities, swimming and poolside play. Each of the cheerful and contemporary rooms has a private balcony, with a view of the surrounding mountains, golf courses and desert.
560 rooms. Restaurant, bar. Business center. Fitness center. Pool. Golf. Tennis. $151-250

WHERE TO EAT
★★★LE SAINT GERMAIN
74-985 Highway 111, Indian Wells, 760-773-6511; www.lestgermain.com
This is a charming and elegant restaurant where classic French and California flavors fuse to create an eclectic dining experience. Dine on roasted chicken with lemon and honey au jus, or grilled Black Angus beef with a Roquefort crust. There's also an extensive wine list.
French, Mediterranean. Dinner. Closed Sunday, June-August. $36-85

SPA
★★★THE WELL SPA AT MIRAMONTE RESORT
45000 Indian Wells Lane, Indian Wells, 760-341-2200; www.miramonteresort.com
This Tuscan-inspired jewel will awaken your senses with a setting that is distinctive and tranquil. Outdoor and indoor treatment rooms are available to ensure the ultimate spa experience. Services incorporate therapeutic mud, wine extracts, pure essential oils and refreshing waters. A fitness center with an array of classes, full-service salon, spa boutique and smoothie bar round out the relaxing experience.

INDIO
See also Indian Wells, Joshua Tree National Park, Palm Springs
Founded as a railroad construction camp, the town took its name from the large population of Native Americans nearby. The All-American Canal turned the area into fertile ground that now produces 59 types of crops, including 95 percent of all American dates. Visitors must try the date shake, an extra-thick milkshake made with dates. Indio is just five miles east of Indian

Wells (so it's easy to pop over for one of these creamy concoctions if you're staying there.)

WHAT TO SEE
FANTASY SPRINGS CASINO
84-245 Indio Springs Parkway, Indio, 760-342-5000, 800-827-2946; www.fantasyspringsresort.com/

Place a bet at this elegant casino not far from Palm Springs. This casino offers off-track betting, video gaming machines, 1,200-seat bingo room and more than 35 card tables. You will also find entertainment, dining and a resort hotel.

Daily 24 hours.

GENERAL GEORGE S. PATTON MEMORIAL MUSEUM
2 Chiriaco Road, Indio, 760-227-3483; www.generalpattonmuseum.com

General Patton selected this site to prepare his soldiers for combat in North Africa. You'll see Patton memorabilia and artifacts.

Admission: adults $4, seniors $3.50. Daily 9:30 a.m.-4:30 p.m.

SHIELDS DATE GARDEN
80-225 U.S. Highway 111, Indio, 760-347-7768; www.shieldsdates.com

In business since 1924, this all-things-dates market offers a wide variety of products, from gift sets to date cookies to date "sugar." You will also find special varieties of the date, as well as a crystal mix you can use to make your own shakes. Owner Floyd Shields' popular lecture on the date is now a 15-minute movie Romance and Sex Life of the Date that plays all day.

Daily 9 a.m.-5 p.m.

SPECIAL EVENTS
RIVERSIDE COUNTY FAIR AND NATIONAL DATE FESTIVAL
Riverside County Fairgrounds, 82-503 Highway 111, Indio, 760-863-8247; www.datefest.org

This longtime festival was given an Arabian Nights theme by a Hollywood set designer and writer back in the late 1940s. Today, the tradition of celebrating the end of the date harvest is still going strong with more than 70 booths featuring dates of all kinds, entertainment and a pageant.

Mid-late February.

WHERE TO STAY
★★BEST WESTERN DATE TREE HOTEL
81-909 Indio Blvd., Indio, 760-347-3421; www.datetree.com

Sitting on more than five acres of desert, this Best Western is located near downtown Indio and other attractions, including a casino and Joshua Tree National Park. Some rooms feature spa tubs and patios.

118 rooms. Complimentary breakfast. Fitness center. Pool. Pets accepted. $61-150

JOSHUA TREE NATIONAL PARK

See also Indio

Covering more than 1,236 square miles, this park preserves a section of the Mojave and Colorado deserts that is rich in vegetation. The park shelters many species of desert plants. The Joshua tree, which gives the park its name, was named by the Mormons for its upstretched "arms" reaching for heaven. A member of the lily family, this giant yucca attains heights of more than 40 feet. The area consists of a series of block mountains ranging in altitude from 1,000-5,800 feet and separated by desert flats. The summer gets very hot and in the winter, the temperature drops below freezing. Water is available only at the Black Rock Canyon Visitor Center/Campground, Cottonwood Campground, the Indian Cove Ranger Station and the Twenty-nine Palms Visitor Center. Pets are permitted on leash only and not on trails. Take one of the guided tours and campfire programs. Picnicking is permitted in designated areas and campgrounds, but no fires may be built outside the campgrounds.

WHAT TO SEE
HIDDEN VALLEY NATURE TRAIL

74485 National Park Drive, Joshua Tree National Park, 760-367-5500; www.nps.gov/jotr

This trail is a one-mile loop. Access it from the picnic area across Hidden Valley Campground. The valley is enclosed by a wall of rocks.

KEYS VIEW

74485 National Park Drive, Joshua Tree National Park, 760-367-5500; www.nps.gov/jotr

Here you'll get a sweeping view of the Coachella valley, desert and mountain. A paved path leads off the main road.

LOST PALMS CANYON

74485 National Park Drive, Joshua Tree National Park, 760-367-5500; www.nps.gov/jotr

This eight-mile round-trip hike is reachable by four-mile trail from Cottonwood Spring. It shelters the largest group of palms (120) in the park. Daily sunrise-sunset.

OASIS VISITOR CENTER

74485 National Park Drive, Joshua Tree National Park, 760-367-5500; www.nps.gov/jotr

At this visitors' center, you'll find exhibits and a self-guided nature trail through the Oasis of Mara, discovered by a government survey party in 1855. Daily.

SPECIAL EVENT
PIONEER DAYS

73660 Civic Center, Twentynine Palms Chamber of Commerce, 760-367-3445;
www.29chamber.com

This traditional event offers a children's carnival, a parade, a rodeo, concerts, outhouse races and more.
Third weekend in October.

WHERE TO STAY
★BEST WESTERN GARDEN INN & SUITES
71487 Twentynine Palms Highway, Twentynine Palms, 760-367-9141, 800-780-7234;
www.bestwestern.com
A comfortable and affordable place to spend the night after a day in Joshua Tree National Park. The hotel is just five miles from the park.
83 rooms. Complimentary breakfast. Fitness center. Pool. Pets accepted. $61-150

LAKE ARROWHEAD
See also Big Bear Lake, Redlands
People are drawn to this mountainous lake region in the San Bernardino National Forest for the outdoor recreation. Although the lake itself is private (visitors can tour it on the Arrowhead Queen, take waterskiing lessons or use the beach as guests of the Lake Arrowhead Resort), everyone can enjoy hiking, biking, horseback riding and camping. There are also plenty of shops, restaurants and other attractions, including the ice-skating rink where Michelle Kwan trained. In winter, skiers and snowboarders take to the powdery slopes.

WHAT TO SEE
ARROWHEAD QUEEN & LEROY'S SPORTS
28200 Highway 189, Lake Arrowhead, 909-336-6992
Enjoy a 50-minute narrated boat cruise on Lake Arrowhead, past architectural points of interest and historical sites.

WHERE TO STAY
★★★LAKE ARROWHEAD RESORT AND SPA
27984 Highway 189, Lake Arrowhead, 909-336-1511, 800-800-6792;
www.lakearrowheadresort.com
There's much to do around Lake Arrowhead, but this lakefront resort nestled in the San Bernardino forest is so warm and luxurious, visitors may never want to leave. Guest rooms feature plush goose-down comforters, granite bathrooms and private balconies or patios. Guests have access to the private beach as well as golf and tennis privileges at Lake Arrowhead Country Club. The resort's fine dining restaurant Bin 189 offers a menu of contemporary American fare for breakfast, lunch and dinner. Weekly movies featuring films made in Arrowhead are also shown.
173 rooms. Restaurant, bar. Pool. Tennis. Spa. $151-250

LOMPOC
See also Pismo Beach, Santa Barbara
More than two-dozen murals around this community showcase the works of internationally acclaimed artists such as Roberto Delgado and Dan Sawatsky. Located 20 miles west of Solvang, Lompoc is also the flower seed capital of the world. From May to September, the city is bordered by more than 1,000 acres of vivid zinnias, marigolds, sweet peas, petunias and other blossoms.

WHAT TO SEE
LA PURISIMA MISSION STATE HISTORIC PARK
2295 Purisima Road, Lompoc, 805-733-3713; www.lapurisimamission.org
Founded in 1787, this is the 11th of the 21 Spanish missions established in what became California. The mission was moved in 1812 and restored in its current setting.
Daily 9 a.m.-5 p.m.

MURAL WALK
More than 24 giant murals painted by world-class artists adorn the exterior walls of buildings in old downtown.
Daily.

SPECIAL EVENTS
LOMPOC VALLEY FLOWER FESTIVAL
Ryon Park, 414 W. Ocean Ave., Lompoc, 805-735-8511; www.flowerfestival.org
This fest in June has lots of flower power, featuring a floral parade, flower exhibits, an arts and craft show, entertainment plus bus tours of 1,200 acres of flower fields.
June.

WHERE TO STAY
★★EMBASSY SUITES
1117 N. H St., Lompoc, 805-735-8311, 800-362-2779; www.embassysuites.com
This Embassy Suites near Santa Barbara and Solvang has the standard private bedroom with king bed and separate living room (with two televisions). There's also a complimentary reception each night, and the breakfast is cooked-to-order.
155 rooms. Complimentary breakfast. Business center. Fitness center. Pool. $61-150

LOS ANGELES
See also Anaheim, Arcadia, Beverly Hills, Disneyland, Hollywood, Long Beach, Manhattan Beach, Marina del Rey, San Marino, San Pedro, Santa Monica, Thousand Oaks, Valencia, West Hollywood, Westwood, Westwood Village
On September 4, 1781, the governor of California, Don Felipe de Neve, marched to the city and founded the town of Our Lady Queen of the Angels of Porciúncula, later thankfully shortened to Los Angeles.

L.A. has often been described as 40 suburbs without a city. Visitors usually stick to four distinct areas. If it's sun and sand you seek, make a beeline for the beach communities of Malibu, Venice and Santa Monica. Malibu is full of surfers and million-dollar homes right on the water; Venice is funky as ever, especially on the honky-tonk boardwalk; Santa Monica is a cross between the two, with a popular amusement park on the pier and a few more homeless people than the city would like. If you've come to shop, you might never leave Beverly Hills. The super-glitzy stores of Rodeo Drive are here, as are some of L.A.'s most fabulously expensive homes. For shopping on a mere mortal's budget, try the Beverly Center or The Grove, L.A.'s premier malls-cum-entertainment-centers, and home to retailers ranging from Gucci to H&M. L.A. does have an actual downtown, which includes Frank Gehry's Walt Disney Concert Hall, several top-flight museums, Chinatown, Little Tokyo and Mexican marketplace Olvera Street. Downtown is undergoing a renaissance, but the sidewalks still roll up at night, so hotels here cater primarily to business travelers.

West Hollywood is (ironically) the most centrally located part of Los Angeles, and home to the hippest restaurants and nightspots of the moment along Melrose Avenue and the Sunset Strip. And unlike Hollywood proper, which is somewhat seedy, you might see movie stars here. Just don't expect to find parking.

WHAT TO SEE
CENTER THEATRE GROUP
Mark Taper Forum and Ahmanson Theatre at the Music Center, 135 N. Grand Ave., Downtown; Kirk Douglas Theatre, 9820 Washington Blvd., Culver City, 213-628-2772; www.centertheatregroup.org
Center Theatre Group, which includes the Ahmanson Theatre, the Mark Taper Forum and the Kirk Douglas Theatre, is Los Angeles's prized theater company and has been recognized as one of the best in the country. Headed by artistic director Michael Ritchie, the non-profit group has elicited a Tony Award-winning performance in *Angels in America* at the Mark Taper Forum, as well as raves for a *Death of a Salesman* at the Ahmanson. The small, 317-seat Kirk Douglas Theatre in Culver City has put on classics such as *Come Back, Little Sheba*, as well as premieres of new musicals. Show times vary. See Web site for details.

DOWNTOWN LOS ANGELES ART WALK
Gallery Row, Los Angeles, 213-624-6212; www.downtownartwalk.com
In 2003, city officials pushed a motion to designate a section of downtown (known as the Historic Core) as "Gallery Row" in order to formally recognize its blossoming art scene. What was once an area largely dominated by gang activity, homelessness and prostitution is now home to dozens of galleries. The best way to explore the downtown art scene is on the second Thursday of the month, when dozens of local galleries throw open their doors for an art walk—or, if you'd rather not walk (this is L.A., after all), you can hop one of the cool 1940s retro-fitted school buses that shuttle people around to the different galleries (just wave to flag one down). Participating galleries include the Museum of Conteporary Art and the Los Angeles Center for Digital Art, as well as small, independent outfits. The event is self-guided (and free), so start at whichever gallery catches your eye first.
Admission: free. Noon-9 p.m.

LA OPERA
Dorothy Chandler Pavilion, 135 North Grand Ave., Los Angeles, 213-972-7219;
www.laopera.com
Legendary opera singer Placido Domingo leads the company and has been integral to its success; in less than two decades, it has become the fourth largest opera company in the U.S. housed at the Dorothy Chandler Pavilion (former home of the Oscars), the opera's most recent season featured classic performances of Mozart's *The Magic Flute*, Bizet's *Carmen*, as well as

Giuseppe Verdi's *La Traviata*.

LOS ANGELES BALLET

Los Angeles Ballet Center, 11755 Exposition Blvd., Los Angeles, 310-998-7782;
www.losangelesballet.org

The Los Angeles Ballet is relatively new—their premiere performance was a December 2006 production of the The Nutcracker—but they've already won rave reviews, finallygiving this major city a ballet company of its own. (Very wisely, the founders decided that if the people of this sprawling city wouldn't come to them, they'd go to the people—the company performs in six different theaters all over Los Angeles.) It seems the ballet is here to stay, too. The holiday production of TheNutcracker has already become a Southern California tradition.

LOS ANGELES COUNTY MUSEUM OF ART/
BROAD CONTEMPORARY ART MUSEUM

5905 Wilshire Blvd., Los Angeles, 323-857-6000

Set aside a good chunk of time when you visit LACMA—with 100,000 art objects in its catalogue, LACMA is the biggest art museum in the West. The museum's collections span several continents and thousands of years, so you can see an Egyptian sarcophagus and photographs taken by Ansel Adams on the same day. LACMA's newest addition is the Broad Contemporary Art Museum, designed by architect Renzo Piano. On view at BCAM are works by artists including Richard Serra, John Baldessari, Ed Ruscha and Cindy Sherman. Along with having an impressive permanent collection, LACMA also manages to acquire top-notch exhibits. Past shows have included photographs from *Vanity Fair* from 1913 to 2008; portraits, frescoes, sculpture and decorative arts from the lost city of Pompeii; and paintings from Gustav Klimt. Every day, after 5 p.m., admission is "pay what you wish," and on the second Tuesday of each month, general admission to permanent exhibitions is free.

Admission: adults $12, seniors and students $8, children 17 and under free. Monday-Tuesday, Thursday noon-8 p.m., Friday noon-9 p.m., Saturday-Sunday 11 a.m.-8 p.m.

LOS ANGELES FARMERS MARKET

6333 W. Third St., Los Angeles, 323-933-9211, 866-993-9211;
www.farmersmarketla.com

Located at Fairfax Avenue and Third Street is one of the U.S.'s first Farmers Markets, which has been going strong since the 1930s. While there are only a handful of stallsthat sell fresh fruit and vegetables here (the market is dominated by restaurantstalls), it's a great destination for an alfresco lunch. Bennett's (stall 548, 323-939-6786)offers some of L.A.'s best ice cream and sorbet with fun flavors such as cabernetsauvignon and pumpkin; ¡Loteria! (stall 322, 323-930-2211; lighter versions of Mexican fare, like chiles rellenos stuffed with goat cheese and chorizo; Magee's Kitchen, (stall 624, 323-938-4127) one of the oldest stalls in the market, tempts with all-American dishes like roast and corned beef; and Patsy D'Amore's (stall 448, 323-938-4938; www.patsydamore.com) New York-style pizza is legendary. The market is a laid-back yet lively place to eat and people-watch. You'll see hipsters eating

crêpes, kids screaming for treats in front of candy stalls and old-timers dunking their doughnuts in cups of joe.
Monday-Friday 9 a.m.-9 p.m., Saturday 9 a.m.-8 p.m., Sunday 10 a.m.-7 p.m.

LOS ANGELES FASHION DISTRICT

90-block area bordered by Seventh Street, I-10, Main and San Petro streets, Downtown; Santee Alley is between Santee Street and Maple Avenue at Olympic Boulevard; www.fashiondistrict.org

If you've been dying to get your manicured hands on some designer labels, then a trip to Downtown L.A.'s Fashion District is in order. But you can't visit the Fashion District without hitting up Santee Alley (between Santee Street and Maple Avenue). The alley is a cross between a flea market and Middle Eastern bazaar, with people hawking everything from fake designer purses to gold jewelry. Santee Alley contains more than 150 stores, and the weekend is its busiest time, so go early (alley stores open around 10 a.m.) to avoid the crowds and get that look-alike purse. Remember, bargaining is totally acceptable while shopping in the alley. If you're not a fan of designer knockoffs, then consider heading to the Fashion District on the last Friday of the month, when many designer showrooms hold sample sales that are open to the public.

MUSEUM OF CONTEMPORARY ART (MOCA)

250 S. Grand Ave., Los Angeles, 213-621-1741; www.moca.org

MOCA has been providing Los Angeles with cutting-edge contemporary art since 1979. The museum is spread across three facilities (MOCA Grand Avenue, The Geffen Contemporary at MOCA and MOCA Pacific Design Center), but the Grand Avenue location offers the biggest bang for your buck. Besideswelcoming exhibits showcasing world-renowned artists including Jean-Michel Basquiat, Andy Warhol and Robert Rauschenberg, the museum also has animpressive permanent collection. Roy Lichtenstein, Claes Oldenburg, Mark Rothko and Diane Arbus are just a few of the artists whose work can be seen year-round at MOCA. After taking in the art, visit the MOCA Store, which offers modern knickknacks (if you appreciate sleek design), and then grab a bite at the Patinette café, which offers casual, gourmet fare from the Patina Restaurant Group. If you're on a budget, make sure to visit on Thursday between 5 and 8 p.m., when admission is free.

Admission: adults $10, students and seniors $5, children under 12 free.
Monday and Friday 11 a.m.-5 p.m., Thursday 11 a.m.-8 p.m., Saturday-Sunday 11 a.m.-6 p.m.

NATURAL HISTORY MUSEUM OF LOS ANGELES COUNTY

900 Exposition Blvd., Los Angeles, 213-763-3466; www.nhm.org

Confront a Tyrannosaurus rex; look Megamouth, the world's rarest shark, in the eye; and discover more than 300 pounds of gold. Make like Indiana Jones and do all of this at the Natural History Museum of Los Angeles County, the third-largest museum of its kind in the United States. The Natural History Museum is a monument to the natural world. After seeing T. rex bones, aquarium-bound predators and precious metal at the Gem and Mineral Hall, learn some state history in the Lando Hall of California History. Then explore the cultures of native peoples in the Visible Vault: Archeological Treasures from Ancient Latin America, where artifacts from the Mayan, Aztec and Incan empires are on display. If you're still jonesing for some Indy-type adventure, head to the Ralph M. Parsons Discovery Center and get cozy with all kinds of live insects, reptiles and amphibians.

Admission: adults $9, seniors and children 13-17 $6.50, children 5-12 $2, children under 5 free. Daily 9:30 a.m.-5 p.m.

OLVERA STREET
845 N. Alameda St., Downtown, 213-680-2525; www.olvera-street.com

To get a glimpse of L.A.'s Latino heritage, seek out Olvera Street. This area, called El Pueblo de Los Angeles Historical Monument, is considered the birthplace of Los Angeles, so there are many historic buildings to explore in this area. Check out the Avila Adobe (10 E. Olvera St.), which was built in the early 19th century by former mayor Francisco Avila; the Pelanconi House (17 Olvera St.), the oldest brick home in the city, which now houses the Casa La Golondrina Mexican restaurant; and the Victorian-style Sepulveda House (622-624 N. Main St.), built in 1887. Besides touring these local landmarks, you can also shop for traditional Mexican wares and snack on huaraches and other authentic Latin American foods from the dozens of merchants who line the street.

Admission: Free. Avila Adobe: Daily 9 a.m.-4 p.m. Sepulveda House: Daily 9 a.m.-4 p.m.

PAGE MUSEUM AT THE LA BREA TAR PITS
5801 Wilshire Blvd., Los Angeles, 323-934-7243; www.tarpits.org

It's hard to imagine that saber-toothed cats and woolly mammoths once roamed the gridlocked streets of L.A., so to get a better of idea of what prehistoric Southern California was like, take a trip to the La Brea Tar Pits. When you visit the tar pits, or Rancho La Brea, as it's often called, you'll still see (and smell!) the bubbling pools of black asphalt that trapped hundreds of species thousands of years ago. Thanks to the tar, millions of Ice Age fossils were preserved and eventually recovered. After touring the tar pits (which feature life-size replicas of woolly mammoths), head inside the Page Museum, where you can see animal skeletons and watch scientists at work in the Page Museum Laboratory.

Admission: adults $7, seniors and students $4.50, children 5-12 $2, children under 5 free. Daily 9:30 a.m.-5 p.m. First Tuesday of the month free.

PETERSEN AUTOMOTIVE MUSEUM
6060 Wilshire Blvd., Los Angeles, 323-930-2277; www.petersen.org

If you keep tabs on NASCAR, take a detour to the Petersen Automotive Museum. You can travel back in time with antique cars and steam engines, and then fast forward to the future with alternative power forms. If your eyes glaze over at the thought of fuel cells, then head to the Hollywood Gallery, where you can see Herbie from The Love Bug, a bright yellow Pantera driven by Elvis Presley, the Hannibal 8 driven by Jack Lemmon in The Great Race and much more. And don't forget to see which exhibitions are on view—the museum has showcased everything from low riders to Hot Wheels.

Admission: adults $10, seniors, students and active military $5, children

5-12 $3, children under 5 free. Tuesday-Saturday 10 a.m.-6 p.m.

STAPLES CENTER

1111 S. Figueroa St., Los Angeles, 213-742-7340; www.staplescenter.com

If you're looking to rub elbows with thousands of Angelenos—or see athletes throw a couple of elbows—head to the Staples Center. Located in downtown Los Angeles, Staples is home to some of the city's finest sports teams: the Los Angeles Kings, Los Angeles Lakers, Los Angeles Clippers, Los Angeles Avengers and Los Angeles Sparks. Besides being able to cheer along with Jack Nicholson, Tobey Maguire and other famous fans, visitors to the Staples Center can also watch some of the biggest performers in the world onstage. Justin Timberlake, Madonna and Christina Aguilera are just a few of the A-listers who have performed here.

WALT DISNEY CONCERT HALL

111 S. Grand Ave., Los Angeles, 323-850-2000; www.laphil.com

Designed by architect extraordinaire Frank Gehry, Walt Disney Concert Hall is one of L.A.'s newer landmarks, but that hasn't stopped its shiny, stainless steel curves from becoming synonymous with downtown Los Angeles. Aside from being a fascinating example of modern architecture, the hall also provides the city with a performance venue equipped with superior acoustics. So even if you end up sitting way in the back of the hall's honey-colored, wood-paneled auditorium, you'll still get an earful. The WDCH serves as the permanent home of the L.A. Philharmonic (except for when the L.A. Phil decamps to the Hollywood Bowl for the summer), and also welcomes contemporary acts such as Pink Martini and Joanna Newsom throughout the year.

THE WILTERN

3790 Wilshire Blvd., Los Angeles, 213-388-1400; www.livenation.com

The Wiltern definitely stands out among the high-rises along a section of Wilshire in Koreatown; the Art Deco building's exterior pops with a marvelous faded, patina-like green. Previously known as the Pellissier Building and conceived in 1929, the 12-story Los Angeles landmark nicely juxtaposes the retro feel of its 1930s design with the fresh performances of today's hottest bands. The Wiltern also continues to be one of L.A.'s more popular musical venues to see well-known smaller acts such as The Bravery and Snow Patrol.

WHERE TO STAY
★★ELAN HOTEL

8435 Beverly Blvd., Los Angeles, 323-658 6663, 888-611-0398; www.elanhotel.com

Thanks to a recent renovation, Élan Hotel's shabbier beige décor has given way to contemporary lobby pieces in black with mustard accents. It's a good deal for the location; the new rooms are simple (though not fancy) and make more of an attempt toward coolness than others in the same price range by employing furniture with modern lines. Although great views are hard to find—some look out on a tire store—goose-down comforters, luxe cotton bath sheets, room service and complimentary breakfast make the experience comfortable. Plus, the hotel is just one block from the Beverly Center and only five minutes from the newer outdoor mall The Grove and the historic Farmers Market, where food options range from barbecue to Brazilian to Mexican (try the pumpkin-pork tacos).

49 rooms. Fitness center. $151-250

★★★HILTON CHECKERS LOS ANGELES

535 S. Grand Ave., Los Angeles, 213-624-0000; www.hiltoncheckers.com

If you love an evening at the theater but think the experience is reserved for other cities, make a grand entrance at the Hilton Checkers Los Angeles. The refurbished 1920s hotel in L.A.'s newly booming Downtown offers dinner guests complimentary shuttles to the theater district, stopping at places such as the Mark Taper Forum and the Walt Disney Concert Hall. If you're in town for business, relax on the rooftop pool deck between meetings, and absorb the contrasting cityscape or partake in easy-to-squeeze-in "Express" spa treatments.

188 rooms. Restaurant, bar. Fitness center. Pool. Spa. $151-250

★★★LOS ANGELES MARRIOTT DOWNTOWN

333 S. Figueroa St., Los Angeles, 213-617-1133, 800-228-9290; www.marriott.com

The hotel's décor skews a bit corporate, but the Los Angeles Marriott Downtown is perfect for business travelers needing easy access to the L.A. Convention Center, Staples Center, Financial District and more. Recently upgraded, the hotel features plush goose-down bedding, highlighted views of the city skyline and mile-high lobby ceilings with skylights. But forgo the hotel's numerous casual eateries and head to the nearby festive and innovative Latin-fusion restaurant Ciudad. The hot spot offers delicious morsels and great music.

469 rooms. Restaurants, bar. Fitness center. Pool. Spa. $151-250

★★★MILLENNIUM BILTMORE HOTEL LOS ANGELES

506 S. Grand Ave., Los Angeles, 213-624-1011; www.millenniumhotels.com

Long before Downtown resurged with contemporary lofts and trendy new hotels popping up everywhere, Millennium Biltmore made its reputation as one of L.A.'s classiest hotel experiences. Wandering into the lobby is like happening upon a palace or museum, as mile-high ceilings are ornately gilded with images of cherubs. At least it's palatial enough for Hollywood royalty: Eight of the first Academy Awards ceremonies in the 1930s and '40s went down at the Biltmore Bowl, the hotel's opulent ballroom. Whether you belly up to the Gallery Bar and Cognac Room or take high Victorian tea in the Rendezvous Court, you'll feel transported to another era. But modern in-room amenities like MP3 hook-ups plus the innovative Sai Sai restaurant (serving dishes such as a grilled pork chop with sweet potato mash, onion confit, asparagus and pear and lychee compote, or Maine diver scallops with edamame polenta and sake shrimp) shepherd you back to the present day.

683 rooms. Restaurant, bar. Business Center. Fitness center. Pool. $151-250

★★★OMNI LOS ANGELES HOTEL AT CALIFORNIA PLAZA

251 S. Olive St., Los Angeles, 213-617-3300; www.omnihotels.com

As Downtown's most luxe convention hotel, Omni Los Angeles offers standard business-related amenities such as hotel-wide wireless Internet access. But Omni created some unusual services for travelers, too. Because frequent travel can lead to an unbalanced lifestyle and even weight gain, the hotel has an Ideal Living program for eating healthfully, Get Fit suites with exercise equipment such as treadmills, and even Get Fit kits with dumbbells, a yoga mat and more. For families, the hotel offers some lucky children a Kids Fantasy Suite, complete with beanbag chairs, bunk beds and toys galore. For grown-ups, at upstairs fine-dining restaurant Noé (which has a lovely view of California Plaza's Watercourt, a great destination for summer concerts), executive chef Glen Ishii serves lauded contemporary American cuisine. Dishes include shellfish-stuffed Japanese turnip with caviar and ratatouille vinaigrette, and cocktails include pear-lavender martinis and a candied ginger collins.

453 rooms. Restaurants, bar. Business center. Fitness center. Pool. Spa. Pets accepted. $151-250

★★★SHERATON LOS ANGELES DOWNTOWN HOTEL

711 S. Hope St., Los Angeles, 213-488-3500; www.starwoodhotels.com

Once you tear yourself away from meetings at the nearby L.A. Convention Center, Lakers' games at Staples Center and countless events at L.A. Live, you might enjoy hanging out in your room at Sheraton Los Angeles Downtown. Crimson striped carpeting and dark wood welcome you to the highrise, but more important, the hotel's rooms offer luxuries such as signature comfy beds. A decked-out club lounge supplies you with complimentary breakfast and afternoon hors d'oeuvres, if you should choose to upgrade. The Brasserie, The Italian Grill (open seasonally) and The Lobby Bar offer several other dining options, but rather than partake of the hotel's generically named eateries, explore the great culinary scene nearby.

485 rooms. Restaurant, bar. Business center. Fitness center. Pool. $61-150

★★★SLS HOTEL AT BEVERLY HILLS

465 S. La Cienega Blvd., Midtown, 310-247-0400; www.luxurycollection.com

Visionary entrepreneur Sam Nazarian (owner of hospitality giant SBE) has launched most of L.A.'s hottest restaurant and nightlife destinations, from Katsuya to Hyde. A year ago, SBE launched its first hotel, SLS Hotel at Beverly Hills. In Le Meredien's former digs on La Cienega, the hotel aims to change the face of hospitality. Upon entering the Philippe Starck-designed hotel, you'll have the option of coming through two separate lobbies: Tres, the Private Guest Lobby (a serene space with an exclusive lounge), or The Bazaar (a constant party with culinary indulgences by Spanish chef José Andrés as well as cocktails and shopping). To top it all off, guests are afforded preferential access to SBE's restaurants and nightclubs across the city. Continue the VIP treatment at Ciel Spa at SLS, use the fitness center with personal trainer in tow or rent one of the signature Lifestyle Suites, equipped with Technogym's Kinesis personal equipment series (which allows you to do hundreds of exercises on one machine). Each room's comprehensive pillow menu, from hypoallergenic to down, will ensure a good night's sleep, which you'll need after a night out on the town.

297 rooms. Restaurant, bar. Business center. Fitness center. Pool. Spa. Pets accepted. $351 and up

★★★SOFITEL LOS ANGELES

8555 Beverly Blvd., Los Angeles, 310-278-5444, 800-763-4835;
www.sofitellosangeles.com

Renovated practically from top to bottom, the hotel has become a serious Hollywood hot spot thanks to the high-end, innovative comfort food at Simon L.A. restaurant (helmed by head chef Kerry Simon) and a sassy insider crowd at the adjoining Stone Rose cocktail lounge. New LeSpa at Sofitel L.A. also draws bliss-seekers, and guestrooms include rain showers. Everyone mingles in the lobby, reveling in its futuristic parody of contemporary style—complete with a chair made from half dollars. The hotel's central location is a foodie's and shopper's paradise; it sits across from the city's most famed mall, The Beverly Center, and a couple of blocks from stretches of chic celebrity-filled eateries (from Toast to The Ivy) and boutiques on Third Street and Robertson Boulevard. The hotel is only minutes from Beverly Hills, West Hollywood and The Grove farmers' market, movie theaters and an outdoor mall, too. In this notoriously spread-out city, locations don't get more central than the Sofitel.

295 rooms. Restaurant, bar. Fitness center. Pool. Spa. $251-300

★★★THE STANDARD

550 S. Flower St., Los Angeles, 213-892-8080; www.standardhotels.com

It may look like a typical downtown office building from the outside, but step inside The Standard and you're not in corporate America anymore. Its look and feel is equal parts nightlife hot spot and modern art museum. Funky music plays throughout, and live bands jam by the rooftop pool during warmer months. To get away from the hubbub, head to your room—all guest rooms are a study in minimalism with their muted whites and grays, but the amenities are far from spartan, with oversized fluffy towels, mood lighting and plenty of high-tech treats, such as iHomes and complimentary Wi-Fi.

207 rooms. Restaurant, bar. Business center. Pool. $251-350

WHERE TO EAT

★★AOC

8022 W. Third St., Los Angeles, 323-653-6359; www.aocwinebar.com

Small plates remain en vogue in Los Angeles because of tapas eateries like AOC. The charcuterie selection is especially good, with savory offerings like the coppa, sopressata and cacciatorini, as well as the lomo and chorizos. In the fish department, you can't go wrong with the gulf shrimp with smoked tomato butter and cornbread. The staff will help you pair your choices with just the right wines (the list is vast, so let them). Getting a seat at the bustling wine bar itself isn't easy, so try the separate cheese and charcuterie bar instead. Just remember: It gets loud and crowded the later it gets, so follow another local trend—the early-to-bed movement—and make reservations for earlier in the night.

Tapas. Dinner. Reservations recommended. Bar. $36-85

★★ANGELINI OSTERIA

7313 Beverly Blvd., Los Angeles, 323-297-0070; www.angeliniosteria.com

Angelini Osteria is a restaurant in the tradition of the true osteria, the Italian version of a local cantina. Opened in 2001 by chef Gino Angelini, this is the type of place where friends gather for good wine, tasty food and lively conversation. (Though the service can be a bit snooty, which can be a real buzzkill). For dinner, start with the grilled quail with guanciale, mixed baby greens and saba sauce, then move along to a pasta course of pumpkin tortelli with butter, sage and asparagus, and a second course of breaded veal chop alla Milanese with fritto of zucchini and eggplant. For the perfect finish, save room for a little ice cream affogato, a scoop of gelato drowned in a shot of espresso.

Italian. Lunch (Tuesday-Friday), dinner. Closed Monday. Bar. $36-85

★★★BLD
7450 Beverly Blvd., Los Angeles, 323-930-9744; www.bldrestaurant.com

Yes, BLD stands for "breakfast, lunch and dinner," but the offerings here are nothing so quotidian. The pancakes aren't just boring old buttermilk; they're blueberry-ricotta hotcakes with Berkshire maple syrup. Even better, they're served until 5 p.m. on the weekend, along with the rest of the still breakfasty menu, which offers such options as grapefruit brûlée and eggs Florentine. Lunch features delicious salads, sandwiches, burgers and pastas. Try the eggless egg salad sandwich with tofu, celery, red onion, lemon tofu aioli and oven dried tomato spread on multi-grain bread, or the blackened catfish sandwich with horseradish cole slaw, served with a side of Old Bay French fries. In the evening, get creative and go with the Self-Constructive Dinner; you choose a protein, like grilled flatiron steak; a side, like fresh polenta; and a sauce, like arugula pesto—and voila. A meal as easy as the restaurant's name.

American. Breakfast, lunch (Monday-Friday), dinner, Saturday-Sunday brunch. Reservations recommended. Bar. $16-35

★★★CAFÉ PINOT
700 W. Fifth St., Los Angeles, 213-239-6500; www.patinagroup.com/cafepinot

For light fare and a casual dining experience, Café Pinot is just the ticket. The restaurant is situated in the charming front garden of the Los Angeles Public Library, making it a natural choice for the business-lunch crowd. Office workers nibble tasty morsels such as the Maryland crab cake with sweet corn, roasted pepper and black olive relish, and the mustard-glazed rotisserie chicken with fries. But sports fans know that it's also a good spot for a pre-Lakers game dinner. Lunch includes a spa menu based on what's available from the farmers' market.

American. Lunch (Monday-Friday), dinner. Bar. $36-85

★★★CAMPANILE
624 S. La Brea Ave., Los Angeles, 323-938-1447; www.campanilerestaurant.com

Joined to the famed La Brea Bakery, Campanile is something of a mid-city oasis. Housed in a unique, historic structure built by Charlie Chaplin in 1929, the atmosphere is airy and functional, with faded-gray arched doorways, vaulted ceilings, concrete walls and plenty of natural light. But don't mistake an uncomplicated look for unsophisticated taste—in fact, this is an institution for people who are serious about good food. Owner and executive chef Mark Peel is a venerable name on the restaurant scene; he started out peeling vegetables for Wolfgang Puck and went on to open Spago with him in 1982. Peel still scours the local farmer's markets to make beautiful seasonal dishes, and you can taste his favorite finds in his special three-course Monday-night menus.

American, Mediterranean. Lunch (Monday-Friday), dinner (Monday-Saturday), Saturday-Sunday brunch. Reservations recommended. Bar. $36-85

★★LUNA PARK
672 S. La Brea Ave., Los Angeles, 323-934-2110; www.lunaparkla.com

With entertainment publications *Variety* and *The Hollywood Reporter* just down the street, you can bet that there's never a dull moment for eavesdropping on the lively media crowd, which congregates here for three-martini lunches and after-work cocktails. Like nearly every Los Angeles eatery, Luna Park has a nice selection of salads, but we think that some of the best items on the menu are about turn-a-blind-eye indulgence, so put away the calorie counter and order the warm goat cheese fondue appetizer, served with grilled bread and sliced apples. It pairs beautifully with the restaurant's award-winning mojito and the grilled cheezlitz, a grilled cheese sandwich served with mixed greens and tomato soup kept piping hot by a tiny tealight candle. The daily lunch specials are also hard to resist, especially the fried chicken with coleslaw and a buttermilk biscuit one every Tuesday. Good grub and drinks? Now there's something to talk about.

International. Lunch (Monday-Friday), dinner, Saturday-Sunday brunch. Bar. $16-35

★★★★PATINA
Walt Disney Concert Hall, 141 S. Grand Ave., Los Angeles, 213-972-3331; www.patinagroup.com/patina

There are those who still mourn the late, great neighborhood vibe of Patina in its former life on Melrose Avenue. While it has got fancy new digs at the Walt Disney Concert Hall, the haute cuisine here imagined by master chef Joachim Splichal is still exquisite. So go ahead and let the detractors complain—that just means you'll have more room to admire the undulating interior walls and seamless service. You can't go wrong with any of the daily or seasonal tasting menus, which may include a warm lobster salad with a barbecued corn sorbet or seared Kobe beef with root beer and avocado purée. And don't pass up dessert, with options like chocolate coulant cake with cane sugar honey, and housemade strawberry and tomato sorbet. Add to that a show at the Frank Gehry-designed concert venue, and your evening couldn't be more magical than if, you were a 6-year-old at Disneyland.

French. Dinner. Closed Monday. Hours may change during L.A. Philharmonic concerts. Reservations recommended. Bar. $36-85

★VERSAILLES
1415 S. La Cienega Blvd., Los Angeles, 310-289-0392;10319 Venice Blvd., Culver City, 310-558-3168; 17410 Ventura Blvd., Encino, 818-906-0756; 1000 N. Sepulveda Blvd., Manhattan Beach, 310-937-6829; Universal CityWalk, Hollywood, 100 Universal City Plaza, Universal City, 818-505-0093; www.versaillescuban.com

One of Los Angeles' most popular eateries, Versailles offers generous portions of savory Cuban dishes, such as fried fish and roasted garlic chicken, and nearly everything comes with sweet plantains, white rice and black beans. Regulars know to order the addictive Cuban-style roasted pork; it's

arguably one of the most flavorful dishes in the city, and people talk about it with reverence. On your way out, pick up a bottle of Versailles' famous garlic-citrus mojo sauce. It's what makes the roasted pork so special, and it lends a delightfully garlicky and savory flavor to just about anything.
Cuban. Lunch, dinner. Bar. $16-35

LOS ANGELES AREA CITIES
BEVERLY HILLS/BEL AIR
Surrounded by Bel-Air, Westwood, Century City and West Los Angeles, Beverly Hills might just be the most famous six square miles in the United States. It's a neighborhood of mansions, shops and restaurants that has come to symbolize the glitz and glam of Los Angeles.

Looking for movie stars? You'll find them here, or at least see the imposing gates and security cameras outside their glamorous mansions. The maps of the stars' homes are centered on these neighborhoods west of Hollywood and east of the ocean. Los Angeles' toniest addresses are in Beverly Hills, a separately incorporated city with a famous zip code (90210)—you know you've crossed over when blue street signs give way to white ones. It is home to some of the world's most exclusive shopping areas like Rodeo Drive and the Beverly Center. Bel Air is just as posh with some of the most expensive homes in the country.

WHAT TO SEE
MUSEUM OF TOLERANCE
Simon Wiesenthal Center, 9786 W. Pico Blvd., Beverly Hills, 310-553-8403;
www.museumoftolerance.com
When you go to the Museum Of Tolerance, you get a passport featuring the name and picture of a Jewish child who was in the Holocaust. Only at the end of the tour will you discover the heart-wrenching truth about whether or not "your child" survived the horrific ordeal. It's the most eye-opening experience at the museum, which aims to eradicate intolerance thorough education. The Museum uses powerful interactive devices like the passport to illuminate the various ways intolerance has affected and continues to affect society. Special sections are dedicated to archiving the events of the Holocaust, including video and audio presentations as well as like the letters of Anne Frank. After traveling back in time to World War II, you'll be transported back to present day when you visit the museum's Tolerancenter, where you'll learn about modern-day human rights abuses and come face to face with your own prejudices.
Admission: adults $15, seniors $12, children 5-18 $11, children under 5 free. Monday-Friday 10 a.m.-5 p.m., Sunday 11 a.m.-5 p.m. November-March: Friday 10 a.m.-3 p.m.

THE PALEY CENTER FOR MEDIA
465 N. Beverly Drive, Beverly Hills, 310-786-1000; www.mtr.org
If you get the shakes from TiVo withdrawal while on vacation, the Paley Center for Media (formerly known as the Museum of Television and Radio) might help. At this Beverly Hills institution, you can watch thousands of television programs from around the world or rediscover the lost art of radio. But

what the Paley Center does best is programming. The Paley Center's public programs allow visitors to poke the brains of all kinds of entertainment icons, from chef Giada De Laurentiis to actor Kenneth Branagh. To attend one of the Paley Center's events, make sure to get tickets well in advance. That'll give you a fix until you are reunited with your precious TiVo.

Suggested donation: adults $10, seniors and students $8, children under 14 $5. Wednesday-Sunday noon-5 p.m.

RODEO DRIVE
Rodeo Drive, between Wilshire and Santa Monica boulevards, Beverly Hills;
www.rodeodrive-bh.com

If you've never strolled down Beverly Hills' most famous street, then get ready to see designer duds and bling. A tour down Rodeo is like leafing through the pages of Vogue—Gucci, Prada, Fendi, Yves Saint Laurent, Dolce & Gabbana, Christian Dior, Valentino and Cartier are just a few of the names you'll see (and their selections are quite good, so it's worth it to check here if you've been looking for, say, a certain bag for some time). Afterward, swing by the Beverly Wilshire, A Four Seasons Hotel on nearby Wilshire Boulevard, where you can sit at the hotel's street-side patio and drink the afternoon away while you try to spot celebrities.

WHERE TO STAY
★★★AVALON HOTEL BEVERLY HILLS
9400 W. Olympic Blvd., Beverly Hills, 310-277-5221, 800-511-5743;
www.avalonbeverlyhills.com

Wandering into the Avalon Hotel is like taking a trip down Mid-Century modern memory lane, if Kelly Wearstler had been around back then for consultation. The famed interior designer's first pet hotel project is decked out in pieces by George Nelson, Isamu Noguchi and Charles Eames. Just around the corner from stellar shopping strip Beverly Drive (not to be confused with Beverly Boulevard) and staple lunch spot Urth Caffé, the Avalon combines retro-chic style with contemporary aesthetics. Hollywood A-listers and Beverly Hills execs seeking a bit of downtime sip sweet and savory martinis in cushy cabanas by the hourglass-shaped pool. Wearstler revised her original design in 2009 in everything from guest rooms to Oliverio (formerly Blue on Blue), the new restaurant featuring Italian cuisine such as handmade pastas from executive chef Mirko Paderno.

84 rooms. Restaurant, bar. Business center. Fitness center. Pool. $251-350

★★BEST WESTERN CARLYLE INN
1119 S. Robertson Blvd., Beverly Hills, 310-275-4445; www.carlyle-inn.com

While it's pretty far down on the stretch (a 10-minute drive at least), Best Western Carlyle Inn does lie on Robertson Boulevard. If you go north toward the hill, the street becomes fancier and finally turns into one of L.A.'s chicest casual shopping and dining areas, where paparazzi plant themselves outside Kitson and The Ivy restaurant just waiting for stars to emerge. The Carlyle holds a few surprises—it's got a tiny but colorful and cute lobby, and a complimentary breakfast buffet. As far as inexpensive places to crash in Beverly Hills go, this hotel is a tough one to beat.

32 rooms. Complimentary breakfast. Fitness center. Spa. $151-250

★★★★★THE BEVERLY HILLS HOTEL AND BUNGALOWS

9641 Sunset Blvd., Beverly Hills, 310-276-2251, 888-897-2804;
www.thebeverlyhillshotel.com

One of L.A.'s most enduring icons isn't some fame-starved ingenue or mysterious leading man—it's a stately, pale-pink-clad hotel on Sunset Boulevard. The Beverly Hills Hotel has been attracting guests (famous and not) since 1912, and its star power is by no means fading. While celebrities love the hotel for its private bungalows (perfect for canoodling and doing whatever else stars do), civilians love the tropical gardens (gorgeous) and the retro-style pool (movie-star chic). Guest rooms, which are bathed in soft hues, are kitted out in unique English furniture and marble baths. Once you've fully reveled in your good fortune (and the impeccable service and extra-comfy beds), make your way downstairs to the French-colonial inspired outdoor deck. Or take in the scene at the famous Polo Lounge, which still buzzes with handshakes and business deals, or the new Bar Nineteen 12, which has turned into a place to party with the beautiful and affluent people.

204 rooms. Restaurant, bar. Business center. Fitness center. Pool. Spa. $351 and up

★★★★THE BEVERLY HILTON

9876 Wilshire Blvd., 310-274-7777; www.beverlyhilton.com

The Beverly Hilton hosts the Golden Globes every January, but the hotel offers much more than a red carpet for stars to strut their stuff on. You'll be wowed by the lobby's mile-high ceiling, as well as its 1,400-gallon saltwater aquarium, but you'll be thankful for the hotel's pragmatism, too—you'll find ergonomic workstations and wireless Internet, even by the enormous Aqua Star Pool, which is usually filled with sunning executives. Guest rooms (decked out in serene beige-and-brown tones) also boast that nice balance between luxe and practical: For every luxurious amenity (pillow-top mattresses, Penhaligon's bath products), there's a state-of-the-art one (Bose music systems, 42-inch HDTV plasma TVs). In case you want to groom and pamper yourself like the nominees, Aqua Star Spa and Bellezza Salon are on hand and stocked with Sonya Dakar treatments. You'll look award-worthy, even if you're only going to the poolside Trader Vic's Lounge.

570 rooms. Restaurant, bar. Business center. Fitness center. Pool. Spa. $351 and up

★★★★THE BEVERLY WILSHIRE, A FOUR SEASONS HOTEL

9500 Wilshire Blvd., Beverly Hills, 310-275-5200, 800-819-5053; www.fourseasons.com

When Warren Beatty was a swinging bachelor, the Hollywood legend spent 15 years nesting in a palatial suite at the Beverly Wilshire (previously The Regent Beverly Wilshire). And thanks to a $35 million renovation and additions such as an ultra-sleek cocktail lounge and Wolfgang Puck's steakhouse CUT (designed by Richard Meier of Getty Center fame), the lavish 82-year-old historic grand hotel lures today's hottest celebrities, too. The rooms stay as hip as the clientele, with dark woods and moss-green accents. Make like a star and stroll just outside for a shopping spree at Chanel or Prada on Rodeo Drive, or nibble on a Dungeness crab cake by the pool.

395 rooms. Restaurant, bar. Business center. Fitness center. Pool. Spa. $351 and up

★★★THE CRESCENT

403 N. Crescent Drive, Beverly Hills, 310-247-0505; www.crescentbh.com

Ladies who lunch dripping in diamonds troll Rodeo Drive, but just a few blocks away are some of Beverly Hills' more quaint and quiet tree-lined streets. The Crescent sits pretty on one such block. Once a residence for silent film stars such as John Barrymore, Clara Bow and Mary Pickford, the property feels more like a grandiose home. You'll stroll between two palm trees up some steps, and past a boisterous but refined cocktail crowd chatting and snacking on delicious small bites on the left veranda and upon white leather couches and a shag rug inside. Boé Restaurant stretches outdoors to the right and just indoors, and is popular with local executives and guests, as great outdoor dining spaces are surprisingly not always easy to find in L.A. Votives lead the way upstairs to minimal black-and-white guest rooms, where you can listen to the loaner iPod mini.

35 rooms. Restaurant, bar. Pets accepted. $251-350

★★★★FOUR SEASONS HOTEL LOS ANGELES AT BEVERLY HILLS

300 S. Doheny Drive, Beverly Hills, 310-273-2222, 800-819-5053;
www.fourseasons.com

Sitting pretty on quaint tree-lined Doheny, the famous hotel feels like a part of the posh Beverly Hills neighborhood. But don't think the hotel is overrun by stodgy older folks—chic locals make up half the clientele at the lauded spa thanks to excellent facials, like a Kerstin Florian Caviar treatment. After nourishing your skin, do the same for your body. Sit outside at Cabana Restaurant, where chef Ashley James puts out simply flavored Mediterranean-inflected treats such as mahi mahi tacos or the seafood salad. Then sabotage those healthy California-style eats with a cocktail at the must-see Windows Lounge, where celebrity sightings are practically inevitable. A parade of movie junkets at the hotel attracts all entertainment industry types from journalists to actors, who retreat after work to peachy rooms with iPod docking stations, French doors that open to balconies and bathrooms complete with cushy terrycloth robes. With these perks, hardworking industry folks will want to be part of the neighborhood, too.

285 rooms. Restaurant, bar. Fitness center. Pool. Spa. $351 and up

HOTEL BEL-AIR

701 Stone Canyon Road, Los Angeles, 310-472-1211, 888-897-2804;
www.hotelbelair.com

Due to a major renovation, this historic hotel recently closed and is expected to open sometime in 2011. Look for completely refreshed décor, an expanded spa and updated dining options.

★★★MAISON 140 BEVERLY HILLS

140 S. Lasky Drive, Beverly Hills, 310-281-4000, 800-670-6182; www.maison140.com

Originally the apartment of silent film star Lillian Gish in 1939, Maison 140 now mirrors a Left Bank Parisian motel, courtesy of designer Kelly Wearstler. But it still retains a homey, residential feel. Once past the exterior's brick façade, you'll see Bar Noir, where sweet cocktails such as Lady Godiva (as in the chocolate) are plentiful. The lobby lounge—dressed in sultry black and red—is a heady mix of contemporary and vintage, with touches that include Lucite bar stools and mirrored Chinoiserie to crystal chandeliers and Gallic antiques. All the guest rooms—divided by either Parisian or Mandarin designation—showcase Joshua Elias abstracts, but each space is a bit different thanks to eclectic wallpaper and décor in unorthodox patterns, colors and shapes, giving them a certain je ne sais quoi.

43 rooms. Bar. Fitness center. $151-250

★★★★★MONTAGE BEVERLY HILLS

225 N. Canon Drive, Beverly Hills, 310-860-7800; www.montagebeverlyhills.com

A newly constructed resort hotel tucked just steps from the nexus of Beverly Hills, this Spanish Colonial revival-style complex is a luxurious oasis set in one of the country's most high-end neighborhoods. Opened in November 2008, Montage Beverly Hills features 201 rooms and suites designed to bring to life the glamour of the glory days of early Hollywood—from the hand-painted and gilded stucco ceilings throughout the hotel to the top-notch restaurants (there are two, Muse, a fine-dining spot and a more casual eatery, Parq) and white glove service. Rooms are grown up and refined in décor, with flat-screen TVs and spacious mosaic-tiled marble bathrooms, and they're a fine place to escape to. But it's the common areas at this hotel that impress. The rooftop pool, with its mosaic-tiled surface, private cabanas and views of L.A., is relaxing and comfortable, while the sprawling spa, with its men's, women's and unisex lounges and 17 treatment rooms, is the place for personal retreats.

.201 rooms. Restaurant, bar. Business center. Fitness center. Pool. Spa. Pets accepted. $351 and up

★★★★★THE PENINSULA BEVERLY HILLS

9882 S. Santa Monica Blvd., Beverly Hills, 310-551-2888; www.peninsula.com

While the luxe Peninsula is known for its old-school attention to service and swanky accommodations, it's all about the ultra-updated details, from electronic systems through which you control your room's lighting or temperature by pushing a bedside button to new Davi bath products, created by winemaker Robert Mondavi's grandson. On the re-hauled $4 million roof garden, poolside cabanas—surrounded by heated limestone tile flooring for year-round lounging—can be transformed into offices or massage treatment spaces. Opt for the latter, and the Wild Lime Scalp Treatment, a massage for the scalp, neck and shoulders, will lull you into a state of absolute bliss. If you're famished afterward, ignite those taste buds at The Belvedere. Gobble up fresh, farm-to-table delights such as spicy baked oysters with horseradish-parsnip purée and spinach lemon cream. For those seeking immersion into the local customs, the hotel also offers Peninsula Academy, where you can take culturally specific high-end classes out and about in L.A. in everything from movie making to surfing.

212 rooms. Restaurant, bar. Fitness center. Pool. Spa. $351 and up

★★★★★RAFFLES L'ERMITAGE BEVERLY HILLS

9291 Burton Way, Beverly Hills, 310-278-3344, 800-768-9009; www.raffles.com

The high-profile set hides out at Raffles L'Ermitage, a sanctuary that protects guests from prying eyes. The pool and spa are for guests only, which isn't always the case at L.A. hotels. This hotel sets itself apart by its intimate vibe and exclusivity. Each guest is given elegant, personal attention. The rooms are notoriously spacious with cutting-edge technology, large walk-in closets, English sycamore paneled walls and balconies overlooking lovely tree-lined Burton Way, so you might never want to leave (except maybe to swing into the nearby Christian Louboutin boutique). Behind the sparkling façade of twinkling blue lanterns dotting the trees outside, you can enjoy JAAN's updated Californian-French fusion cuisine indoors, at the private Pavilion or in the newly expanded patio garden. Privacy is top priority here, after all.

119 rooms. Restaurant, bar. Business center. Fitness center. Pool. Spa. Pets accepted. $351 and up

★★★THOMPSON BEVERLY HILLS

9360 Wilshire Blvd., Beverly Hills, 310-273-1400; www.thompsonbeverlyhills.com

Just as insiders know 60 Thompson as one of Manhattan's most elite hot spots, this West Coast sibling pulls in throngs of beautiful people. Images by famed fashion photographer Steven Klein abound amid soft-hued leather and wood décor, mixing California modernism with eclectic elements from the late '80s and '90s. As you enter the lobby, you can't (and shouldn't) miss L.A.'s annex of Jonathan Morr's famed Japanese eatery BondSt. Upstairs, platform beds in rich wood are finished with highly contrasted black-and-white bedding and unusual pieces like jet-black leather and mirrored headboards that extend to the ceiling. But you want to go where the action is. Head to the roof deck, named ABH (for Above Beverly Hills), where wood and greenery intermingle to create a Zen vibe surrounding a Swarovski-embedded pool. There you can get on-demand spa treatments, snacks and exotic cocktails.

107 rooms. Restaurant, bar. Fitness center. Pool. $351 and up

WHERE TO EAT

★★★THE BAZAAR

SLS Hotel at Beverly Hills, 465 S. La Cienega Blvd., Beverly Hills, 310-247-0400; www.thebazaar.com

Super-trendy Bazaar, located in the SLS hotel, is perhaps the most exciting restaurant in L.A. right now. The restaurant is divided into four sections: tapas bar, restaurant, bar and patisserie (and you can transfer your check to any part). The menu is also divided into modern and traditional tapas, and while they're both excellent, the modern tapas are thrilling. Take the foie gras lollipops, for example, in which a piece of foie gras is wrapped in vanilla-scented cotton candy. At first you experience the sweetness and aroma of the cotton candy, and then your mouth is filled with the cold and creamy foie gras. The "not your everyday Caprese" salad is, indeed, unlike any Caprese salad you've ever had—it's in a cup and you drink it. The watermelon "nigiri" is with hamachi, red wine, soy and jalapeno, and is another taste sensation. After dinner head over to the patisserie, decorated in a sugary pink as pretty as the confections lined up on the counter in front of the open kitchen, or to the sexy bar for a nightcap.

Tapas. Dinner. Bar. Reservations recommended. $36-85

★★★★THE BELVEDERE

The Peninsula Beverly Hills, 9882 S. Santa Monica Blvd., Beverly Hills, 310-788-2306;
www.beverlyhills.peninsula.com

One of Los Angeles' most venerable fine-dining restaurants, the acclaimed Belvedere at the Peninsula Beverly Hills has long catered to the city's most discerning crowd. Über-agencies CAA and ICM might have moved from their down-the-street digs to Century City, but the Belvedere dining room is still a deal-sealing destination in Beverly Hills serving exceptional modern American food. For a more laid-back experience, head there for Sunday brunch and grab a table on the cheerful patio, where you can sit amid flowers and trees and soak up the sun with a glass of Perrier Jouêt and the Peninsula's special croque madame (a rich combination of truffled brioche with aged country ham, fontina cheese and organic eggs).

Contemporary American. Breakfast, lunch, dinner, Sunday brunch. Reservations recommended. Bar. $86 and up

★★★BONDST

Thompson Beverly Hills, 9360 Wilshire Blvd., Beverly Hills, 310-601-2255;
www.thompsonhotels.com

Angelenos simply love their sushi restaurants, and now they can finally taste the goods of one of Manhattan's favorite sushi dens, Jonathan Morr's trendy BondSt (so trendy, its name pays no mind to punctuation or space bars), whose first West Coast foray is in the new Thompson Beverly Hills hotel. But BondSt is less about the sushi and more about the scene; expect lots of black-clad people who look like they work in the industry, and scads of pretty young things gabbing on their iPhones. But even scenesters have to eat sometime, and many go for the seaweed salad, a tongue teaser of an appetizer rife with varied, crunchy textures. Those who aren't in a decision-making mood should go with the omakase menu and let the chefs guide the meal; they're likely to suggest something unique that many Angelenos might never have considered—like the possibility that an East Coast import could become their favorite sushi destination (note: sushi is not served at lunch on the weekends).

Japanese. Breakfast, lunch, dinner. Bar. Reservations recommended. $36-85

★★CHAYA BRASSERIE

8741 Alden Drive, Beverly Hills, 310-859-8833; www.thechaya.com

After an especially long shopping session along nearby über-trendy Robertson Boulevard, Chaya feels like a comforting hug with its welcoming, skylight-illuminated dining room and airy French-Japanese cuisine. The roomy bar is a neighborhood hot spot; locals gather here for the lively happy hour. Sundays are another popular time, when a brunch entices Angelenos with eggs Benedict with smoked salmon and ricotta blueberry lemon pancakes. The best quick pick-me-ups are the pastries, made from scratch every day in the bakery upstairs—the dessert sampler, for one, which includes a fallen chocolate cake, warm chocolate croissant bread pudding and a French apple tart.

French, Japanese. Lunch (Monday-Friday), dinner, Sunday brunch. Bar. $16-35

★★CRAZY FISH
9105 W. Olympic Blvd., Beverly Hills, 310-550-8547

People have been lining up for a table at this casual sushi joint for years, and it's definitely not for its pastel 1990s décor or the soft-rock soundtrack. They come for the wide assortment of quirky and generous rolls, such as the sashimi tempura roll, which includes just about every kind of fish and is deep-fried to perfection. The ama ebi, or sweet shrimp, sashimi is another standout—with deep-fried shrimp heads included for an extra crunch. Japanese. Lunch (Monday-Friday), dinner. Bar. $16-35

★★★CRUSTACEAN
9646 Little Santa Monica Blvd., Beverly Hills, 310-205-8990; www.anfamily.com

Distinguished Vietnamese restaurant Crustacean, in the heart of Beverly Hills, is perhaps best known for its winding aquarium walkway and famous garlic noodles, but this gorgeous French Colonial-style eatery offers far more. Book a romantic dinner for two (with sommelier service) in the exclusive Opium Cellar, or make merry in the remodeled, Hanoi-chic main dining room. Menu favorites include the grilled rack of lamb flambéed in chardonnay, while the suit-and-tie crowd favors the healthful lunchtime "business express" menu, guaranteed to have you in and out in 45 minutes. Cocktails are a treat, too—we love the Beverly, made with fresh orange and pomegranate juices, peach Cointreau and a squeeze of lime. Vietnamese. Lunch (Monday-Friday), dinner. Bar. $36-85

★★★CUT
Beverly Wilshire, A Four Seasons Hotel, 9500 Wilshire Blvd., Beverly Hills, 310-276-8500; www.wolfgangpuck.com

Does Wolfgang Puck ever miss? Apparently not—the man's got another hit on his hands, this time with CUT, located in the posh Beverly Wilshire hotel across the street from the Rodeo Collection shopping center. Designed by celebrity architect Richard Meier of Getty Center fame, CUT is stark and sleek, with a skylight that plays up the moonlight glow after dark. The cuisine here is steakhouse fare with imagination, such as the starter of warm veal tongue, marinated artichokes, autumn shelling beans and salsa verde. Start with the Maryland blue crab and Maine lobster cocktail with spicy tomato horseradish, and follow it with the 14-ounce New York sirloin—it's Nebraska corn-fed and dry-aged for 35 days. And don't cut yourself off before dessert; the nougat semifreddo (Italian for "half-cold" or chilled) with strawberry sorbet and wild strawberries is superb. Steak. Dinner. Closed Sunday. Reservations recommended. Bar. $86 and up

★★★GRILL ON THE ALLEY
9560 Dayton Way, Beverly Hills, 310-276-0615

Although the Grill is in an alley near Wilshire Boulevard, you can simply follow the streams of fans filing in to find it. Modeled after the great grills of New York and San Francisco, the focus is on classic American food, including steaks and comfort foods like chicken pot pie, meatloaf and pasta dishes. The décor is also classic American, with mirrored walls, large chandeliers, dark wood flooring and semi-private booths. Steak. Lunch, dinner. $36-85.

★★★IL CIELO
9018 Burton Way, Beverly Hills, 310-276-9990; www.ilcielo.com

It makes sense that countless pricey weddings have taken place in this Beverly Hills institution, which opened in 1986. Arguably the most romantic restaurant in Los Angeles, Il Cielo is deserving of its name, which means "the sky," because patrons dine in the outdoor garden beneath the open blue and a canopy of twinkling lights. Dining here will put you in the mood for love—it seems that every couple in the place makes eyes at each other over plates of housemade pasta and focaccia—so give in and order the antipasto Il Cielo, described as "good for two."

Italian. Lunch, dinner. Reservations recommended. Bar. $36-85

★★IL PASTAIO
400 N. Canon Drive, Beverly Hills, 310-205-5444; www.giacominodrago.com

Master chef Celestino Drago and his brother, executive chef and partner Giacomino Drago, are dead serious about pasta. If it takes more than the bottle-necking crowd engulfing the host to convince you, all you'll need is a bite of the mezzelune—a platter of housemade half-moon ravioli stuffed with lobster and topped with finely-diced zucchini and yet more lobster—to turn you into a believer. So secure a reservation, get seated, and order from the a la carte menu or opt for the chef's six-course tasting menu, which comes with a little bit of everything: soup; salad; ravioli; your choice of pasta or risotto; meat or fish; and, of course, a housemade dessert or ice cream (selections change daily).

Italian. Lunch, dinner. $16-35

★★THE IVY
113 N. Robertson Blvd., Beverly Hills, 310-274-8303

The Ivy is a Los Angeles institution, and we're not just saying that because celebrities are seen leaving here all the time. The restaurant is located on a strip of Robertson Boulevard that's home to some of the most unique boutiques in the city, which is why you'll often spot paparazzi trolling the sidewalk for a glimpse of the latest "it girls" as they power-lunch over salads and cocktails (and not much else). Despite the circus, the Ivy maintains a surprisingly laid-back ambiance, complete with a white picket fence surrounding the patio, which is adorned with flowers that the owners grow in their gardens at home. The reliable menu includes standbys such as the melt-in-your-mouth lobster ravioli, which co-owner and executive chef Richard Irving makes by hand every day.

American. Lunch, dinner. Reservations recommended. Bar. $86 and up

★★LA PAELLA
476 S. San Vicente Blvd., Los Angeles, 323-951-0745; www.usalapaella.com

La Paella is about as homey and charming an eatery as you could ask for, with quaint trinkets lining the walls and a staff that's sure to make you feel welcome. The terrific tapas menu—packed with tasty hot options like the patatas bravas (fried potatoes tossed with spicy tomato sauce) and cold ones like aceitunas rellenas (traditional Spanish olives stuffed with anchovies)—makes it difficult to save room for the main course. But exercise a little restraint nonetheless, because you don't want to miss the paella Valencia mixta, which tosses saffron, meat, vegetables, seafood, rosemary and red peppers into an aromatic, tasty dish. You'll probably be stuffed after that, but throw caution to the wind and order the light, orange-kissed delicate flan de naranja.

Spanish-Mediterranean. Lunch (Monday-Friday), dinner. Closed Sunday. Bar. $16-35

★★MAKO

225 S. Beverly Drive, Beverly Hills, 310-288-8338; www.makorestaurant.com

For epicures craving a meal with more variety than that of your usual sushi restaurant, head to five-year-old Mako. The simply designed restaurant—the space is bathed in soft lighting and outfitted with blond wood walls—offers a small-plates menu of ippin-ryouri, or individually sized portions; they allow diners to pick and choose from executive chef Makoto Tanaka's mouth-watering contemporary Asian dishes. Standouts include Mako's version of pad thai and the bluefin tuna sashimi served with mixed greens, avocado and jalapeño with soy olive oil dressing. Mako also offers multiple-course bento boxes to go; they make for a delightful picnic dinner at the Hollywood Bowl.

Contemporary Asian. Lunch (Tuesday-Friday), dinner. Closed Sunday-Monday. Reservations recommended. Bar. $36-85

★★★MASTRO'S STEAKHOUSE

246 N. Canon Drive, Beverly Hills, 310-888-8782; www.mastrossteakhouse.com

Looking for good grub with a side of classic L.A. mayhem? Then head to this reliable steakhouse, which is equal parts food and scene. Mastro's two floors are dimly lit and on the noisy side; the first floor is decidedly old school, but the upstairs is livelier, with a central bar packed with Hollywood ingénues and the hangers-on who dote on them. Once you figure out where you fit in, take a seat and start with the seafood tower; it's always fresh and loaded with succulent oysters, shrimp, crab legs and the like. The point of a meal at Mastro's, of course, is the steak, which arrives perfectly cooked on a piping-hot plate, and goes beautifully with the gorgonzola mac and cheese.

Steak. Dinner. Reservations recommended. Bar. $86 and up

★★MR. CHOW

344 N. Camden Drive, Beverly Hills, 310-278-9911; www.mrchow.com

One of Michael Chow's six famed Mr. Chow locations, this 36-year-old Beverly Hills stalwart is kitted out in a stark black-and-white color scheme, complete with checkered floor and soaring vaulted ceilings, and remains one of the most striking (if not vaguely '80s) dining rooms in town. What's more, Mr. Chow is still one of Los Angeles' most notable see-and-be-seen restaurants for high-powered Hollywood types (hence the throngs of paparazzi outside), which means that often it's more about the people-watching than the food. If you drop in on an off night, shift your focus to solid signature dishes such as the green prawns sautéed with peppers and cashews, and lobster served fresh from a live tank.

Chinese. Lunch (Monday-Friday), dinner. Bar. Reservations recommended. $36-85

★★★★MUSE

Montage Beverly Hills, 225 N. Canon Drive, Beverly Hills, 310-860-7800;
www.montagebeverlyhills.com

Ascend an elegant stairway to find this mahogany lined and intimate restaurant. Sit near the railing and hear the lively piano player from the neighboring hotel lounge. Chef John Cuevas selects only the freshest seasonal items to create the menu at this innovative American restaurant. Dishes might include a poached farm fresh egg with thick and crispy pork belly and Parmesan; or plate of seared scallops with braised bacon and an unusual popcorn tuile. The chef has a delicate hand with fresh seafood, such as the line caught Loup De Mer with cuttlefish and Spanish sausage. Finish with desserts such as Greek yogurt cake with lemon basil and peaches, and served with honey ice milk, or the heirloom chocolate tart made with frozen chocolate brittle, caramel krispies and aged rum.

American. Dinner. Closed Sunday-Monday. Reservations recommended. $86 and up

★NATE 'N AL DELICATESSEN RESTAURANT

414 N. Beverly Drive, Beverly Hills, 310-274-0101; www.natenal.com

For more than half a century, Nate 'n Al has been one of the city's go-to spots for classic deli food, from Reubens and melts to corned beef hash and smoked whitefish. The diner's Formica-heavy décor, deli counter and charismatic servers in kitschy uniforms have remained unapologetically the same all these years, and customers wouldn't have it any other way.

American. Breakfast, lunch, dinner. Bar. $16-35

★★★★ORTOLAN

8338 W. Third St., Beverly Hills, 323-653-3300; www.ortolanrestaurant.com

Executive chef Christophe Émé may be better known as the husband of sultry blond actress Jeri Ryan, but gourmands know him from his years at L'Orangerie. His wife's sex appeal may have rubbed off on the couple's restaurant Ortolan, with its cream-colored tufted banquettes, cozy fireplace and a bevy of sparkling chandeliers, but it's Émé's haute cuisine (along with stellar service) that keeps patrons coming back for more. Named after a rare bird historically eaten as a delicacy in the south of France, Ortolan offers tempting à la carte options such as the signature scrambled eggs with caviar and two prix fixe menus—appropriately dubbed Seduction and Plaisir, which is French for "pleasure."

French. Dinner. Closed Sunday-Monday. Reservations recommended. Bar. $36-85

★★★POLO LOUNGE

The Beverly Hills Hotel, 9641 Sunset Blvd., Beverly Hills, 310-276-2251;
www.thebeverlyhillshotel.com

There are few more pleasant ways to while away a summer evening than by sitting amid the carefully tended garden on the patio of the Polo Lounge, cocktail in hand, while live jazz plays in the background. Located at the Beverly Hills Hotel, where Cary Grant's tuxedo collar still hangs on the wall, the Polo Lounge remains a place for deal-making businessmen. The rest of the crowd—keen on classics such as the roasted prime beef tenderloin, braised short rib and pan-seared diver scallops—is more old-Hollywood than new, which makes for a classy atmosphere befitting the historic digs any time of the year.

American. Breakfast, lunch, dinner, Sunday brunch. Reservations recommended. $36-85

THE RESTAURANT AT HOTEL BEL-AIR

Hotel Bel-Air, 701 Stone Canyon Road, Bel Air, 310-472-5234; ww.hotelbelair.com

Due to a major renovation to the Hotel Bel-Air, this classic restaurant will be closed until mid-2011. Check back then for updated interiors and new menus—the classic, polished service will remain the same.

★★★SPAGO BEVERLY HILLS

176 N. Canon Drive, Beverly Hills, 310-385-0880; www.wolfgangpuck.com

Wolfgang Puck is perhaps the most recognizable name in and outside of the culinary world, and Spago Beverly Hills is the flagship of his empire. This Los Angeles institution continues to draw the biggest names in town, from Tom Cruise to Sidney Poitier. Celebs pack the house nightly, looking to talk show business and indulge in the fine American cuisine from executive chef Lee Hefter, who uses only fresh (and often local) produce on the seasonal menu. Famous restaurateur and interior designer Barbara Lazaroff created the elegant and colorful dining room, where patrons enjoy the likes of iced Kumamoto and Fanny Bay oysters, grilled prime New York steak and, of course, Puck's signature pizzas.

American. Lunch (Monday-Saturday), dinner. Bar. $86 and up

ALSO RECOMMENDED

PARQ

Montage Beverly Hills, 225 N. Canon Drive, Beverly Hills, 310-860-7800; www.montagebeverlyhills.com

Taking a cue from the hotel in which it is housed, Parq is a sunny spot located inside the Spanish Colonial-inspired Montage Beverly Hills, filled with mosaic tiles and large windows. You can dine outside on the patio overlooking the gardens or inside in one of the large half-moon booths. A mix of studio executives, creative types meeting over breakfast and a variety of guests come here to dine on the creative American cuisine, which runs the gamut from heavenly pancakes for breakfast to the juicy Parq burger at lunch and comfort foods like flaky lobster pot pies for dinner. Afterward, make time for a drink at the cozy bar, which specializes in classic cocktails. Service is crisp and professional, making a visit here even more enjoyable.

American. Breakfast, lunch, dinner. Bar. $36-85

SPAS

★★★AQUA STAR SPA AT THE BEVERLY HILTON

The Beverly Hilton, 9876 Wilshire Blvd., Beverly Hills, 310-887-6048; www.beverlyhilton.com

A star spa calls for a star skincare line. Facial treatments here exclusively use the botanical-based products of Sonya Dakar, who has spent 30 years working with celebrity skin, making sure stars like Gwyneth Paltrow and

SHOPPING TOUR: BEVERLY HILLS

Even if people don't chase you down for an autograph, spending a day in Beverly Hills can make you feel like a star (and, by the end of the day, you'll certainly be dressed like one). However, to get the most out of your day in this most famous of zip codes, you'll need a game plan.

First, fuel up at Nate 'n Al Delicatessen Restaurant in the form of a bagel and smoked whitefish or any of the other classic deli items on the menu. Next, go south from the deli to hit up the ritzy enclave's smaller, independent boutiques first, including Planet Blue (409 N. Beverly Drive, Los Angeles, 310-385-0557; www.shopplanetblue.com).

Keep heading south from Planet Blue to Taschen (354 N. Beverly Drive, 310-274-4300; www.taschen.com), an upscale bookstore, then go across the street to Gearys Beverly Hills (351 N. Beverly Drive, 310-273-4741; www.gearys.com) where you'll find a well-edited selection of jewelry.

Take a break for some pampering at The Spa at Beverly Wilshire (9500 Wilshire Blvd., 310-385-7023; www.fourseasons.com/beverlywilshire), just keep trekking south until you get to Wilshire Boulevard, then hang a right. The spa's High Heel Appeal ($80) relieves tired legs with a 20-minute treatment that includes a foot soak, exfoliation and massage. Afterward, you don't have to walk far (or even out of the building) for lunch. Sit down for some eats at Wolfgang Puck's CUT, with skylighting that allows you to enjoy your 14-ounce Nebraska corn-fed New York sirloin beneath sunny rays.

Now it's time to walk over to the stores that are a must-shop for any fashionista worth her Jimmy Choos. Head west on Wilshire and scour the racks of Saks Fifth Avenue (9600 Wilshire Blvd., 310-275-4211;) and Neiman Marcus (9700 Wilshire Blvd., 310-550-5900; www.neimanmarcus.com).

After your warm-up at the department stores, it's time to let loose on California's shopping mecca: Rodeo Drive. Make your way back toward the Beverly Wilshire, head north on Rodeo and start gawking at the gorgeous garb in the shop windows. Start at Tiffany & Co. (210 N. Rodeo Drive, 310-273-8880; www.tiffany.com) to take home a sparkly souvenir in one of those trademark blue boxes. You can opt to go on a detour through Via Rodeo, a cute little European-inspired cobblestone street lined with haute shops such as Versace. Otherwise, keep going north on Rodeo, stopping at big-name shops such as Louis Vuitton, Dolce & Gabbana and Prada, which are all lined up next to each other. Keep going north and spend the rest of the afternoon and early evening browsing Chanel, Hermès and Ralph Lauren.\

Right along the Drive among all the shops, you'll find the Rodeo Collection shopping center (421 N. Rodeo Drive; www.rodeocollection.net). Enter the mini-mall, one of the few in Beverly Hills, and check out BCBG Max Azria, La Perla and Stuart Weitzman. When you're all shopped out, grab a bite at the white, mustard and dark-wood-filled Prime Grill (310-860-1233; www.theprimegrill.com), a kosher steakhouse. Take a seat in one of the sunken booths, but leave the gossamer purple curtains open; you'll want to peer out while you sip your kosher wine and gnaw on your carnivorous meal (you can get a juicy steak, but since you likely gobbled one for lunch, order from the extensive sushi dinner menu) and see if you spot any celebrities.

Fergie are always ready for their close-ups. This all-natural line of moisturizers, masks, age-renewing gels and more is made from ingredients like green tea extract, ginger root, almond and omega-3 oils. Aqua Star's team will whip up just the right potion for your complexion. No matter your skin type, you can't go wrong with the Flawless Facial ($170), which includes a deep cleanse, exfoliation and moisture mask. It'll leave you looking camera-ready.

★★★★THE BEVERLY HILLS HOTEL SPA BY LA PRAIRIE

The Beverly Hills Hotel, 9641 Sunset Blvd., Beverly Hills, 310-887-2505;
www.thebeverlyhillshotel.com

In a town where face-lifts are as common as Fendi bags, a spa like La Prairie, which focuses on anti-aging treatments, is an in-demand destination for those looking for a little pampering without the pain. The spacious spa caters to both the elegant old-money elite as well as young spa addicts who love to spoil themselves. You, too, can indulge in the high life with a luxe treatment like the Caviar Intensive Eye Lift ($100), which uses real roe to help reduce fine lines and dark circles. Fish eggs on your face may seem unappetizing, but the rich proteins in the caviar are said to boost collagen production. To really fight Mother Nature (or crow's feet), the 60-minute Microdermabrasion Facial ($300) blasts away dead skin (and with it, fine lines) to reveal a super-smooth surface that makes you look younger. Seek relief in the Jet Lag Therapy Package ($415), which includes 30 minutes of aromatherapy massage, 30 minutes of foot/hand reflexology and a 30-minute de-stressing facial.

★★★★THE PENINSULA SPA

The Peninsula Beverly Hills, 9882 S. Santa Monica Blvd., Beverly Hills, 310-712-5288,
800-462-7899; www.beverlyhills.peninsula.com

Marilyn confirmed for us the obvious: Diamonds are a girl's best friend. But at the Peninsula, ladies (and gents) can get their fill of rubies, emeralds and sapphires, too. The spacious indoor/outdoor spa is the first in North America to use Shiffa precious gem oils, which contain micro-fine fragments of the aforementioned sparklers. The Shiffa services on the menu ($195-$385)—massages and body scrubs—can be customized with your gem of choice, each of which comes with its own special healing powers: Diamond is for balance and harmony, emerald for stability and strength, ruby for stimulation and vitality, and sapphire for peace and tranquility. We're not sure if all that bling actually works wonders on your skin (let's face it, some of these treatments were created for the very rich, who get very bored), but a scrub-down with diamond dust sure feels luxurious.

★★★★THE SPA AT BEVERLY WILSHIRE

Beverly Wilshire, 9500 Wilshire Blvd., Beverly Hills,310-385-7023;
www.fourseasons.com

A lot of spas deal in luxury for the sake of luxury. This retreat specializes in treatments most of us really need. In addition to a range of massages, facials and body treatments, the spa offers a special rub-down for stiletto-worshippers (the High Heel Appeal, $80)—a massage designed to soothe four-inch-heel-addicted feet and legs. There's also the Techie Neck ($80), a stretching massage that goes to work on the place where most of us hold our tension. And for the super stressed (who says shopping all day on Rodeo isn't stressful?), there's the Mind Unwind ($80), a pressure-points-targeted scalp massage along with a neck and shoulder rub that aims to relieve the sinuses and help you focus.

★★★★THE SPA AT FOUR SEASONS HOTEL LOS ANGELES

Four Seasons Hotel Los Angeles at Beverly Hills, 300 S. Doheny Drive, Beverly Hills,310-786-2229; www.fourseasons.com/losangeles

The Four Seasons in Beverly Hills is the place for celebs and industry business (someone is always taping an interview somewhere in the hotel). The concierge service will cater to your every whim, not only letting you choose the type of massage you'd like but where you'd like to have it. In your suite? In one of the outdoor cabanas? Word is that celebs love the all-over body polishes. The traditional Turkish Scrub ($165) is applied in two steps: For the first, a mix of thermal salts and minerals are rubbed into clean skin. Then comes the loofah, which leaves no dead skin cell behind.

★★★★SPA MONTAGE

Montage Beverly Hills, 225 N. Canon Drive, Beverly Hills, 310-860-7800; www.montagebeverlyhills.com

This sprawling spa housed in the luxury Spanish-style Montage Beverly Hills offers a variety of relaxing—and effective—treatments in a peaceful and glamorous environment. The 17 individual treatment rooms are decorated like lavish suites in a private house, with mosaic tiles, plush, padded treatment tables and deep club chairs for relaxing post-treatment. Massages and facials can be tailored to your needs, and the water therapies, will wash away all your troubles and can be tacked on to any treatment. Before a massage, try a hydrotherapy bath with essential oils and underwater massage to loosen you up. Afterwards, put your locks in the very capable hands of the stylists at the onsite Kim Vo salon (he's famous for coloring the tresses of Goldie Hawn, Britney Spears and scores of other stars). The fitness center is brimming with cutting-edge machines, freeweights and more, and private or group pilates and yoga classes are also available.

CENTURY CITY/WESTWOOD/CULVER CITY

Century City is a corridor of office buildings, apartments and hotels. Westwood is the home of UCLA, while Culver City, south of the 10 Highway, is L.A.'s newest dining scene. A revitalization plan has brought live theater, cineplexes and dozens of exciting new restaurants to Culver's city center.

WHAT TO SEE
HAMMER MUSEUM

10899 Wilshire Blvd., Westwood, 310-443-7000; www.hammer.ucla.edu

While it's technically not on the UCLA Campus, the Hammer Museum is under the jurisdiction of the university, so if you're taking a tour around the campus, be sure to include the Hammer in your itinerary. The museum's permanent art collection features heavyweights like Claude Monet, Camille Pissarro, Vincent van Gogh and Rembrandt van Rijn. Otherwise, the Hammer is very much dedicated to featuring revolutionary contemporary art—the museum's ongoing "Hammer Projects" exhibitions highlight the work of up-and-coming artists. But what makes the Hammer unique is its eclectic free programming. The museum attracts literary minds such as Joan Didion and James Ellroy, as well as creative powerhouses such as Oliver Stone, Miranda July and Brian Grazer. As if that weren't enough, you can watch cinematic treasures from the UCLA Film & Television Archive in the Billy

Wilder Theater, and hear everything from progressive jazz to indie rock in the museum's courtyard.

Admission: adults $7, seniors $5, children under 17 and students free. Free Thursday. Tuesday-Wednesday, Friday-Saturday 11 a.m.-7 p.m., Thursday 11 a.m.-9 p.m., Sunday 11 a.m.-5 p.m.

MILDRED MATHIAS BOTANICAL GARDEN

UCLA Campus, at Hilgard and Le Conte avenues, Westwood, 310-825-1260;
www.botgard.ucla.edu

Smack-dab in the middle of the bustle of Westwood is a real oasis: the Mildred E. Mathias Botanical Garden. This seven-acre garden is a good choice for those who don't want to make the long trek to the L.A. Arboretum. The garden was started in 1929, around the same time that UCLA began classes in Westwood, and is still used for some botanical experiments, although today the garden mostly serves as a peaceful place for visitors to enjoy. Walk among 5,000 different species, including tropical and sub-tropical plants, and be sure to stroll the garden's Metasequoia (the tallest dawn redwoods in North America) and its Eucalyptus grandis trees, planted here more than 40 years ago, long before the trees popped up all over the region.

Admission: free. Monday-Friday 8 a.m.-5 p.m. (in winter months, until 4 p.m.), Saturday 8 a.m.-4 p.m.

SONY PICTURES STUDIO TOUR

10202 W. Washington Blvd., Culver City, 310-244-8687;
www.sonypicturesstudiostours.com

Sony Pictures Studios will show you behind-the-scenes Hollywood. But don't expect to spy any movie stars strolling around the lot. Instead, you may see the sets of Jeopardy! and Wheel of Fortune, sans Alex Trebek and Vanna White, that is. You'll also get a chance to look at Academy Awards earned by films like Lawrence of Arabia; it's not the most exciting part of the tour, unless you happen to love a nice piece of hardware. Be prepared: This is a two-hour walking tour. So, if you're looking to sit back and relax on a tram ride, you're better off going to Universal Studios.

Tours: $28. Monday-Friday 9:30 a.m., 10:30 a.m., 1:30 p.m. and 2:30 p.m.

WHERE TO STAY

★★★HOTEL PALOMAR LOS ANGELES-WESTWOOD

10740 Wilshire Blvd., Westwood, 310-475-8711; www.hotelpalomar-lawestwood.com

They say that art imitates life, but at the new Hotel Palomar Los Angeles-Westwood, hospitality imitates film. Event spaces have been named for festivals, ranging from Sundance to Cannes and even Outfest, while casting couches in each room and planned movie breaks with popcorn go all but overboard with the theme. Guest rooms ignite neutral tones like charcoal and chocolate with striking accents of turquoise and patterns evoking everything from peacock feathers to French bordello-chic florals. Accents include with black faux fur throws, iHome docking stations, in-room Kerstin Florian spa treatments and, in the bathroom, spa tubs and L'Occitane products. Head to buzzed-about restaurant BLVD 16, where chef Simon Dolinky serves seasonal specials such as white corn ravioli stuffed with Maine lobster and roasted mushrooms, using sustainable, organic produce from local farms. The green doesn't stop there, as the hotel chain has gone eco-friendly with recycling bins in the rooms, new energy and water-conservation mechanisms. Suddenly, saving the world is easier than it seems in the movies.

268 rooms. Restaurant, bar. Fitness center. Pool. Pets accepted. $351 and up

★★★HYATT REGENCY CENTURY PLAZA
2025 Avenue of the Stars, Century City, 310-228-1234; www.hyatt.com

When presidents come to town, they check into the enormous Hyatt Regency Century Plaza. After just completing a significant renovation, the swanky spot now features brand-new suites, which include the use of the Regency Club, a private lounge with complimentary refreshments as well as a new pool and pool deck with posh cabanas. You can hang out in the new Lobby Court and Patio for afternoon coffee or evening cocktails, or hit the new X bar to nibble on tapas amid outdoor fire pits and greenery. The best perk is the adjoining multi-tiered Equinox Fitness Club + Spa, the company's West Coast flagship gym (although there is a $20 fee to access the club, unless you have a spa treatment booked). The cutting-edge classes and some of the city's best aestheticians offering almost a dozen different massage techniques draw high-level executives from surrounding offices, but it's also fit for a commander-in-chief.

726 rooms. Restaurant, bar. Business center. Fitness center. Pool. Spa. $351 and up

★★★INTERCONTINENTAL LOS ANGELES CENTURY CITY
2151 Avenue of the Stars, Century City, 310-284-6500, 877-348-2424;
www.intercontinental.com

The InterContinental sits among Century City's swank high-rises, housing major agencies such as CAA and ICM and entertainment bigwigs like 20th Century Fox. Executives often powwow at the Park Grill over organic California cuisine and at Park Grill Lounge, where cocktails are named for Fox characters and programs, including the American Idoltini and the Jack Bauer and Coke (after *24*, if you've been living under a rock). But another reason to visit the hotel is the Spa InterContinental. Treatment rooms lie within three villas, each of which include an Infiniti Kohler jet tub, shower, flat-screen TV, lounging area and outdoor patio; guests are greeted with a signature aromatherapy ritual in order to de-stress before their treatment. If you don't feel like fighting for swimming space in the new pool, plunge into your oversized in-room tub instead.

364 rooms. Restaurant, bar. Business center. Fitness center. Pool. Spa.$351 and up

★★★W LOS ANGELES – WESTWOOD
930 Hilgard Ave., Westwood, 310-208-8765; www.starwoodhotels.com

Adrift in Westwood's sea of UCLA students, chain restaurants and nondescript luncheonettes, the W is incongruously trendy. You'll wander from the elaborately sleek lobby, past the outdoor Backyard café to the retro-chic pool area, full of sunglasses-clad cool kids, and wonder how this scene landed amid so many sub shops. Stroll over to the nearby weekly Thursday Farmers' Market for fresh fruit and tamales and to snag finds such as ridiculously inexpensive and Diddy Riese cookies (grab an ice-cream cookie sandwich), but the W is mostly a self-contained experience, complete with summer poolside film screenings, hipster lobby art openings, Bliss Spa treatments and Whiskey Blue cocktail hours. Thom Filicia of *Queer Eye for the Straight Guy* helmed a recent redesign of bungalow rooms and poolside cabanas (hooked up with "Intellichaise" technology, so sun worshippers can order refreshments and peruse local offerings without effort). New executive chef Monique King elevates food at eateries NINETHIRTY and The Backyard— the latter is a perfect outdoor spot to sip a cocktail.

258 rooms. Restaurant, bar. Fitness center. Pool. Spa. $$$$

WHERE TO EAT

★★LA CACHETTE

10506 Santa Monica Blvd., Los Angeles, 310-470-4992; www.lacachetterestaurant.com

Only a tried-and-true L.A. staple like La Cachette, beloved for its fine French cuisine, could have survived the upheaval that Santa Monica Boulevard has undergone in recent years. But you no longer have to navigate major roadwork to dine at this lauded establishment from chef-owner Jean Francois Meteigner. Start with the decadent sautéed foie gras with brioche, rhubarb gelee and pearl, and follow up with the country dish of the week (whatever it is, it won't disappoint). Try to catch one of La Cachette's "Cooking with Jean Francois" classes while you're in town, so you can re-create some of his mouthwatering morsels at home, as often as you like.

French. Lunch (Monday-Friday), dinner. Closed Sunday. Reservationsrecommended. Bar. $86 and up

★★TENGU

10853 Lindbrook Drive, Westwood, 310-209-0071; www.tengu.com

Being a college town—Westwood is home to plenty of inexpensive California roll sushi joints. But for something hip and upscale (and not exactly fit for a college-student budget), Tengu is the place. With bamboo accents, mood lighting, shoji screen partitions and DJs spinning mellow but uptempo tunes, the vibe here is equal parts Zen and lounge. For libations, opt for the signature house sake, which is infused with fresh Maui pineapples; it makes for the ideal counterbalance to the standout sashimi picante, a tuna, yellowtail and salmon trio with jalapeño and ginger-garlic ponzu sauce.

Japanese. Lunch (Monday-Friday), dinner. Bar. $36-85

★SUNNIN LEBANESE CAFE

1779 Westwood Blvd., Westwood,310-477-2358; 5110 E. Second St., Long Beach, 562-433-9000; www.westwood.sunnin.com

For authentic, delicious and reasonably priced Lebanese fare, there's no place like the tiny, spare Sunnin. The restaurant is owned and run by "famous chef, much-loved Em Toni" (according to the menu), and after tasting the falafel here, you'll feel the love. (That, and the fact that on several occasions, she can be spotted toiling over an enormous rotating vertical spit of her mouthwatering beef shawarma.) The only thing you may not be so crazy about is the parking here, which is nearly impossible. Then again, it may just signal that the menu was right on the fame thing, too.

Lebanese. Lunch, dinner. $16-35

SPA
★★★THE SPA AT EQUINOX CENTURY CITY
Hyatt Regency Century Plaza, 10220 Constellation Blvd., Century City, 310-286-2900; www.equinoxfitness.com

If you've been to an Equinox gym, you know it's a great place to get in a workout. At this location, you can also head to the attached spa afterward to relax. For a great post-workout treatment, try the Lemon Sugar Body Polish ($70), a body scrub, which uses raw cane crystals and lemon to give you baby soft and glowing skin. Or try the Body Melt ($210), a customized wrap/massage/detox treatment that's supposed to shed inches from flab-prone areas: you choose to focus on your abs, glutes, arms, chest or thighs. We've never taken out a tape measure afterward to see if it actually works, but 80 minutes of targeted treatment does have a way of making you feel "lighter."

HOLLYWOOD
Films are rarely made in Hollywood anymore, but that doesn't stop visitors from flocking to the corner of Hollywood and Vine, gawking at the cement prints of the stars in front of Grauman's Chinese Theatre or hunting for their favorite celebrities along the Walk of Fame. Once a year, the red carpet goes down in front of the gorgeous Kodak Theatre for the Academy Awards; on the other 364 days, the Hollywood & Highland entertainment complex is the central attraction in an otherwise seedy neighborhood. It's also an excellent place to take a photograph with the famous Hollywood sign in the background.

WHAT TO SEE
BARNSDALL ART PARK
4808 Hollywood Blvd., Hollywood; www.barnsdallartpark.com

Heiress Aline Barnsdall donated the Barnsdall Art Park to the city in the 1920s to provide an arts center for the community, and that she did. The park's biggest attraction is the Hollyhock House, which was designed for Barnsdall by Frank Lloyd Wright. The house, which was inspired by the architecture of Colombia's Mayan temples, was Wright's first project in Los Angeles. The architect specifically designed the structure with Southern California's climate in mind, but Hollyhock still manages to evoke his signature style. Besides touring Hollyhock House, you can peruse artworks at the wonderful Los Angeles Municipal Art Gallery, see Shakespeare in the park and catch a show at the Barnsdall Gallery Theatre, a low-priced rental house for theater, dance, music and more. The park also overlooks the city of Los Angeles, providing beautiful views.

Hollyhock House Tours: adults $7, seniors $3, children 17 and under $2. Wednesday-Sunday 12:30 p.m., 1:30 p.m., 2:30 p.m. and 3:30 p.m.

CBS TELEVISION CITY
7800 Beverly Blvd., Hollywood, 323-575-2458

The West Coast studios of CBS Television is the source of many of its network telecasts. Write for free tickets well in advance (specify dates and shows preferred) and enclose a self-addressed, stamped envelope. Tickets may also be picked up at the information window (daily) on a first-come,

first-served basis. Age limits for admittance vary and are specified on tickets; children under 16 not admitted to any broadcast.
Monday-Friday.

GRAUMAN'S CHINESE THEATRE

6925 Hollywood Blvd., Hollywood, 323-464-8111; www.manntheatres.com/chinese
Grauman's Chinese Theatre is the heart and soul of Hollywood Boulevard. Since it opened in 1927, the theater has become one of the city's most iconic landmarks and a favorite venue for celebrity-studded film premieres. And thanks to the celeb hand and foot prints cast in cement outside the theater's entrance, it's also a favorite spot for tourists. But if you think the theater's elaborate design and architecture is just another testament to movie magic, think again. When it was constructed, authentic temple bells, pagodas and stone figures were imported all the way from China to decorate the theater—many of those pieces can still be seen today. While Grauman's is a crowded tourist trap, you can't help be a little moved by all the prints outside this legendary theater, so go ahead and see how your hands size up with the likes of Brad Pitt's.
Tickets: adults $12.75, children 3-12 $8.75, seniors $8.50.

GREEK THEATRE

Griffith Park, 2700 N. Vermont Ave., Los Angeles, 323-665-5857;
www.greektheatrela.com
Don't expect to see plays like Sophocles' Oedipus Rex and Antigone here. Despite its name, the Greek Theatre is an amphitheater-style concert venue featuring everything from pop and classical to blues and rock. Many of the biggest names in entertainment have played here, including Stevie Nicks, Sting and Paul McCartney. It's the diverse offerings and intimate setting—the 5,801-seat theater, with great views from any angle, is surrounded by towering trees in a canyon in Griffith Park—that make the Greek so loved.

HOLLYWOOD BOWL

2301 N. Highland Ave., Hollywood, 323-850-2000; www.hollywoodbowl.com
"As the sky turns first pink, then purple, then midnight blue, and the music rises to meet the first stars of the night, you'll realize there is only one place on earth to experience such magic," according to an anonymous quote inscribed at the Hollywood Bowl Museum's entrance, professing how the setting sun complements whatever happens on stage. The Hollywood Bowl may sound like a sports arena, but it's far from it. Nestled among the hills south of the Cahuenga Pass, this musical concert hall is especially busy during summer, when the Los Angeles Philharmonic and other musical delights perform. Its outdoor stadium seating makes it the perfect venue for savoring all varieties of music from rich classical concerts to mariachi to pop music performances by Radiohead and John Mayer. But what makes this open-air amphitheater truly lovely is its stage, known as "the shell." Composed of concentric half circles (rainbow style), it resembles the interior of a smooth, white shell during the day and a glowing kaleidoscope after dark. Picnic tables dot the Bowl's entrance, where many show-goers scarf down an alfresco dinner prior to the concert, so pack a gourmet meal and a couple of bottles of wine to enjoy before going up the hill for the show.

HOLLYWOOD FOREVER MEMORIAL PARK

6000 Santa Monica Blvd., Hollywood, 323-469-1181;www.hollywoodforever.com

The Hollywood Forever Memorial Park is the final resting place for such legendary stars as Douglas Fairbanks, Jayne Mansfield and Cecil B. DeMille. During the day you can take a guided tour (www.cemeterytour.com) of the cemetery grounds, which includes mausoleums, exhibitions, monuments and gardens. Once the sun goes down the park hosts another iteration of its name via biweekly summer movie screenings. The outdoor screenings, which are organized by Cinespia (www.cinespia.org), feature cult favorites such as Vertigo, Harold and Maude and The Exorcist. Make like the locals and bring picnic dinners, blankets and lawn chairs (seating is not provided). Tours: $12

HOLLYWOOD SIGN

Mount Lee Perch, Hollywood; www.hollywoodsign.org

What was once a glorified real estate sign has turned into one of the world's most recognizable icons. The Hollywood sign has been tampered with a number of times (to read "Hollyweed" and "Ollywood") since it was erected in 1923, but has since been restored to its original glory. Thanks to a combined force of gates, security cameras and park rangers, the sign will be safe and sound for years to come. Since it's illegal to get anywhere near the famous white letters, you'll have to be content to gaze from afar (assuming the smog isn't too bad that day). Good views of the sign can be found near Lake Hollywood—but if you don't feel like schlepping to the lake, you can see those big block letters from most streets in Hollywood.

HOLLYWOOD WALK OF FAME

Hollywood Boulevard from Gower Street to La Brea Avenue; Vine Street, fromYucca Street to Sunset Boulevard, Hollywood, 323-469-8311;www.hollywoodchamber.net

Nothing marks the Entertainment Capital of the World better than the Hollywood Walk of Fame. Conceived in 1958, the Walk of Fame was designed to immortalize Hollywood's elite. While many enjoy seeing the stars engraved with the name of their favorite contemporary actors (Halle Berry, Matt Damon and Sean Combs are some recent inductees), many visit the Walk to pay homage to silver-screen greats like Charlie Chaplin, Marilyn Monroe, James Dean, Elvis Presley and Cary Grant. Keep an eye out for the more unconventional stars—Godzilla, Lassie, Big Bird and Bugs Bunny all have a plaque on the Walk as well.

HOLLYWOOD WAX MUSEUM

6767 Hollywood Blvd., Hollywood, 323-462-5991; www.hollywoodwax.com

It's not exactly Madame Tussauds, but if you have a yearning to see plastic celebrities immortalized in wax, then head to this museum. You'll see shoddy likenesses of tabloid favorites including Angelina Jolie and Tom Cruise, as well as efforts to celebrate such film icons as Marilyn Monroe and Clint Eastwood. While the waxwork isn't especially skillful, it's sort of interesting to see reproductions of clothing worn by celebrities like Hugh Hefner. Across the street at the Guinness World Records Museum, you can also see a display of Michael Jackson's gold records—the late star gave these to the museum in exchange for a wax figure of Roddy McDowell as Cornelius from the film *Planet of the Apes.* Try to purchase your tickets online because you'll pay less than you would at the box office. Also, combo tickets to both are available online.

Hollywood Wax Museum (box office): adults $15.95, seniors $13.95, children 5-12 $8.95, children 4 and under free. Hollywood Wax Museum (online): adults $12.95, seniors $10.95, children 5-12 $5.95, children 4 and under free. Hollywood Wax Museum (box office): adults $17.95, seniors $15.95, children 5-12 $10.95, children 4 and under free. Hollywood Wax Museum and Guinness World Records Museum (online): adults $14.95, seniors $12.95, children 5-12 $7.95, children 4 and under free. Monday-Thursday 10 a.m.-midnight, Friday-Saturday 10 a.m.-1 a.m.

KODAK THEATRE
6801 Hollywood Blvd., Hollywood, 323-308-6300; www.kodaktheatre.com

If you've always dreamed of thanking the Academy, practice your acceptance speech at the Kodak Theatre, home of the Oscars. Every year the 3,332-seat venue is flooded with thousands of Hollywood's best and brightest stars, and not just for the Academy Awards—the Daytime Emmys, BET Awards, ESPY Awards and (most important) the American Idol finals have all been hosted at the Kodak. If you're not lucky enough to see the interior of the venue during a performance (artists Prince and the Dixie Chicks have played at the theater), take a guided tour. You can see a real Oscar statuette; find out who sat where at this year's Academy Awards; and take a peek at VIP areas, including the George Eastman VIP Room, a first-floor bar where stars order drinks to get them through the lengthy awards ceremonies.

Tours: adults $15, seniors and children 17 and under $10, children under 3 free. Daily 10:30 a.m.-2:30 p.m. June-August, Daily 10:30 a.m.-4 p.m.

THE LAUGH FACTORY
8001 Sunset Blvd., Hollywood, 323-656-1336; www.laughfactory.com

Legendary comedians like Jerry Seinfeld, Jim Carrey, Chris Rock and Robin Williams have all performed here, making it L.A.'s go-to place for stand-up. Before you and your pals head to the club for some laughs, check out the garden party option, which allows groups to dine outside under a tent before seeing the comedians. If you think you can assemble your own Laugh Factory-worthy bit, test it out at the club's Tuesday open mike (sign-up is at 5 p.m.).

Daily; show times vary. See Web site for details.

MULHOLLAND DRIVE
Hollywood

The best way to view Los Angeles' beautiful Santa Monica Mountains is to go for a spin on Mulholland Drive. This 21-mile road runs along the top of the range from Hollywood to Ventura, dipping through the peaks and canyons of the Hollywood Hills. The views of the San Fernando Valley and the Los Angeles Basin are breathtaking—as are the celebrity homes you'll spot along the way.

PANTAGES THEATER

6233 Hollywood Blvd., Hollywood, 213-480-3232; www.pantages-theater.com

Southern California's version of Broadway is the Pantages, where musical theater is king. The historic Art Deco theater, which sits a few steps from the famous intersection of Hollywood Boulevard and Vine Street, opened in 1930. In 1949, billionaire Howard Hughes purchased the theater and turned it into an RKO movie house. Under Hughes' ownership, the Pantages became the venue for the Academy Awards—the awards show was held there for more than 10 years. Today, productions such as The Lion King, Wicked, Mamma Mia!, The Producers and Rent bring their razzle-dazzle to this famous stage.

RUNYON CANYON

2000 N. Fuller Ave., Hollywood, 213-485-5572; www.lamountains.com

To give your lungs a break after inhaling the exhaust fumes on Hollywood Boulevard, head north of Hollywood's busy streets to Runyon Canyon Park. Runyon, whose rugged terrain sprawls across 130 acres, offers awesome views of the city (on a clear day you can see from Downtown to Santa Monica) and a network of trails that will tone your legs better than a StairMaster. Another reason why Runyon is packed almost every day of the week is because it serves as an off-leash dog park (just remember to clean up after your pooch). Runyon will be a breath of fresh air for both you and your canine. Runyon Canyon can be accessed from the north via Mulholland Drive, or from the south at Fuller Avenue.

SUNSET RANCH

3400 Beachwood Drive, Hollywood, 323-469-5450; www.sunsetranchhollywood.com

If your trip out West is giving you the urge to saddle up, then mosey on down to Sunset Ranch, where you can rent a horse or take a riding lesson. What makes Sunset Ranch better than your average stable is its Dinner Ride. The ride starts off in Griffith Park and takes riders to Burbank, where they wine and dine at the Viva Fresh Mexican Restaurant. (If you would rather take a trip during the day, there are other trips to choose from. See Web site for details.) After dinner, you're treated to a moonlit ride back to Griffith Park. Be sure to wear comfortable clothes during your ride and sensible shoes (this means no flip-flops). Remember to keep the margarita drinking to a minimum during dinner; you don't want to fall off your horse.

Dinner Ride: $105 for first person, $75 for every additional person. Sunday-Friday, 4 p.m., 4:30 p.m., 5 p.m. Office: Daily 9 a.m.-5 p.m.

UPRIGHT CITIZENS BRIGADE THEATRE

5919 Franklin Ave., Hollywood, 323-908-8702; www.ucbtheatre.com

The Upright Citizens Brigade (or UCB) began in Chicago and is now in both L.A. and New York. The troupe's completely unpredictable sketch comedy, led by Matt Besser, Amy Poehler, Ian Roberts and Matt Walsh, is often sidesplittingly funny. Tickets can be hard to come by, so reserve yours early and take advantage of bargain shows like UCB's weekly $5 "Comedy Death Ray," which features a lineup mixed with seasoned and novice stand-up comedians. The UCB also hosts Not Too Shabby, a free gig that offers the stage to the audience (calling all aspiring comedians!) and starts after midnight, going into the wee hours. Daily; show times vary. See Web site for details.

TOURING THE STARS' HOMES

L.A. celebrity home tours are as impossible to resist as guilty-pleasure supermarket tabloids. So if you're going to see where the stars live, do it right (you'll be sorry if you pick up one of those shoddy star maps on a Sunset Boulevard corner; they're often out of date). Starline Tours (800-959-3131; www.starlinetours.com) offers one of the most comprehensive tours out there. The company operates a "Movie Stars Homes" tour that will shuttle you past the mansions of blockbuster stars like Tom Cruise and Angelina Jolie as well as the former estates of film icons like Elvis Presley, Marilyn Monroe, Frank Sinatra, Lucille Ball, Judy Garland and Humphrey Bogart. Be aware, however, that many of these homes are protected by shrubberies and gates, so you might end up just seeing some roof shingles—but hey, at least they're famous roof shingles.

In addition to spying celebrities' permanent homes, you'll also get to see some of their temporary ones. The tour bus swings by famous spots like the Beverly Hills Hotel—which has housed the likes of Howard Hughes and Elizabeth Taylor—and the Chateau Marmont, which has seen more than its fair share of celebrity drama. At the Chateau, John Belushi died in a bungalow, Jim Morrison allegedly fell off one of the hotel's balconies, and Benicio Del Toro and Scarlett Johansson are rumored to have done something scandalous in one of the elevators after the 2004 Oscars. Besides seeing celebrity digs, you'll also get a guided tour of the legendary Sunset Strip, where you'll be able to catch a glimpse of celeb-studded clubs like the Viper Room and the legendary Whisky A Go-Go, as well as Beverly Hill's shopping nexus, Rodeo Drive. The odds of seeing a real, live celebrity on Rodeo Drive are slim, but you can quickly scan all the designer boutiques including Gucci, Prada, Fendi and Dior.

The tour operates all year long and departs every half hour (from 9:30 a.m. to sundown) from Grauman's Chinese Theatre and various hotels in the area (call or check the Web site for a full list). The tour clocks in at about two hours, and tickets cost around $40 for adults and $30 for children—you'll save a few bucks if you get picked up at Grauman's Chinese Theatre.

WHERE TO STAY
★★★HOLLYWOOD ROOSEVELT HOTEL

7000 Hollywood Blvd., Hollywood, 323-466-7000; www.hollywoodroosevelt.com

The Roosevelt is the perfect example of how inevitably L.A. life comes full circle. When the hotel opened in 1927, huge names of the time, from Marilyn Monroe to Clark Gable, set up residence at the swanky place, where the first Academy Awards ceremony was held. For a while it fell into disrepair, but then reemerged as a premium hot spot in 2005. Now, renovated but still retaining its original charm, the lavish Art Deco lobby hosts after-parties for premieres; refurbished old Hollywood celebrity suites are used by current A-listers for award show preparation; and tastemakers head to Dakota restaurant for haute cuisine (where you might catch a sight of Brad and Angie) or to 25 Degrees for custom hamburgers and half bottles of wine. The Tropicana Bar—by the famous pool depicted by artist David Hockney—still draws scenesters and starlets, including Tom Hanks, Kate Hudson and the cast of *Entourage*. Teddy's—the elite bar out front—is one of L.A.'s most difficult doors to get through, though many a celebrity glides right on in (Leo DiCaprio is a regular there).

300 rooms. Restaurant, bar. Fitness center. Pool. Pets accepted. $351 and up

★★★RENAISSANCE HOLLYWOOD HOTEL & SPA

1755 N. Highland Ave., Hollywood, 323-856-1200, 800-769-4774;
www.renaissancehollywood.com

There's no shortage of stimulation at the Renaissance Hollywood Hotel, housed inside L.A.'s elaborate Hollywood & Highland shopping complex, above frenetic visitors' destination Hollywood Boulevard and next door to the famous Grauman's Chinese Theatre. The hotel is also across from the Academy Awards' Kodak Theatre and many a starlet has primped in one of the hotel's Mid-Century modern rooms and then sneaked through secret passages to the red-carpet area. A new lobby lounge, Caffé Fama, serves Italian Illy café espresso to give you that jolt to tackle all of the tourist attractions, and later, celebrity-designed signature cocktails are available to help you unwind after a tiring day of sightseeing. Spa Luce adds another layer of luxury (and another potential activity on your to-do list), with treatments that use upscale products from celebrity skincare experts such as Sonya Dakar, Red Flower and Somme Institute. It'll give you a nice break from the flurry of activity outside.

632 rooms. Restaurant, bar. Business center. Fitness center. Pool. Spa. $ 251-350

WHERE TO EAT

★★★CITRUS AT SOCIAL

6525 Sunset Blvd., Hollywood, 323-462-5222; www.citrusatsocial.com

Everyone in Hollywood wants to be an insider, and at Citrus at Social, hobnobbing with the glitterati is as easy as making a reservation. Located in the historic Hollywood Athletic Club, where Charlie Chaplin and Rudolf Valentino once kicked back, Citrus at Social has a fittingly citrus-green and yellow color palette. Chef Michel Richard turns out palate-pleasing dishes such as 72-hour short ribs, Colorado lamb with jalapeño sauce and lobster burgers with crème fraîche.

American, French. Dinner. Closed Sunday-Monday. $36-85

★★★DAKOTA

Hollywood Roosevelt Hotel, 7000 Hollywood Blvd., Hollywood, 323-769-8888;
www.dakota-restaurant.com

With renowned chef Jason Johnston at the helm, this steakhouse in the storied Hollywood Roosevelt Hotel is nothing short of grand. There's the expansive dining room with its carved-beam ceilings; the prompt and professional service; and, most important, the food. In that department, Dakota puts other steakhouses to shame, serving up some of the city's most flavorful cuts of beef (pair yours with the buttery black truffle cream sauce) and comfort-food sides, like mac and cheese and potato purée, as well as delectable seafood including succulent diver scallops. Appetizers are inventive and addictive, such as the crispy pork belly with fried quail egg and pomegranate glaze—put the fork down or you'll be stuffed by the time the main course arrives. The wine list is long, but if you prefer cocktails, head outside to the Tropicana Bar for a nightcap beside the pool and check out the underwater mural by David Hockney.

Steak. Dinner. Reservations recommended. Bar. $36-85

★★★GRACE
7360 Beverly Blvd., Hollywood, 323-934-4400; www.gracerestaurant.com
With respected executive chef Neal Fraser at the helm, Grace has done what few high-profile restaurants manage to do: turn deafening early buzz into long-term success. Foodies from around town keep returning for the simple but divine roasted beet salad with Humboldt Fog goat cheese, grilled radicchio, pistachios, onion marmalade and arugula—it's the perfect prelude to the grilled tenderloin of wild boar served with roasted Brussels sprouts, herbed Yukon gold potato spaetzle and violet mustard sauce. It's no wonder that even after six years, reservations at Grace are still a must.
American. Dinner. Closed Monday. Reservations recommended. Bar. $36-85

★★LA POUBELLE
5907 Franklin Ave., Hollywood, 323-465-0807;www.lapoubellebistro.net
Resting on the same hipster-overrun stretch of Franklin Avenue as the long-standing Bourgeois Pig coffee house is La Poubelle, which means "the trash can." The moniker actually refers to the menu—there's a little bit of everything here, from classic bistro fare such as pommes frites and escargot to a healthy array of pasta dishes and even tapas. It's always packed, and the cavernous acoustics make it a bit raucous, but if you can get a table, opt for a specialty of the house, such as the coq au vin, chicken stewed in burgundy with carrots, onions and mushrooms; or the bouillabaisse, a classic kitchen-sink Mediterranean fish stew with white fish, shrimp, mussels, clams and scallops.
French. Dinner, Friday-Sunday brunch. Bar. $16-35

★★MUSSO AND FRANK GRILL
6667 Hollywood Blvd., Hollywood, 323-467-5123; www.mussoandfrankgrill.com
Not much has changed since this historic institution opened in 1919 (the famed "Round Table" of Saroyan, Thurber, Faulkner and Fitzgerald met here). You can still order Welsh rarebit and enjoy what many swear is the most perfect martini on the planet. The dining room is as frozen in time as the menu, with lots of dark mahogany wood, lumpy booths and archival photos. Oak-beamed ceilings, chandeliers donned with tiny shades, and red-coated waiters, some of whom have been there since the 60s, add to the warm and cozy setting. Hollywood old-timers and up-and-comers alike meet here to do deals, or to simply get a taste of old Hollywood and enjoy a nice steak.
American. Lunch, dinner. $36-85

★★★OSTERIA MOZZA
6602 Melrose Ave., Hollywood, 323-297-0100; www.mozza-la.com
The "casual tavern" side of Mozza (the other side of this trendy Italian eatery is Pizzeria Mozza), Osteria Mozza was hyped to death long before it even opened in mid-2007. It's still one of the hottest restaurants in town, and it's easy to see why: The restaurant is the brainchild of Nancy Silverton (of Campanile and La Brea Bakery fame), celebrity chef Mario Batali and winemaker Joseph Bastianich, who know a thing or two about the business. If you're a free-spirited sort, your best bet is to try to nab a seat at the central

mozzarella bar; it's pretty much your only hope of eating here without a reservation. You'll end up sipping a glass of cabernet and nibbling on the crispy pig's trotter with cicoria and mustard, while watching Silverton herself dish up small bites of delectable mozzarella and burrata dishes. Try the pasta—the egg and ricotta raviolo is particularly good.

Italian. Dinner. Reservations recommended. Bar. $36-85

★★PIZZERIA MOZZA
641 N. Highland Ave., Hollywood, 323-297-0101; www.mozza-la.com

Getting a table at Pizzeria Mozza, the sister establishment of Osteria Mozza, remains a competitive sport among Los Angeles foodies, despite the fact that the place opened three years ago. The crowds just keep on coming—regardless of the noisiness or the location, which has seen numerous eateries come and go—but you'll realize it's not all hype when you taste the rustic gourmet pies, which are handmade before your eyes in an open kitchen and baked in wood-burning ovens. The pizza topped with clams, bursting with the fresh flavors of garlic, oregano, Parmigiano and pecorino, is one of the best. Just remember to put the reservations line on speed dial, and sharpen those elbows before you show up.

Pizzeria. Lunch, dinner. Bar. $16-35

★★★PROVIDENCE
5955 Melrose Ave., Hollywood, 323-460-4170; www.providencela.com

Co-owner Donato Poto and partner-executive chef Michael Cimarusti sure know how to paint a pretty picture. Providence offers some of the most artful dishes we've seen; in fact, each is something of an edible sculpture. But, they're more than just nice to look at—they're also delicious. Choose from the market menu, which changes daily and acts as a canvas for creations by Cimarusti, who works with the freshest fish from around the world, or the à la carte menu, with raw and cold starters like Maine lobster with pink grapefruit, hearts of palm, avocado and coriander, hot ones like "chowda" with smoky bacon, manila clams and a silky broth, and main courses like wild king salmon with beets, Neuske's bacon and mustard emulsion. No wonder Providence is a favorite with Los Angeles gourmands.

Seafood. Lunch (Friday), dinner. Reservations recommended. Bar. $36-85

★★STREET
742 N. Highland Ave., Hollywood, 323-203-0500; www.eatatstreet.com

Go around the world at chef Susan Feniger's new restaurant. Feniger is one of the "Two Hot Tamales" (which ran on the Food Network for four years), co-founder of Border Grill in Santa Monica and, along with Mary Sue Milliken, fought her way into kitchens back in the 70s, when women weren't exactly welcome. Feniger's love of street food continues at her first solo venture with a menu that spans the globe and has a casual atmosphere to match. You know you've found the place when you see the neon sign out front on an otherwise near-empty block. Graffiti on the walls, a small outdoor area with a fire pit and staff dressed in black hoodies greet you inside. This is the place to be adventurous and try things. Servers describe dishes in detail and propel you forward by telling you how delicious everything is. The lunch menu is divided into tea cakes and dumplings, handhelds and

★
★
★
★

more. The lamb tacos are one of the most popular items at lunch—crispy and spicy, and filled with refried white beans and cucumber mint sour cream. Dinner is the same sort of affair—with a variety of tea cakes and dumplings (Chinese sesame cakes, Kaya toast), noodles and curries and big plates such as Korean barbecued short ribs and lamb kofta.

International. Lunch, dinner, Sunday brunch. Bar. Reservations recommended. $16-35

LOS FELIZ/SILVER LAKE/ECHO PARK

These largely residential neighborhoods still retain their bohemian character, though rising real estate prices are always a threat to the funky coffee shops, eccentric art galleries, offbeat restaurants and gritty music clubs. The area is home to Griffith Park, an expanse so large and wild that mountain lions have been spotted nearby, and not just in the Los Angeles Zoo.

WHAT TO SEE
AUTRY NATIONAL CENTER

4700 Western Heritage Way, Los Feliz, 323-667-2000;www.autrynationalcenter.org

Co-founded by "America's Favorite Singing Cowboy," actor and singer Gene Autry, the Autry National Center is composed of the Museum of the American West, the Southwest Museum of the American Indian and the Institute for the Study of the American West. The Autry isn't dedicated to exhibiting how the West was won, but rather to telling the stories of how the diverse peoples of the American West influenced the rest of the country and the world. Expect to see an impressive collection of art and artifacts, including textiles created by Navajo and Pueblo Indians, movie paraphernalia from Western films and television shows, and one of the largest collections of arms and armor in the western United States. Not into guns and knives? The museum also offers a wide range of more family-friendly activities. You can pan for gold like an original 49er; watch old Gene Autry flicks during the summertime series, Dinner and a Movie; and buy works from Native American artists at the annual Intertribal Arts Marketplace.

Admission: adults $9, students and seniors $5, children 3-12 $3, children under 3 free. Tuesday-Friday10 a.m.-4 p.m. Saturday-Sunday 11 a.m.-5 p.m. Thursdays July-August 10 a.m.-8 p.m.

DODGER STADIUM

1000 Elysian Park Ave., Echo Park, 323-363-4377; www.ladodgers.com

What an iconic sports team in Los Angeles needs is an equally iconic sports venue, and that is exactly what the Dodger Stadium delivers. The downtown stadium has some of the city's best visual backdrops, from a view of downtown and the forests of the Elysian hills to the heights of the distant but visible San Gabriel Mountains. Fans pile into the stadium to cheer on their favorite cerulean-clad ballplayers and to devour the famous foot-long Dodger Dogs. Built in 1962, the stadium is undergoing major renovations to modernize the ballpark, including a new promenade with restaurants and shops.

GRIFFITH OBSERVATORY

2800 E. Observatory Road, Los Feliz, 213-473-0800; www.griffithobservatory.org

The Griffith Observatory came into being in 1935 after "Colonel" Griffith J. Griffith (who adopted the title of colonel despite not being a military man as a superior alternative to his repetitive name)) donated $100,000 to the city to build a public observatory on Mount Hollywood. And $93 million worth of renovations later, the observatory now combines Art Deco charm with superior technology. While the exterior's neo-classical architecture and the foyer's Foucault pendulum (which was one of the observatory's original exhibits) are testaments to the structure's history, the state-of-the-art planetarium and interactive exhibits are evidence of its foray into the future. You can find out how much you weigh on other planets, see real meteorites and explore the Milky Way without leaving the comfort of planet Earth. Free. Tuesday-Friday noon-10 p.m., Saturday-Sunday 10 a.m.-10 p.m.

GRIFFITH PARK

4730 Crystal Springs Drive, Los Feliz, 323-913-4688; www.laparks.org

Don't come to this park (which happens to be the largest municipal park with an urban wilderness area in the United States) expecting to see a larger version of Central Park. Griffith Park is real wilderness—lots of dirt, naturally occurring fauna and some dangerous wildlife, including coyotes and rattlesnakes. But at more than 4,000 acres, Griffith also has tamer offerings, including miles of trails for hikers and horseback riders, picnic areas, tennis courts, a swimming pool, and athletic fields for soccer, rugby, baseball and badminton. The area, which was once inhabited by Native Americans, was purchased in the 19th century by Welsh immigrant "Colonel" Griffith J. Griffith. In 1896, Griffith gave the city the 3,015 acres of the park that now bears his name.

Daily 6 a.m.-10 p.m.

LOS ANGELES ZOO

5333 Zoo Drive, Los Angeles (in the center of Griffith Park), Los Feliz, 323-644-4200; www.lazoo.org

When gridlocked Los Angeles traffic brings out the beast in you, decompress among your fellow creatures at the L.A. Zoo. It's home to animal species from all around the world, but the special habitats are what make the zoo stand out. The best of the special habitats belong to the resident primates, so make sure to swing by the Red Ape Rain Forest, Campo Gorilla Reserve and the Chimpanzees of the Mahale Mountains. If you're more of a hands-on type (or if you have kids in tow), the Winnick Family Children's Zoo gives you the opportunity to pet and groom barnyard animals, including goats and sheep.

Admission: adults $13, seniors $10, children 2-12 $8, children under 2 free. Daily 10 a.m.-5 p.m.

TRAVEL TOWN

5200 Zoo Drive, Los Feliz, 323-662-5874; www.ci.la.ca.us

This outdoor transportation museum is on the northeast corner of Griffith Park, so take that into consideration if you're planning a visit to the park or the L.A. Zoo. Travel Town lives up to its name with an impressive collection of locomotives, freight cars, passenger cars and motorcars dating all the way back to the 19th century. While the museum is for people of all ages, it shouldn't come as a big surprise that Travel Town is highly trafficked by kids who want to see trains or who are big fans of Thomas the Tank Engine. Admission is free, but if you want to ride the miniature train that circles the premises you'll have to fork over a little cash.

Monday-Friday 10 a.m.-4 p.m., Saturday-Sunday 10 a.m.-5 p.m.

WHERE TO EAT
★★★EDENDALE GRILL
2838 Rowena Ave., Silver Lake, 323-666-2000; www.edendalegrill.com

Located in trendy Silver Lake, the Edendale Grill occupies what was once Los Angeles Fire Station No. 56. And though the owners retained the brick façade and cavernous feel, along with a pressed-tin ceiling and beautiful wood floors, the space has been lovingly updated with a classy dining room, expansive bar and cozy heated patio. The food is equally warm; try the Edendale meatloaf wrapped in applewood-smoked bacon with a tomato-brown sugar glaze and mashed Yukon gold potatoes. While this might not be NYC, the bartenders here make a mean Cosmo. Sadly, it's not all good news: Service can be spotty, but that's nothing the decadent blue cheese-tarragon French fries can't fix.

American. Dinner, Sunday brunch. Bar. $16-35

★★EL CHAVO
4441 Sunset Blvd., Los Feliz, 323-664-0871; www.elchavorestaurant.com

A longtime Los Feliz favorite for its tangy margaritas, authentic Mexican cuisine and quirky décor, El Chavo was recently remodeled, but breathe easy—the glow-in-the-dark portrait of Dolly Parton still hangs in the corner, and the ceiling of the bar is still festooned with Day-Glo sombreros. It's a little louder now due to the expanded dining room, but menu favorites—such as the enchiladas rancheras and chiles rellenos—remain the same.

Mexican. Dinner. Bar. $16-35

★★FIGARO BISTRO
1802 N. Vermont Ave., Los Feliz, 323-662-1587; www.figarobistrot.com

You can expect a slice of the City of Light at this Los Feliz restaurant, where local hipsters head for classic bistro fare and true turn-of-the-century Parisian décor. (Think long banquettes and ornate iron overhead lamps.) If you can't find a spot at the tightly packed sidewalk tables (just as if you really were in Europe), grab a stool at the zinc bar and spend a happy hour (or two) with a chilled glass of rosé and some escargots, then indulge in the sole meunière with green beans and lemon sauce. Breakfast at Figaro is also a special Gallic treat; the croissants, baguettes and an array of pastries—baked fresh daily in the adjoining bakery—will have you ooh-la-laing in no time.

French. Breakfast, lunch, dinner. Bar. $36-85

★FRED62
1850 N. Vermont Ave., Los Feliz, 323-667-0062; www.fred62.com

In a city where most restaurants stop serving by 10 p.m., this 24-hour eatery is a godsend. Decked out like a retro diner, with bulbous midcentury light fixtures and chrome toasters everywhere, this trendy Los Feliz outpost has an appropriately hip-and-happenin' (and tasty) menu, with nouveau-diner offerings such the Mrs. Loaf sandwich (housemade turkey meatloaf served on a toasted roll with mozzarella and housemade marinara), the Mac Daddy and Cheese (a spicy version of the comfort dish) and the Super Rico sandwich (a beer-battered tuna patty stuffed with pasilla chiles, onion and cheddar cheese). Whether you're here seeking alcohol-sopping grub or a hearty breakfast, make sure to order the onion rings; they're fluffy, golden and the best in the neighborhood.

American. Breakfast, lunch, dinner. Bar. $16-35

MANHATTAN BEACH

This once-quiet beach enclave has become a vibrant neighborhood that constantly buzzes with new construction and an influx of increasingly wealthy inhabitants. Just blocks from the beach, rolling hills are dotted with quaint homes and the mini-mansions of such luminaries as Tiger Woods.

Still, a mellow beach atmosphere prevails. You'll see groups of surfers walking down the street or families in flip-flops from the beach shopping in the local markets. The main zone of activity is Manhattan Beach Boulevard and the Pier, which are crammed with trendy nightclubs, surf shops and restaurants. Along the strand, in-line skaters, beach volleyball players, bikers and dog lovers make for an active scene.

WHERE TO STAY

★★★MANHATTAN BEACH MARRIOTT
1400 Parkview Ave., Manhattan Beach, 310-546-7511, 800-228-9290;
www.marriott.com

Located three miles south of LAX, this 26-acre property offers vacationers and business travelers a convenient South Bay location. The property is within walking distance of shopping, restaurants and theater and is just a short ride to the local beaches. Newly renovated guest rooms feature the Marriott Revive bedding. Duffers will like the nine-hole golf course onsite.

385 rooms. Restaurant, bar. $151-250

★★★SHADE HOTEL
1221 N. Valley Drive, Manhattan Beach, 310-546-4995; www.shadehotel.com

Before Manhattan Beach visitors could take refuge in the Shade, the beach town didn't have a luxury hotel (for shame). Half a block from the area's main drag—littered with quaint old-fashioned ice cream shops, beach stores, independent boutiques and ethnic restaurants such as Greek destination Petros—Shade is like a bastion of trendy in a universe of cozy. And the combination is ideal. In deep amber woods and white leather upholstery, lobby bar Zinc Lounge has become the place to party in Manhattan Beach. You could stay busy for days in the rooms, too: Cuddle up on an idyllic Tempur-Pedic bed, turn on the Heat & Glo Cyclone fireplace (basically, a cool-looking electric version), brew some java with an in-room Lavazza espresso machine, then soak in the tub with connected chromatherapy lights that throw off different colors depending on your mood (which will inevitably be good). A complimentary breakfast—a step above most—seals the deal.

38 rooms. Restaurant, bar. Complimentary breakfast. $351 and up

WHERE TO EAT
★★★MANGIAMO

128 Manhattan Beach Blvd., Manhattan Beach, 310-318-3434;
www.mangiamorestaurant.com

This quiet, romantic restaurant is just steps from the Pier 9 beach. Nab a table in the intimate wine cellar or sit up front to catch a view of the sunset. The Northern Italian menu features many seafood selections, as well as dishes like osso buco and three-mushroom farfalle.

Italian. Dinner. Reservations recommended. Bar. $36-85

MARINA DEL REY

As its name suggests, this community, located next to Venice and only four miles from LAX, attracts many boating and sport fishing enthusiasts. The dominant feature is the largest man-made harbor in the world, with more than 5,000 slips. Sail and power boat rentals, ocean cruises and fishing expeditions are available. Besides boating, there's biking and jogging in front of the marina, numerous restaurants, shops and beaches.

WHAT TO SEE
FISHERMAN'S VILLAGE

13755 Fiji Way, Marina del Rey, 310-823-5411; www.visitthemarina.com

Modeled after a turn-of-the-century New England fishing town and located on the main channel of the largest man-made small craft harbor in the country, this area and its well-known lighthouse have appeared in many television and movie productions. Cobblestone walks complement the nautical atmosphere and provide a panoramic view of the marina. You can find boat rentals, fishing charters and harbor cruises here, as well as shops, boutiques and restaurants. Entertainment is provided throughout the year, including free jazz concerts on Saturday and Sunday. Daily.

WHERE TO STAY
★★★MARINA DEL REY MARRIOTT

4100 Admiralty Way, Marina del Rey, 310-301-3000, 800-228-9290;
www.marriott.com/laxmb

The Marina del Rey Marriott pioneers a new trend of dispensing signature fragrances throughout the hotel by emitting floral "Zanzibar Mist" aromatherapy in lobbies, hallways and anywhere else your nose may wander. Don't worry: It's not as overpowering as it sounds. Neither is the interior, though it offers big personality in the form of oversized cartoonish lime-green love seats and a high ceiling held up by large red pillars. Stones Restaurant and The Lobby Bar are serviceable, but the property's pride and joy is Glow Bar. The outdoor lounge—with plush banquettes, fireplaces and a large illuminated archway—regularly hosts a parade of DJs spinning house and dance remixes, not to mention a young crowd sipping light cocktails that taste more like fresh fruit, such as the Cucumber Collins and Summer Lemonade. Nearby is Venice's Main Street and Abbot Kinney, the best blocks for strolling among bohemian bookstores and shops.

370 rooms. Restaurant, bar. Business center. Fitness center. Pool. Spa. Golf. $ 151-250

★★★THE RITZ-CARLTON, MARINA DEL REY

4375 Admiralty Way, Marina del Rey, 310-823-1700; www.ritzcarlton.com

The Ritz-Carlton, Marina Del Rey is constantly putting on the ritz. Now, the stylish hotel—with L.A.'s only waterside palm-tree-lined pool—has added more. The new Spa Chakra and fitness center includes high-end beauty products from Guerlain and a new treatment menu featuring facials, body treatments, massages, manicures, pedicures and more. Signature afternoon tea service (at Jer-Ne Restaurant + Bar) is bumped up a contemporary notch with new artisan hand-blown glass Sontu teapots and flavorful brews from Tea Forte (made from rough-cut herbs). You can also hop over to Chaya Venice, if you want to mix with the local Westside scenester set. But if you're more into rescue than ritziness, you can opt to spend an afternoon helping to restore the salt marshes and dunes of nearby Ballona Wetlands. 304 rooms. Restaurant, bar. Business center. Fitness center. Pool. Spa. Pets accepted. $251-350

SANTA MONICA/BRENTWOOD/MALIBU

Here is Los Angeles at its finest: beautiful ocean beaches at the fringe of one of the World's largest metropolises. Malibu is a surfer's paradise. Multi-million-dollar homes line the oceanfront, but visitors without their own screenplay are welcome on dozens of public beaches up and down the coast. Santa Monica is literally and figuratively halfway between the two. Its recreation path along the beach welcomes bikers, skaters and runners by day, while its amusement park on the pier lights up the area after dark. For a peerless view of it all, Brentwood's mansion-packed hills are just the spot.

WHAT TO SEE
CALIFORNIA HERITAGE MUSEUM

2612 Main St., Santa Monica, 310-392-8537; www.californiaheritagemuseum.org

Located on charming Main Street, the California Heritage Museum adds even more culture and flair to the neighborhood with its unique displays of American decorative art, fine art and folk art. This renovated Victorian house, built along the palisades in 1894, was moved to its present site and restored to represent four decades of design. The museum features unusual and entertaining themes and exhibits, such as "Aloha Spirit—Hawaii's Influence on the California Lifestyle."

Admission: adults $5, seniors and students $3, children under 13 free. Wednesday-Sunday 11 a.m.-4 p.m.

THE GETTY CENTER

1200 Getty Center Drive, Brentwood, 310-440-7300; www.getty.edu

Home to the J. Paul Getty Museum and a beacon for Los Angeles' art and cultural sensibility, the Getty Center contains some of the U.S.'s finest and most valuable European art. Designed by architect Richard Meier, the Center is a real beauty that sits high atop the Santa Monica Mountains; its slabs of pale stone perfectly reflect the rosy light of the rising and setting sun. In addition to browsing the art inside, take a walk along the charming Central Garden, part of which is designed like a maze with flower-fringed pathways. Beauty aside, the Center isn't without its share of intrigue. In 2005, accusations surfaced that several pieces of its antiquity collection, largely handled by former Getty curator Marion True, were illegally obtained from Italy. The Getty Trust has since worked with Italian officials in returning 40 artworks, including a highly coveted 2,400-year-old limestone statue of Aphrodite. So head to the free museum quickly, before the rest of the collection gets shipped back to the boot.

Admission: Free. Tuesday-Friday 10 a.m.-5 p.m., Saturday 10a.m.-9 p.m., Sunday 10 a.m.-5:30 p.m.

THE GETTY VILLA

17985 Pacific Coast Highway, Pacific Palisades,310-440-7300; www.getty.edu

West of the Getty Center, the free Getty Villa is an additional treat for art-hungry eyes. J. Paul Getty purchased 64 acres of seaside property in Pacific Palisades to house his collection of Greek and Roman antiquities. Using a 1st-century Roman country house (specifically the Villa dei Papiri in Herculaneum, Italy) as his inspiration, construction of the Getty Villa began in the 1970s. Now you can see the villa's hundreds of Greek, Roman and Etruscan antiquities, including statues, terra cotta urns, gold jewelry and bronze armor. Among those on display is Statue of a Victorious Youth, a treasured bronze sculpture that dates back to 300 to 100 B.C. Make sure to leave enough time to tour the villa's magnificent gardens—the Outer Peristyle is the largest and the most impressive. Modeled after an ancient Roman garden, the Outer Peristyle features plants native to the Mediterranean, pools of aqua water, vibrant murals and replicas of bronze statues found at the Villa dei Papiri.

Admission: Free. Thursday-Monday 10 a.m.-5 p.m.

MAIN STREET

Main St., Santa Monica; www.mainstreetsm.com

The Third Street Promenade is not the only shopping district Santa Monica calls its own. For those looking for a slightly edgier, more urban feel, head just a few blocks south to Main Street. Here you'll find dozens of restaurants ranging from Joe's Diner to the California-French cuisine at the Frank Gehry-designed Rockenwagner. Shops include everything from Betsey Johnson to Patagonia, plus locally owned specialty shops and boutiques.

PALISADES PARK

Ocean Ave. from Colorado Ave. to San Vicente Blvd., Santa Monica, 310-458-8644

Within walking distance of Third Street Promenade, this beautiful stretch of bluff top lawn and walkways overlooking the Pacific offers some of the best spots to catch the California sunset.

SANTA MONICA MOUNTAINS NATIONAL RECREATION AREA

West of Griffith Park in Los Angeles County and east of the Oxnard Plain in Ventura County, 805-370-2301; www.nps.gov

This mountain range is home to some of L.A.'s most beautiful hiking, biking and horseback riding trails (try Malibu Lake Riders—818-510-2245;www.malibulakeriders.com—for the latter). The Santa Monica Mountains can be accessed from a number of locations throughout L.A., and since it's the biggest urban park in the United States, there are plenty of trails from which to choose. You'll probably want to pick a trail close to where you're staying, but here are some popular trails and where to find them: Runyon Canyon (Hollywood), Fryman Canyon (Studio City), Temescal Canyon Park (Pacific Palisades), Topanga State Park (Topanga), Malibu Creek State Park (Calabasas) and Point Mugu State Park (Malibu).

Daily 9 a.m.-5 p.m.

SANTA MONICA PIER

Ocean and Colorado avenues, Santa Monica, 310-458-8900; www.santamonicapier.org

Sometimes there's nothing like some good old-fashioned fun. The Santa Monica Pier delivers that—along with great ocean views—with Pacific Park, a pint-size amusement park. Hop aboard the world's only solar-powered (you're in California, remember?) Ferris wheel, feel your stomach drop on the West Coaster (the West Coast's only oceanfront, steel roller coaster) and spin in circles on Inkie's Scrambler. If you've forgotten to pack Dramamine, make a beeline for the park's games section, where classic amusements like Wac-A-Mole, ring toss and skeeball await. But to make your theme park experience authentic, hit up the vendors selling hot dogs, popcorn, cotton candy and funnel cake.

Admission (unlimited rides): adults and children 8-18 $20.95, children 7 and under $12.95. May-September, Sunday-Thursday 11 a.m.-11 p.m., Friday-Saturday 11 a.m.-12:30 a.m.; January-May, September-December, Monday-Thursday noon-6 p.m., Friday noon-midnight, Saturday 11 a.m.-midnight, Sunday 11 a.m.-9 p.m.

SANTA MONICA PIER AQUARIUM

1600 Ocean Front Walk, Santa Monica, 310-393-6149;www.healthebay.org

You won't see any exotic fish at the Santa Monica Pier Aquarium, but you will see species native to the Santa Monica Bay. Get up close with a number of slimy ocean dwellers in the touch tanks and tide pools—just remember to be careful while handling the tenant sea stars, crabs, sea urchins, snails and sea cucumbers. Also on view (but not available for touching), are octopuses, eels, lobsters and sharks. If you can swing it, go to the aquarium on a popular Shark Sunday, when you can watch the staff feed the resident sharks.

Admission: adults $5 (suggested donation), children under 13 free.

Tuesday-Friday 2-6 p.m., Saturday-Sunday 12:30 a.m.-6 p.m.

SANTA MONICA PLACE

Fourth St. and Broadway, Santa Monica, 310-394-1049; www.santamonicaplace.com

With almost 150 shops, this three-level shopping center is just a few blocks from the famous Santa Monica Pier.

Monday-Saturday 10 a.m.-9 p.m., Sunday 11 a.m.-6 p.m.

SOUTH BAY BICYCLE TRAIL

Temescal Canyon Road, Santa Monica

There's nothing like exploring a city on a bike. And the South Bay Bicycle Trail provides a beautiful scenic tour, starting out at Will Rogers State Beach in Pacific Palisades and winds 22 miles down the coast to Torrance County Beach in Torrance. Most of the path is along the beach (except for a few spots where the trail ends and you have to take the streets), so it makes for

MALIBU BEACHES

Spanning 21 miles along the Pacific coastline, Malibu is home to countless movie stars and great beaches, including Zuma Beach, Surfrider Beach, Westward Beach and Topanga State Beach. All of these are public beaches, although some, including Zuma, charge a fee. Surfrider, which is next to the Adamson House (the unused home of the original builders of Malibu) and the Malibu Lagoon, is known for its long waves and so attracts surfers, as well as those looking to soak up a little California sunshine. (It was the site of many surfer movies filmed in the 60s). The Malibu pier is on Surfrider Beach. Zuma Beach is one of the most famous beaches in Los Angeles County. The white sandy beach that stretches for three miles hosts volleyball tournaments and lifeguard competitions.

a nice, low-key ride (especially since you don't have to worry about getting run over). There are many places along the bike path to stop and grab a drink or a bite to eat, so you can turn your biking adventure into a leisurely trek instead of an arduous workout. The trail gets crowded near the Santa Monica Pier and Venice Beach, so watch out for pedestrians and rollerbladers.

THIRD STREET PROMENADE
Third St., Santa Monica, 310-393-8355; www.thirdstreetpromenade.com
A few blocks from the beach is a shopping haven filled with retailers, restaurants, bars and movie theaters. Third Street Promenade is an outdoor, pedestrian-friendly mall where you can peruse hundreds of shops while enjoying the Santa Monica sun. If you're looking for a specific store, chances are it's on the Promenade—GAP, Anthropologie, Urban Outfitters, Barnes & Noble are just a few of the many shops here. And as far as dining options go, there are restaurants and bars as well as the usual food court staples. After you finish your shopping, stroll the Promenade and watch the impromptu street performances, in which you'll see people of all ages singing, dancing and playing musical instruments.

WILL ROGERS STATE HISTORIC PARK
1501 Will Rogers State Park Road, Pacific Palisades, 310-454-8212; www.parks.ca.gov
In the 1920s, cowboy entertainer Will Rogers bought more than 100 acres in Pacific Palisades. Eventually, Rogers' purchase became the site of 31-room ranch house, stable, corrals, riding ring, roping arena, polo field, golf course and hiking trails. When Rogers' widow died in the 1940s, the ranch was turned into a state park, where the public could be one with nature and learn about the life and career of Rogers. You can tour the ranch house, take horseback riding lessons and hike on one of the many trails surrounding the park. If you're visiting on a weekend during the spring, summer or fall, you'll be able to see the Will Rogers Polo Club in action. Aside from being a movie star, humorist, rope-trick expert and cowboy, Rogers also was an accomplished polo player.
Daily 8 a.m.-sunset. Tours: Tuesday-Sunday 11 a.m., 1 p.m. and 2 p.m.

WHERE TO STAY
★★★THE AMBROSE
1255 20th St., Santa Monica, 310-315-1555; www.ambrosehotel.com
The Ambrose's green-living initiatives are certainly ambrosia for travelers

★★
★★
★★
★★

concerned about their carbon footprints, but this intimate hotel with a fantastic location still offers plenty for those who want a little comfort with their conservation. From the hybrid car rentals to the organic breakfasts, it's no wonder it's the first hotel in the U.S. to earn the prestigious LEED certification for sustainability. There's also an all-concierge staff and 24-hour room service from the popular Urth Caffe, which offers organic coffees and teas. 77 rooms. Complimentary breakfast. Fitness center. $151-250

★★CHANNEL ROAD INN
219 W. Channel Road, Santa Monica, 310-459-1920; www.channelroadinn.com
Channel Road Inn feels more like a country bed and breakfast with feminine touches—flowers and girly floral bedding—than a boutique hotel in a big city like L.A. Many of the homey rooms—which were recently renovated—have fireplaces, Jacuzzis, balconies and romantic canopy beds. The little house, which sits on the cusp of the Pacific Palisades and Malibu, just off Pacific Coast Highway and the beach, doesn't offer dining options. But you're near some of the area's best eateries, including casual spots such as Café Delfini and Sam's By the Beach, and the more upscale (and celebrity favorite) Il Ristorante di Giorgio Baldi, widely considered to be one of the best Italian restaurants in L.A.
15 rooms. Complimentary breakfast. $ 251-350

★★DOUBLETREE GUEST SUITES SANTA MONICA
1707 Fourth St., Santa Monica, 310-395-3332; www.doubletree.com
In the simple, but nice and lightly hued rooms at Doubletree Guest Suites Santa Monica, you'll find all the basics, from wet bars to HBO. And wireless Internet service is complimentary throughout the hotel. Uncommon business amenities, including a notary public, are available, as are light bites from French-colonial-style Café Pronto in the hotel atrium and full meals from 4th Street Grille. The Jazz Loft upstairs provides a place to mingle and relax with a cocktail, although countless spots are just outside the hotel, as well. While you'll encounter plenty of touristy options on Third Street Promenade (including an annex to famous music industry spot Barney's Beanery), you're better off making the quick trip to Main Street for a more authentic experience.
253 rooms. Restaurant, bar. Business center. Fitness center. Pool. $ 151-250

★★★THE FAIRMONT MIRAMAR HOTEL & BUNGALOWS
101 Wilshire Blvd., Santa Monica, 310-576-7777, 800-441-1414; www.fairmont.com
Although the Fairmont Miramar Hotel & Bungalows sits a block from the beach and from overcrowded and touristy Third Street Promenade, it's a secluded oasis reminiscent of a great estate, separated from the street performers and harried shoppers by waterfalls, lush greenery and 32 new private bungalows. The addition of Exhale Spa (a Santa Monica mainstay) ensures relaxation. The acclaimed spa is known not only for great treatments, but also for signature Core Fusion and Core Energy Flow fitness classes (tough, but definitely effective). The longtime celebrity fitness secret uses Qigong techniques to tone and strengthen. Once you've worked up an appetite, head to the new Fig restaurant for organic and sustainable seasonable California cuisine and then to the Lobby Lounge, which overlooks the koi fish pond, for cocktails.
300 rooms. Restaurant, bar. Business center. Fitness center. Pool. Spa. $351

and up

★★★THE GEORGIAN HOTEL
1415 Ocean Ave., Santa Monica, 310-395-9945, 800-538-8147;
www.georgianhotel.com

If The Georgian Hotel was good enough for the Kennedy family matriarch (Rose Kennedy summered here for years), then it's good enough for us. Marking its 75th anniversary in 2008, the beachside (and Santa Monica Pier-adjacent) hotel opened in 1933—when Prohibition speakeasies lined Pacific Coast Highway—and was dubbed "Lady" for its infamously successful owner, Mrs. Rosamond Borde. Rich Hollywood history pervades the Art Deco details, from archways to ornate bathroom tiles. And although the hotel recently underwent a $2 million makeover to include modern amenities including complimentary wireless Internet, flat-screen TVs and MP3 alarm clocks, the historic landmark's deep character and charm have been meticulously preserved. The rooms' décor is both modern and reflective of the hotel's original aesthetic, while The Veranda restaurant draws a buzz for both its food and California wines. Though there's no pool to lounge around, activities ranging from surfing lessons to Santa Monica Pier visits are easily arranged. Plus, the big blue expanse of the Pacific Ocean is just a minute away.
84 rooms. Restaurant, bar. Business center. Fitness center. Pets accepted. $251-350

★★HOLIDAY INN SANTA MONICA BEACH - AT THE PIER
120 Colorado Ave., Santa Monica, 310-451-0676; www.ichotelsgroup.com

The newly renovated Holiday Inn Santa Monica Beach rests at the entrance to Santa Monica Pier, the famous boardwalk that juts out into the Pacific Ocean and is lined with carnival games, fairway food and several rides (take a spin on the famous Ferris wheel, which was recently replaced with a state-of-the-art, partially solar powered one). The Holiday Inn's guest rooms are well kept, with blue-and-brown bedding and upholstered furniture accented with white ribbing. While Windows Restaurant and Lounge is the hotel's onsite dining spot (where kids eat free), there are plenty more exciting culinary and scenic experiences just steps away, ranging from Latin fusion destination Border Grille to star-studded Ivy at the Shore to good old junk food galore on the Pier.
132 rooms. Restaurant, bar. Business center. Fitness center. Pool. $ 151-250

★★★HOTEL CASA DEL MAR
1910 Ocean Way, Santa Monica, 310-581-5533, 800-898-6999;
www.hotelcasadelmar.com

Casa Del Mar originally opened its Renaissance Revival doors and became the place to be seen in 1926, but it reemerged on the contemporary hospitality radar in 1999 after the classic beachside hotel underwent a $50 million renovation. Now, the original sophisticated digs have been rejuvenated. The sparkling new décor is fresh and romantic, revolving around vintage-style four-poster walnut beds à la 1920s chic, with ivory sateen drapes and sea-blue walls. The rooms also boast modern amenities, including 42-inch plasma TVs and iPod docking stations. And though executive chef Michael

Reardon—a La Bernardin vet—offers innovative and delicious seafood and sushi at new restaurant Catch, it may be the incredible view overlooking the beach that stays with you after enjoying a meal at the upscale but mellow addition. Be sure to grab a cocktail at the bar around sunset.

129 rooms. Restaurant, bar. Fitness center. Pool. Spa. $351 and up

★★★HOTEL OCEANA SANTA MONICA

849 Ocean Ave., Santa Monica, 310-393-0486, 800-777-0758;
www.hoteloceanasantamonica.com

After a $16 million renovation, Hotel Oceana is like a home away from home (if your house happens to sit directly across from the Pacific Ocean and embody a refreshingly eclectic slant on Cape Cod chic). Formerly the residence of Stan Laurel of comedy duo Laurel and Hardy, Oceana now is one of L.A.'s most amazing finds. The mellow enclave with apartment-style rooms makes you feel like nesting for the long haul. Rejecting the long-enduring trend of cool minimalism, Oceana has an accessible, breezy freshness with warm, feel-good colors and playful patterns that don't overwhelm. Spacious suites surrounding the courtyard offer practical oversized wooden desks, while chess tables and other thoughtful touches give rooms a distinct personality. In-room amenities such as two HDTVs in several suites, Aveda toiletries, iPod docking stations and Egyptian cotton sheets further elevate this luxe boutique hotel (which has a sister property in Santa Barbara). Electric-blue chaises line the courtyard pool, as do tables spilling out from the casual yet high-end Ocean Lounge helmed by consulting chef Jonathan Morr of BondSt and executive chef Joseph Feldman. There's no place like (this) home.

70 rooms. Restaurant, bar. Fitness center. Pool. $351 and up

★★★THE HUNTLEY

1111 Second St., Santa Monica, 310-394-5454; www.thehuntleyhotel.com

Location, location, location—that's the secret to The Huntley's popularity amidst sun-seekers. The boutique hotel is not just unmistakable due to its location inside a tall, 18-floor building just one block away from the beach, but also for its striking, art-gallery-like lobby, which is outfitted in the cool whites and warm chocolate-and-beige browns of California-contemporary design. The guest rooms feature 42-inch plasma TVs, pillow-top beds and Egyptian cotton linens, and Gilchrist & Soames bath products. When you've had enough of your room's gorgeous bird's-eye ocean views, keep taking advantage of the location and head to the beach or to Third Street Promenade, which is also just steps outside the door. If you want to stay on your high, head to the top of the building for gorgeous vistas, dinner and drinks at The Penthouse restaurant—just be mindful that you're not the only one to recognize a well-situated stomping ground when you see one, so expect a packed dining room on weekends.

209 rooms. Restaurant, bar. Business center. Fitness center. $251-350

★★★LE MERIGOT

1740 Ocean Ave., Santa Monica, 310-395-9700; www.lemerigothotel.com

Just down from Ivy at the Shore (one of several chic Westside eateries, where celebrities are drawn like bees to honey), Le Merigot sits in a slightly busier section of beach-adjacent Ocean Avenue. It's worth upgrading to a deluxe or at least an ocean-view room at this pet-friendly hotel, so that you're ensured a patio with water in sight. If the soundtrack of the ocean's lapping doesn't untangle your nerves (driving in this city knots them right up), the signature Italian linens and goose-down pillows will coax you to a mellow state. If you're still wound up, head over to The Spa for globally inspired treatments, from Epicuren's Chai Soy Mud Wrap to soothe post-sun exposure, to aromatic Moroccan Rassoul Wraps, where you get slathered in mud and seep in all the good enzymes. Then, once you're lulled into a relaxed stupor, let executive chef Desi Szonntagh at Cézanne ply you with French fare that includes black truffle mac and cheese with lobster, roasted pear salad with fennel, spiced pecans, pomegranate, Point Reyes blue cheese and balsamic vinaigrette, and seafood cocktail served with red and green chili sauce.

175 rooms. Restaurant, bar. Business Center. Fitness center. Spa. Pool. $351 and up

★★★LOEWS SANTA MONICA BEACH HOTEL

1700 Ocean Ave., Santa Monica, 310-458-6700, 800-235-6397;
www.santamonicaloewshotel.com

One of the bigger hotels in the area, Loews Santa Monica Beach Hotel stands tall along the ocean. From your room, look out onto white sand and blue water, sparkling cityscape or even, from the Presidential Suite, the entire Santa Monica Pier, complete with nostalgia-inducing Ferris wheel and all (even if you can't remember a time when Ferris wheels were all the rage). In your room you'll find many tactile treats: 300-thread-count cotton sheets, 100 percent combed and ring-spun cotton terry towels and the hotel's signature amenity, the sinfully soft "Ultimate Doeskin" robe by Chadsworth & Haig. The bathroom is filled with natural Lather products, made from plant and herb extracts—great for the environment, but note they don't foam as much because they're chemical-free. Dining options, in addition to the many lining Ocean Avenue, include Papillon lounge for tapas, fireplaces and ocean views; Ocean & Vine for farmers'-market-fresh cuisine (Santa Monica's Wednesday farmers' market is highly esteemed by chefs throughout the country); and a poolside menu for a bite while soaking up the sun. Speaking of relaxing, Ocean Spa's Beachcomber massage uses tiger clam shells from the ocean, heating them with kelp and sea water for a heated massage in the spa's eco-friendly treatment rooms.

342 rooms. Restaurant, bar. Fitness center. Spa. Pool. $351 and up

★★★MALIBU BEACH INN

22878 Pacific Coast Highway, Malibu, 310-456-6444, 800-462-5428;
www.malibubeachinn.com

Before its 2007 overhaul, the Malibu Beach Inn was as bland as any chain. After David Geffen's $10 million renovation, the "Billionaire's Beach"—which sits on the ocean—is worth the excursion (even for east siders looking to get away from it all and see how the other half lives). The hotel doesn't look showy from the outside, but upon entering the lobby, you'll see the ocean through a windowed back wall and restaurant deck (where later you'll sip limited-run California wines). In rooms upstairs (well-appointed, but sometimes small), you'll find treats such as Trina Turk robes, 400 CDs, 350-thread-count linens and a refreshment center filled with snacks. Swanky options for food and shopping at Malibu Country Mart are worth a gander (for star sightings as well), but you can also enjoy less touristy activities ranging from seafood shack fare at the once endangered Reel Inn (kept open thanks to local protest) to waterfall hikes near where Sunset Boulevard and Pacific Coast Highway meet.

47 rooms. Restaurant, bar. Spa. $351 and up

★★★MALIBU COUNTRY INN

6506 Westward Beach Road, Malibu, 310-457-9622, 800-386-6787;
www.malibucountryinn.com

Despite Malibu's major draws—from sandy beaches to upscale restaurants and shops at Malibu Country Mart (including Nobu and L.A. favorite Ron Herman)—there are few hotels in the area. So although it's not fancy, Malibu Country Inn is a bed-and-breakfast-style abode just off Zuma Beach that fills that need. You'll forget that Hollywood is in the vicinity while you're tucked away in this oceanside residence that's a far cry from too-cool hotels on the east side. The mellow, beachy Collection Restaurant & Bar—which technically isn't part of the hotel but is undeniably linked by close proximity—offers standard American fare for breakfast, lunch and dinner as well as views of the ocean from its rooftop. Surf's up all the time here.

16 rooms. Restaurant, bar. Pool. $151-250

★★★SHUTTERS HOTEL ON THE BEACH

1 Pico Blvd., Santa Monica, 310-458-0030, 800-334-9000;
www.shuttersonthebeach.com

For in-the-know locals (including major names whom the hotel prefers to keep hush-hush), Shutters is a frequent destination. It is Santa Monica's most beloved spot for everything from seaside brunches and cocktails to poolside basking, especially since fine dining restaurant One Pico and the famed pool deck both got a makeover (by designer, Michael Smith, who did Obama's White House no less). As you enter the lobby, you're embraced by the sea air and a nautical vibe; you'll see cozy spaces near fireplaces and art from beloved California greats like David Hockney and Claes Oldenburg. Charmingly bleached-out and airy guest rooms are adorned in pure whites, sea blues and deep woods and outfitted with everything from an LCD TV in the bathroom to beachfront patios with light wicker furniture. At One Pico, below lofted ceilings decorated with antique boat hulls and art nouveau lanterns casting warm light, you'll sample chef Michael Reardon's new seasonally driven menu—upscale, but never stuffy. Casual sand-side eatery Coast Beach Café and Bar is another option, as are refreshments at the Lobby Lounge. As celebrity-spa guru Ole Henriksen is steering the ship, One the Spa is a treat for out-of-towners who might not be accustomed to L.A.'s excessive spa services. Make like a local and get a Moon Glow facial and a cucumber-rich Nature Baby signature body treatment.

198 rooms. Restaurant, bar. Fitness center. Pool. Spa. $351 and up

★★★VICEROY SANTA MONICA

1819 Ocean Ave., Santa Monica, 310-260-7500, 800-670-6185;
www.viceroysantamonica.com

As luxurious as Santa Monica is, it never quite had a handle on hip until Viceroy exploded onto the scene. Located a block off the beach, this ultra-sleek, modern yet romantic hotel—where there's always music and mingling—attracts the Westside's young beautiful set. The lobby is done up in tongue-in-cheek, slightly Mad Hatter-ish décor, with old-fashioned embellishments like candelabras updated in kitschy sleek white. You'll find the same eclectic details in the rooms, along with custom-designed beds with linens so pretty you won't want to ruffle them. By the pool, you can savor some snacks and drinks, but Viceroy takes poolside activities to another level: There are three dining cabanas which can be reserved for private dinners and the hotel can even turn the spaces into mini movie theaters complete with popcorn and cocktails for a respite from the sun or manicure/pedicure stations, if you'd like some extra pampering.

162 rooms. Restaurant, bar. Pool. Pets accepted. $351 and up

WHERE TO EAT

★★BORDER GRILL

1445 Fourth St., Santa Monica, 310-451-1655; www.bordergrill.com

The place for hearty, tasty Mexican in Santa Monica is Border Grill, a popular restaurant that grew out of a "taco stand" run by the "two hot tamales" of Food Network notoriety. Nibble on the plantain empanadas before digging into the grilled chicken chilaquiles, and be sure to wash it down with one of the house margaritas. The only thing better? If you happen to be around during one of the specials. Happy hour is on Monday through Friday from 4 p.m. to 7 p.m. (or Saturday and Sunday after 10 p.m.) and includes $3 tacos with freshly mashed guacamole. The $10 quick lunch (11:30 a.m. to 3:30 p.m. Monday through Friday) is another sweet deal that includes a green corn tamale appetizer, iced tea or soda and a delicious dish depending on the day, like the Monday Mexican Cobb Salad.

Mexican. Lunch, dinner. $16-35

★★★CAPO

1810 Ocean Ave., Santa Monica, 310-394-5550; www.caporestaurant.com

Keep your eyes peeled or you'll easily speed right past this tiny, hospitable eatery. Capo means "boss" or "chief," which is fitting, as the cuisine is upscale Italian and the atmosphere is elegant in that old-school sort of way, with a blazing fireplace, gentle candlelight and a crowd that comprises both wealthy Westside gourmands and real-deal industry types who'd rather not shout to be heard. The wine list is comprehensive, and the risottos—made with either porcini, Dungeness crab or lobster or lobster—are creamy perfection. Finish up with the vassoio da formaggio. Don't speak Italian? Then practice fast because this place is authentic all the way.

Italian. Dinner. Closed Sunday. Reservations recommended. Bar. $36-85

★★★CATCH RESTAURANT & SUSHI BAR

Hotel Casa del Mar, 1910 Ocean Way, Santa Monica, 310-581-7714;
www.catchsantamonica.com

Catch captures the best aspects of Santa Monica. The restaurant, located at the recently renovated Hotel Casa del Mar, features enviable ocean views that have inspired us to enjoy more than one leisurely meal here, happily relaxing amid the beachfront-chic décor with its hints of seafoam green and a central bar inlaid with mother-of-pearl and accented by gnarled driftwood branches. The service, too, is classy but welcoming—a refreshing change from the overwrought minimalism of so many Los Angeles restaurants. What will really nab your attention, however, is the restaurant's simple and delicious seafood. Indeed, executive chef Michael Reardon's love of seafood is obvious; the menu is packed with fresh sushi offerings like red snapper and an excellent selection of crudo, including one with tuna, red grapefruit and fennel.

Seafood, sushi. Lunch, dinner. Bar. $36-85

★★★CÉZANNE
1740 Ocean Ave., Santa Monica, 310-395-9700; www.lemerigothotel.com
Try to snag one of the high-backed banquettes for the best people-watching while chef Desi Szonntagh charms you with French fare that includes black truffle mac and cheese, roasted pear salad with fennel, spiced pecans, pomegranate, Point Reyes blue cheese and balsamic vinaigrette, and seafood cocktail served with red and green chili sauce. A bold décor sets the stage for the impeccable French California-style dishes.

American, French. Breakfast, lunch, dinner. $36-85

★★★CHINOIS ON MAIN
2709 Main St., Santa Monica, 310-392-9025; www.wolfgangpuck.com
A longtime Wolfgang Puck mainstay, Chinois on Main has been serving up delectable Asian-fusion cuisine—executed with French technique and California flair—since 1983. Pull up a chair at the counter and watch the magic happen in the open kitchen while you sip on a vintage from the extensive wine list. But as fitting as this spot is for private tête-à-têtes, it's even better for big groups, since the offerings—such as the whole sizzling catfish with ponzu dipping sauce and the pork shoulder with wild sticky rice and tamarind sauce—are served family-style and at communal tables. Once you take a bite, you'll see that sharing is actually a very selfish motive.

Asian-fusion. Dinner. Bar. $36-85

★★GEOFFREY'S MALIBU
27400 Pacific Coast Highway, Malibu, 310-457-1519; www.geoffreysmalibu.com
Geoffrey's is as classic Malibu as it gets—it began as the Holiday House, a Richard Neutra-designed resort and restaurant that opened in 1948 and catered to the era's biggest Hollywood stars, including Frank Sinatra, Lana Turner and Marilyn Monroe. The restaurant became Geoffrey's in 1983 and didn't miss a beat. Perhaps its success has something to do with its enviable location atop a bluff overlooking the Pacific—or perhaps it's the deliciously classic California fare. We especially love this spot for its Sunday brunch; the stunning ocean views make for the perfect accompaniment to favorites like eggs Benedict topped with prosciutto, housemade hollandaise sauce and rosemary potatoes, and chicken picatta with sautéed vegetables, mashed potatoes and a lemon-caper butter sauce.

American. Lunch (Monday-Friday), dinner, Saturday-Sunday brunch. Reservations recommended. Bar. $36-85

★★★INN OF THE SEVENTH RAY

128 Old Topanga Canyon Road, Topanga, 310-465-1311;
www.innoftheseventhray.com

Topanga Canyon is one of the last remaining flower-child enclaves of Los Angeles; its residents love its proximity to the beach and its woody natural beauty, and many of them have lived in the neighborhood since the '60s. The canyon's single fine-dining establishment, the Inn of the Seventh Ray, fits perfectly into its serene atmosphere, with tables overlooking a gentle creek and a menu of healthy and almost entirely organic fare. The restaurant goes the extra mile for the latter, baking its own organic-grain bread daily and using only naturally raised, range-fed chickens and natural meats from animals that were never fed hormones or antibiotics. The kitchen, presided over by new chef Bradley Miller, also uses as many local ingredients in dishes such as lamb chops with fresh vegetables, fennel purée and home-made blackberry jam.
American. Lunch (Monday-Saturday), dinner, Sunday brunch. Bar. $36-85

★★★JOSIE

2424 Pico Blvd., Santa Monica, 310-581-9888; www.josierestaurant.com

Located on the unprepossessing corner of Pico Boulevard and 24th Street in Santa Monica, Josie is the creation of chef Josie Le Balch, who's done time in the kitchens of Remi and the Saddle Peak Lodge. Le Balch is known for combing the city's farmers' markets for fresh seasonal ingredients, and the daily specials change based on what's been inspiring her lately. Still, there's a slew of reliable favorites on the cards, such as the buffalo burger with truffle fries or the whole boneless trout with corn, green beans and asparagus in a lemongrass nage.
American. Dinner. Reservations recommended. Bar. $36-85

★★THE LOBSTER

1602 Ocean Ave., Santa Monica, 310-458-9294; www.thelobster.com

This longtime Santa Monica fixture located at the end of the pier serves crowd-pleasing seafood, whether it's a whole Maine lobster you're craving or a crunchy shrimp salad, while offering some of the best (and only) water views in Santa Monica. You might consider it a tourist trap but the food from chef Allyson Thurber is classic yet sophisticated. The place is always packed and the bar scene kicks in well before happy hour.
American, seafood. Lunch, dinner. $36-85

★★LA CACHETTE BISTRO

1733 Ocean Ave., Santa Monica, 310-434-9509; www.lacachettebistro.com

L.A. staple La Cachette, beloved for its fine French cuisine, recently relocated to Santa Monica and is now a more casual bistro than a fine-dining spot. You'll find hardwood floors, booths, French posters and an outdoor patio. The setting may have changed but chef-owner Jean Francois Meteigner's wonderful French cooking and wines haven't. Start with the creamy foie gras terrine with rhubarb and brioche, and follow up with the coq au vin. Or stop in for happy hour and have some fried organic chicken breast with ginger plum sauce, or perhaps an organic burger with grilled onions, fig chutney and mixed blue cheeses (both are just $6 during happy hour), with a Mexican or Italian beer (the list is well rounded).

French. Lunch (Monday Friday), dinner, Saturday Sunday brunch. Reservations recommended. Bar. $36-85

★★★★MELISSE

1104 Wilshire Blvd., Santa Monica, 310-395-0881; www.melisse.com

Named after an aromatic, calming Mediterranean herb also known as lemon balm, Melisse is a favorite spot for Westside gourmands. Chef Josiah Citrin opened this elegant but unpretentious eatery in 1999, creating contemporary American dishes with French influences, like the tasting menu's 48-hour short rib with celery confit, dijonnais and herbed bordelaise sauce. The dishes here are artfully presented and innovative but not overly intellectual, and ingredients are always fresh, as Citrin takes advantage of southern California's year-round growing season and frequents local farmers' markets to find the best produce to soothe those Westside foodies' ravenous appetites.

French. Dinner. Closed Sunday-Monday. Bar. $86 and up

★★★MICHAEL'S

1147 Third St., Santa Monica, 310-451-0843; www.michaelssantamonica.com

Many Los Angeles restaurants claim a celebrity clientele, but Michael's in Santa Monica, (there's also one in New York that's a media favorite for lunch), arguably the birthplace of California cuisine, is the real deal. Under the direction of Michael McCarty, Michael's keeps a database of its famous clients, right down to what they do for a living, how many times they've been in and what they've ordered. (Mel Brooks is among the many regulars.) Indeed, the 30-year-old Michael's has seating arrangements down to a science; they're tweaked multiple times a day (to accommodate dueling agents, of course). Like many loyal (and not necessarily famous) Michael's patrons, however, we prefer to dine in the lovely garden with a retractable ceiling; it's just the place to seal a deal while enjoying a juicy Michael's burger with applewood-smoked bacon.

American. Lunch (Monday-Friday), dinner. Closed Sunday. Bar. $ 36-85

★★MOONSHADOWS

20356 W. Pacific Coast Highway, Malibu, 310-456-3010;
www.moonshadowsmalibu.com

Despite its gorgeous, ridiculously perfect vistas—schools of dolphins cruising the horizon, beautiful sunsets—Malibu suffers from a strange dearth of ocean-view restaurants, which makes Moonshadows and its trendy Blue Lounge an oasis right off the Pacific Coast Highway. Diners swarm the outdoor patio at sunset, sucking down cocktail after cocktail while nibbling on such delectables as oysters on the half shell and the Snake River Farm Kobe beef burger. The scene really heats up after dark, when DJs, including local favorite Raul Campos of KCRW, spin an eclectic mix for a hip crowd.

Contemporary American. Lunch, dinner, Saturday-Sunday brunch. Reservations recommended. Bar. $36-85

★★★NOBU

3835 Cross Creek Road, Malibu, 310-317-9140; 903 N. La Cienega Blvd., West Ho-
wood, 310-657-5711; Matsuhisa, 129 N. La Cienega Blvd., Beverly Hills, 310-659-9639;
www.noburestaurants.com

In 1999, Nobu Malibu opened its doors in the too-cool-for-everyone Malibu Country Mart shopping center at Cross Creek Road and the Pacific Coast Highway, and reservations have been hard to come by ever since. Thankfully, Nobu Los Angeles has finally taken over the space formerly occupied by L'Orangerie—not to mention Matsuhisa Beverly Hills has opened as well—so sushi lovers can choose from more than one location for a mouthful of chef Nobuyuki Matsuhisa's signature yellowtail sashimi with jalapeño. Nobu's acclaimed new-style Japanese cuisine shows the influence of Matsuhisa's experiences in Peru when he was in his mid-20s (with dishes like tiradito and ceviche), and fans and foodies have already ensured that all locations are booked up.

Japanese, sushi. Lunch (Monday-Friday), dinner. $86 and up

★★★ONE PICO

Shutters Hotel on the Beach, 1 Pico Blvd., Santa Monica, 310-587-1717;
www.shuttersonthebeach.com

Located on a spot of Los Angeles' priciest beachfront real estate, One Pico, the acclaimed eatery inside Shutters Hotel on the Beach, actually sits on the sand, with the psychedelic colors of the Santa Monica Pier's new Ferris wheel spinning in the distance. The restaurant was recently renovated, but the fare remains reliably delicious. One Pico is helmed by chef Michael Reardon, who also heads up nearby Catch at the Casa del Mar. Reardon's menu hinges on what's fresh and in season; the dishes boast a light touch with an Italian sensibility incorporating an array of spit-roasted meats and whole fish, as well as mouthwatering starters like the roasted market beets with black truffle goat cheese and lemon. The view can't be beat, and the décor has been redone in perfect beachy-chic fashion by in-demand designer Michael S. Smith, who has created interiors for everyone from Cindy Crawford and Dustin Hoffman to most recently, President Obama at the White House.

American. Lunch, dinner, Sunday brunch. Bar. $36-85

★★PECORINO

11604 San Vicente Blvd., Brentwood, 310-571-3800; www.pecorinorestaurant.com

Pecorino, in the space formerly occupied by Zax, is a triple threat: there's the friendly, doting service; the warm but elegant dining room, complete with beam ceilings and an exposed brick wall; and, last but not least, the food. There are plenty of hearty classics on offer, from lasagna and ravioli to spaghetti and fettucini alla Bolognese. The agnello Cacio e uovo—a deboned New Zealand rack of lamb casserole with artichokes, eggs and pecorino—is particularly tender and savory. For the finale, indulge in the tiramisu with amaretto liqueur; it's deliciously creamy. Or make like a real Italian and try the delightful cheese platter for dessert—with a variety of pecorinos, of course.

Italian. Lunch (Monday-Saturday), dinner. Bar. $36-85

★★★THE PENTHOUSE

The Huntley Hotel, 1111 Second St., Santa Monica, 310-393-8080;
www.thehuntleyhotel.com

Poised high atop the stylish Huntley Hotel on Santa Monica Beach, the Penthouse is a tasteful jewel box rendered life-sized. The curvy white chandeliers, paper-thin white curtains and pale-blue upholstered chairs with backs shaped like ocean waves will inspire a trip to your interior decorator. The restaurant is accessible through the hotel's interior elevator, or you can take the glass-encased exterior lift. The restaurant provides stunning views of the Pacific through a wall of windows, while executive chef Seth Greenburg's creations draw inspiration from France, Spain and beyond. Try a black truffle omelet with goat cheese and wild mushrooms for breakfast; a braised brisket sandwich with horseradish, mustard, tomato and watercress for lunch; or the spicy seafood stew with clams, black sable, calamari, crab, chorizo and white wine broth for dinner.

American. Breakfast, lunch, dinner, Sunday brunch. Bar. Reservations recommended. Bar. $36-85

★★SUSHI ROKU

1401 Ocean Ave., Santa Monica, 310-458-4771; www.sushiroku.com

This hip sushi spot packs them in nightly, thanks to beautifully presented, fresh sushi and an outdoor patio with views of the ocean. You'll find some creative rolls on the menu, including one with baked lobster with creamy miso sauce. The hot items, including spicy jumbo shrimp with homemade potato chips and rib eye with a grilled soy garlic sauce, are also nice. Anything pairs well with a choice from the extensive sake list.

Japanese. Lunch, dinner. $36-85

★★TAKAO

11656 San Vicente Blvd., Brentwood, 310-207-8636

In the heart of Brentwood, Takao continues to please the taste buds of the city's many notoriously finicky sushi aficionados. For their part, these serious foodies know not to look twice at the spartan, unmemorable décor of the smallish eatery— which is easy to miss if you don't look closely—because Takao focuses on quality sushi, not a trendy scene. Many consider the meaty cold cuts here to be some of Los Angeles' best and freshest raw fish. Regulars order the omakase, entrusting themselves to the chef for a culinary flight that might be a bit pricey, but is nearly guaranteed to tickle your taste buds. Just keep in mind that for this menu, the staff will only inquire about your preferences—the chef will decide what gets brought to the table, and while nothing here is a bargain, several levels of slightly different pricing are available.

Japanese, sushi. Lunch (Monday-Saturday), dinner. Bar. $36-85

★★★TAVERN

11648 San Vicente Boulevard, Brentwood, 310-806-6464; www.tavernla.com

You can't go wrong at any of Suzanne Goin's restaurants (Lucques and Hungry Cat are among her other L.A. places). Her latest, Tavern, serves the same outstanding seasonal cuisine in a manor-like setting with wingbacked chairs and a sun-drenched atrium filled with olive trees. Lunch includes salads, sandwiches, burgers and main courses, while dinner includes entrées such as the pork chop with cornbread, chorizo and spiced maple syrup. You'll also find a nice list of desserts and cocktails. Or simply pop into the larder, a storefront café where you can pick up cupcakes, salads and fresh-baked bread.

American. Breakfast (Monday-Friday), lunch, dinner, Saturday-Sunday brunch. $36-85

★★★VALENTINO

3115 Pico Blvd., Santa Monica, 310-829-4313; www.pieroselvaggio.com

For almost three decades, Valentino owner Piero Selvaggio has provided diners with premier Italian food accompanied by a wine list composed of the best that both Italy and California have to offer. The food is classic with dishes like linguine with clams and sweet garlic, or a veal chop with prosciutto, cream and Marsala.

Italian. Dinner. Closed Sunday. $86 and up

★★★WHIST

Viceroy Santa Monica, 1819 Ocean Ave., Santa Monica, 310-260-7500;
www.viceroysantamonica.com

Whist is super-quirky and cool. What else could you expect from a restaurant named after an old-school card game? Inside, it's like the Mad Hatter decorated for a grown-up tea party: lime-green walls, row after row of English china and accents of silver damask wallpaper. But as charming as the dining room is, it may not compare with the Santa Monica sun for some, which is why you can also take it outside to one of the luxe poolside tables or cabanas. Ditch the tea party altogether and have a coffee klatch by pairing one of the sinful desserts—such as the cherry upside-down cake with candied walnuts, vanilla and malt—with Whist's broad selection of java.

American. Breakfast, lunch (Monday-Saturday), dinner, Sunday brunch. Bar. $36-85

THE VALLEY

If you're planning to visit one of the TV tapings in Burbank or Universal Studios Hollywood (home to a movie studio, a theme park and the CityWalk entertainment complex), you'll need to venture northwest of the city into the largely residential San Fernando Valley (known colloquially as The Valley), which includes Studio City and Burbank.

WHAT TO SEE
GIBSON AMPHITHEATRE

100 Universal City Plaza, Universal City, 818-622-4440; www.hob.com/venues

Though this mammoth theater seats about 6,000, it's known for its good sight lines and acoustics. Every chart-busting music act has entertained here at one time or another. Gibson is part of the Universal City complex, so you're just steps from Universal Studios Hollywood and Universal City-Walk, a popular entertainment center with an IMAX 3D theater, restaurants, shops and nightclubs.

GREAT WALL OF LOS ANGELES

Oxnard Street and Burbank Boulevard, San Fernando Valley, 310-822-9560;
www.sparcmurals.org

Conceived by Judith Baca, director and founder of the Social and Public Art Resource Center in 1974, the Great Wall of Los Angeles has become one of the most famous and respected murals in the world. The wall portrays the beginnings of California history to the present. From the 1522 Spanish arrival to the birth of rock and roll to gay rights, you will get a glimpse of the diverse California culture.

NBC STUDIOS TOUR

3000 W. Alameda Ave., Burbank, 818-840-4444; www.nbc.com

Get a behind-the-scenes look at NBC's television operations. The tour shows where sets are designed and gives visitors a peek at wardrobe and makeup. It's a limited tour, but the nice price tag ($7.50)—and the fact that the other networks don't offer studio tours—makes this an appealing destination. Admission: $7.50. Monday-Friday 9 a.m.-3 p.m.

RONALD REAGAN PRESIDENTIAL LIBRARY AND MUSEUM

40 Presidential Drive, Simi Valley, 805-577-4000, 800-410-8354;
www.reaganfoundation.org

Ronald Reagan owned a ranch high in the Santa Barbara Mountains. Stop by his comprehensive library, located just eight miles off the 101 (take CA-23 North toward Fillmore and follow signs). Perched on a mountaintop with views of the mountains, valleys and Pacific Ocean, this 100-acre site has exhibits that follow Reagan from childhood to the glamorous world of Hollywood stardom, to his inauguration as the 40th President of the United States. Key events of his two terms are revealed through documents, photographs and artifacts, including a full-scale replica of the Oval Office and Cabinet Room, a nuclear missile that was deactivated after the president and Mikhail Gorbachev signed the INF treaty and a section of the Berlin Wall. Admission: adults $12.00, seniors $9, children 11-17 $6, children under 11 free. Daily 10 a.m.-5 p.m.

UNIVERSAL STUDIOS HOLLYWOOD

100 Universal City Plaza, Universal City, 818-622-3801;
www.universalstudioshollywood.com

Universal Studios lets you kill several birds with one stone: Not only can you go on a tour of a living, breathing movie studio, but you can also jump aboard theme park rides, enjoy urban nightlife at Universal CityWalk and see world-famous music acts at the Gibson Amphitheatre. On the studio tour you'll be shuttled around the Universal lot on a tram, where you'll get to see the sets of *War of the Worlds*, *Desperate Housewives* and *CSI: Crime Scene Investigation*. Then scream your head off on Revenge of the Mummy—The Ride, Jurassic Park—The Ride, and The Simpsons Ride. After spending the day at the park, unwind at CityWalk, where you can eat, drink, shop, see a movie at the IMAX, go rock 'n' roll bowling or ride the Saddle Ranch's mechanical bull.

Tickets: $67, children under 48" $57. Monday-Friday 10 a.m.-6 p.m., Saturday-Sunday 9 a.m.-6 p.m.

WARNER BROTHERS STUDIOS VIP TOUR

4000 Warner Blvd., Burbank, 818-972-8687; www.studio-tour.com

During the two-hour, 15-minute tour of the Warner Bros. Studios backlot, you'll see sound stages, craft shops and exterior sets from TV shows of the past and present, such as Two and a Half Men. Tours vary depending on which shows are shooting that day, but count on seeing the sets from Friends and ER as well as special effects demonstrations, costumes and much more. If that's not enough, you can upgrade to the Deluxe Tour, which clocks in at five hours, includes lunch with the group in the Studio's Commissary Fine Dining Room and offers a more in-depth look at how the studio works. Deluxe tour: $195. Monday-Friday 10:20 a.m.; VIP tour: $45. Monday-Friday 8:20 a.m.-4 p.m.

WHERE TO STAY

★★★HILTON LOS ANGELES/UNIVERSAL CITY

555 Universal Hollywood Drive, Universal City, 818-506-2500, 800-445-8667;
www.hilton.com

While the nearby studios and entertainment destinations are a clear draw for any hotel in Universal City, rooms at this towering Hilton offer plush beds with down comforters and pillows that mold to your head, and floral-scented Crabtree & Evelyn's LaSource toiletries. If you're a parent on a family trip, use the hotel's babysitting service, whether you just hop down to onsite Café Sierre for the signature seafood buffet and Chinese chow, the Lobby Lounge for a light bite and cocktail, or out and about to any of the surrounding restaurants. If you like sushi, run over to Sushi Nozawa (a restaurant from the chef known as the "Sushi Nazi") or the original Katsuya for some of the city's best sashimi and cooked Japanese food. If you end up making it a late night, grab java from the hotel's Starbucks Coffee Corner the next day to help you get through the morning of sightseeing with the kids.

491 rooms. Restaurant, bar. Business center. Fitness center. Pool. $151-250

★★★HOTEL AMARANO BURBANK

322 N. Pass Ave., Burbank, 818-842-8887; www.hotelamarano.com

Tourists like that the hotel is 10 minutes from major movie studios like Warner Bros., Disney and Universal, while business travelers appreciate the complimentary wireless Internet, oversized desks and iPod docking stations. Both will enjoy the popular cocktail-hour tapas and tipples at chef Jose Sanchez's Library Lounge restaurant. The simple rooms have a 1930s modernism aesthetic (cue the low-slung, clean lined-furniture and glass-topped tables) and offer cool Molton Brown bath products. Although a sundeck with Jacuzzi will get you outdoors, a hop, skip and a jump to Griffith Park for a hike is definitely worth the trip. Tip: If you stay here, bypass the chaos of LAX and fly into the nearby Burbank Airport instead.

100 rooms. Restaurant, bar. Fitness center. Business center. $251-350

★★★SHERATON UNIVERSAL HOTEL

333 Universal Hollywood Drive, Universal City, 818-980-1212, 877-599-9810;
www.sheraton.com

It's hard to be more immersed in "the biz" than in Universal City. This extremely touristy area of L.A. is all about the movie industry and Sheraton

Universal is at the epicenter. After a $30 million renovation in summer 2008, the hotel offers newly refreshed rooms with Shine by Bliss bath products, Starbucks coffee and iPod docking station/clock radios. Check out the re-done Starview Room's panoramic view from its rooftop location (it's a perfect spot for a meeting or private event). Wheeler-and-dealer types will be too busy for sightseeing in the Link@Sheraton business center, which looks like a futuristic coffee shop with casual décor and cushy seating, creating a more pleasant working space than the business office norm.

451 rooms. Restaurant, bar. Business center. Fitness center. Pool. $351 and up

WHERE TO EAT

★★★ASANEBO
11941 Ventura Blvd., Studio City, 818-760-3348
Forget the strip-mall ambience and concentrate on the jaw-dropping array of beautifully crafted delicacies served by a super-fast and helpful staff. Besides superior sushi, there are special dishes like Dungeness crab made sashimi-style and monkfish liver in ponzu sauce.
Japanese. Lunch, dinner. Closed Monday. $16-35

★★★PINOT BISTRO
12969 Ventura Blvd., Studio City, 818-990-0500; www.patinagroup.com
Los Angeles celebrity chef Joachim Splichal of Patina fame has spun off Pinot Bistro, a less expensive, more accessible taste of his signature French cooking. The menu hews to bistro classics such as duck confit and roasted chicken, while the extensive wine list defies French-only conventions. This Studio City favorite offers dining in several distinct areas, such as the Fireplace Room. The décor is warm and inviting throughout, with wood accents, checkered floors, art-covered walls and cozy banquettes.
French. Lunch (Monday-Friday), dinner. $36-85

★★SUSHI KATSU-YA
11680 Ventura Boulevard, Studio City, 818-985-6976; www.sushikatsu-ya.com
Before splashy locations opened up in Hollywood and Brentwood, people from all over the Los Angeles area descended on this storefront for the city's best sushi. There's still a line snaking out the door at the place where Katsuya Uechi first began playing with texture, temperature and spice to create signatures like this albacore sashimi with frizzled onions and crispy rice topped with spicy tuna—a dish that is now copied by sushi restaurants all over the country. Some say this location is the best, but if you're looking for more of a scene, you can also visit Katsuya (www.sbe.com/katsuya), which has locations in Brentwood and Hollywood.
Japanese, sushi. Lunch (Monday-Saturday), dinner. $36-85

★★WINE BISTRO
11915 Ventura Blvd., Studio City, 818-766-6233; www.winebistro.net
If you love wine, this is the place. Settle in at the bar and enjoy a glass with your pick of tapas, such as the marinated artichoke melt with dipping vinaigrette or dollar size Kobe beef burgers with Belgian fries. Or sit down for multiple courses of the French bistro menu.
Lunch (Tuesday-Friday), Dinner. Closed Monday. $36-85

VENICE

Venice has its canals and beaches, but it is probably best known for its bohemian vibe and boardwalk. A visit here might feel like a flashback to the 1960s counterculture. People-watching doesn't get any better than in this funky beach community. The boardwalk that fronts the ocean stretches for two miles and every inch of it is packed with a colorful cast of characters. In-line skaters, power-walkers, runners and bikers mingle with street performers, local artists, massage therapists, preachers, tattoo artists and anyone else who shows up for a day in the California sun.

WHAT TO SEE
VENICE BEACH AND BOARDWALK
1800 Ocean Front Walk, Venice; www.laparks.org

Venice Beach probably hasn't changed much since the swinging '60s and '70s, when skateboarders and hippies ruled the boardwalk. Although many of the area's homes are now owned by wealthy yuppie types, Venice is as zany as ever. Skateboarders still flood the Venice Skatepark, artists still make their mark on the Venice Beach graffiti wall, and bodybuilders still pump iron at Muscle Beach's legendary outdoor gym. The Venice Boardwalk is inundated with shopkeepers peddling all kinds of wares, from cheap sunglasses to snarky T-shirts to smoking pipes. The area also attracts a variety of street performers, everything from human statues to jugglers who favor chainsaws over clubs. With this cast of characters, it's a great spot for people-watching.

WHERE TO EAT
★★AXE
1009 Abbot Kinney Blvd., Venice, 310-664-9787; www.axerestaurant.com

Pronounced "ah-shay," this swanky and sparse space has gleaming polished concrete floors, strict angular furniture, tiny votives in simple dishes, and unadorned white walls—save for a drippy torso-sized candle, there is no décor to speak of. This minimalism serves the strictly organic menu, which uses the freshest ingredients to create dishes like coconut curry lamb stew and roasted trout with balsamic cabbage. The crowd consists of local couples on spontaneous dates, girlfriends playing catch-up, and toned folks on the way home from yoga.
American. Lunch, dinner. $16-35

★★CAPRI
1616 Abbot Kinney Blvd., Venice, 310-392-8777

Abbot Kinney Boulevard offers a competitive culinary lineup, and Capri is no slouch. The eatery's sparse, whitewashed, pseudo-industrial interior—warmed by romantic candlelight and expensive-looking paintings—provides a canny counterpoint to its sumptuous northern Italian fare. Proud shore-dwellers, sneaker-clad tourists, and the occasional celebrity tend to linger over the handwritten menu, which, in addition to a selection of second-course pastas, features New Zealand rack of lamb, muscovy duck, and halibut steak with grilled red onion and radicchio
Italian. Dinner. $36-85

★★HAL'S BAR AND GRILL

1349 Abbot Kinney Blvd., Venice, 310-396-3105; www.halsbarandgrill.com

Among trendy clothing boutiques, antique furniture stores and yoga studios, Hal's stands out as the ultimate upscale neighborhood restaurant, where a hipster beach crowd dresses up to meet friends and family. The loftlike, whitewashed space is adorned with commanding modern art pieces, dotted with spacious booths, and lined with an ever-crowded and lively bar. Sushi hand rolls and osso buco are crowd pleasers, but the turkey burger and Caesar salad win raves as well. Live jazz on Saturdays and Sundays draws in the beautiful people.

American. Lunch (Monday-Friday), dinner,Saturday-Sunday brunch. $ 36-85

★★JAMES' BEACH

60 N. Venice Blvd., Venice, 310-823-5396; www.jamesbeach.com

This sand-adjacent joint is a restaurant and a nightclub rolled into one. Like a swanky beach house, the décor is simple and chic, save for the illuminated boxer shorts hanging from the ceiling, which are rumored to have been left there over the years. A tan and toned crowd clad mostly in black swigs cocktails and flirts, but not before enjoying California comfort food like turkey burgers and fried calamari. Sinful homemade chocolate chip cookies cap off the meal before the party really begins.

American. Lunch (Wednesday-Friday), dinner, Saturday-Sunday brunch. Bar. $16-35

★★JOE'S

1023 Abbot Kinney Blvd., Venice, 310-392-5655; www.joesrestaurant.com

Regarded as the culinary pinnacle of Abbot Kinney Boulevard, Joe's still retains a neighborhood charm, where beach-dwelling locals rub elbows with celebrities and gourmands who travel miles and miles to dine on excellent California/French country fare. Architecturally, Joe's runs the gamut from a mod blue-lit bar to a rustic provincial farmhouse to a Zen-like patio with a river-rock waterfall, united only by a distinctly Californian aura. Foie gras paired with ahi tuna and red snapper with "potato scales" are a couple of specialties of the eclectic and avant-garde menu.

French, American. Lunch (Tuesday-Friday), dinner, Saturday-Sunday brunch. Closed Monday. $16-35

★★PRIMITIVO

1025 Abbot Kinney Blvd., Venice, 310-396-5353; www.primitivowinebistro.com

Always teeming with eye-catching professionals, this wine bistro and tapas bar resembles an elegant swap meet, with candles resting in Depression-era glass, antiqued chandeliers, and bolts of fabric decoratively strewn about. The funky charm of the shabby-chic dining room is offset by the colorful and bold tapas, like zucchini blossoms stuffed with goat cheese and chorizo-stuffed quail. The high-energy bar is a great choice for impromptu dates and solo dinners. Wine fans take note: there is an excellent selection of half bottles for easy sampling.

Mediterranean. Lunch (Monday-Friday), dinner. Reservations recommended. Bar. $36-85

★★WABI-SABI
1635 Abbot Kinney Blvd., Venice, 310-314-2229; www.wabisabisushi.com

This festive sushi restaurant is funky, Zen-like, modern, always packed, open late and full of lookers. And it serves up great fish. In short, it's the ultimate neighborhood joint. A grand sushi bar graces the long dining room, which opens into an outdoor patio, which then becomes a glossy-white back dining room. Fresh sushi, sashimi, and oyster specials rotate daily, and entrées like miso black cod and tempura are favorites. An approachable cold sake list helps diners wash it all down.

Japanese, sushi. Dinner. $16-35

WEST HOLLYWOOD

This tiny city-within-a-city boasts stylish home design shops, fashionable boutiques and fine restaurants. Robertson Boulevard features antiques, designer duds and celeb-heavy lunch spots like The Ivy. La Cienega is home to restaurant row and the Beverly Center Mall. Santa Monica Boulevard is the center of the city's gay community, with hip fast-food joints, nightclubs, gyms and crowded streets at all hours.

Locals take advantage of the breakfast spots, cheap manicures, tiny boutiques and swanky cocktail lounges on Beverly Boulevard and Third Street, while those with an unquenchable thirst for fashion flock to Melrose Avenue, which is more couture west of Fairfax and more punk rock to the east.

WHAT TO SEE
THE GROUNDLINGS
7307 Melrose Ave., West Hollywood, 323-934-4747; www.groundlings.com

This L.A. institution has been cracking up audiences since 1975, thanks to all the hilarious actors who train at the Groundlings School of Improvisation. Lisa Kudrow, Phil Hartman, Jon Lovitz and many others have all practiced their improvisational skills here. Many alumni have also gone on to write for our favorite funny TV shows, including Cheers, Taxi and Golden Girls. Drop by on a Thursday night to see L.A.'s longest running improv show (since 1992), Cooking with Gas, which is based entirely on audience suggestions. Shows take place five days a week.

Wednesday-Thursday 10 a.m-8 p.m., Friday 10 a.m.-10 p.m., Saturday 2:30 p.m.-10p.m., Sunday 2 p.m.-7:30 p.m.

THE ROXY THEATRE
9009 W. Sunset Blvd., West Hollywood, 310-278-9457; www.theroxyonsunset.com

The Roxy goes way back: Neil Young played the venue's first show in 1973, Bruce Springsteen gave a now-classic performance here in 1975 and Guns N' Roses rocked the house before making it big. (Unfortunately, the Roxy is also known as the place where John Belushi partied before he overdosed and died.) These days, everyone from Tori Amos to Jay-Z plays at the legendary club. Kick back in a booth and order a drink before hitting the dance floor. Box office hours: Monday-Friday noon-6 p.m. Venue hours vary by show times.

TROUBADOUR

9081 Santa Monica Blvd., West Hollywood, 310-276-1158; www.troubadour.com

What do musicians Neil Young, Joni Mitchell, Elton John, the Pointer Sisters, Metallica and Guns N' Roses all have in common? They all made their debuts at the Troubadour. Since 1957 this West Hollywood club has been making music history. Tom Waits was discovered at the Troubadour during an amateur night, Carly Simon first met James Taylor at a Troubadour show, and Janis Joplin partied at the Troubadour the night before she died. Today, the venue welcomes up-and-coming acts from around the world, but veteran musicians still hold the venue in high esteem, so don't be surprised when you hear about big-name bands headlining shows here. Coldplay, Red Hot Chili Peppers and The Killers have all ripped up the Troubadour's stage in recent years.

Check Web site for ticket and performance information

WHISKY A GO-GO

8901 Sunset Blvd., West Hollywood, 310-652-4202;www.whiskyagogo.com

The Whisky A Go-Go opened its doors on the Sunset Strip in 1964—just in time to book acts like the Doors, the Byrds and Led Zeppelin. In the 1980s, the venue became a haven for punk music and bands like The Germs and X. Nowadays, the Whisky usually hosts acts that are of the hard-rock variety, so you'll see lots of tattoos and piercings at this nightspot. But since the club is also open to all ages, you can also expect to see a fair share of high schoolers. While the Whisky typically caters to local artists, chart-toppers like Velvet Revolver and Avril Lavigne stop in from time to time.

PINK'S HOT DOGS

709 N. La Brea Blvd., West Hollywood, 323-931-4223; www.pinkshollywood.com

In 1939 Paul Pink opened a hot dog cart at the location where the famous Pink's hot dog stand still sits. Times may have changed but Pink's hot dog recipe hasn't. Eat inside, among dozens of autographed star photographs, or outside under the shade of an umbrella. Don't be deterred by the long line—it's constant, but the people behind the counter move customers through faster than you can say, "I'll have a Three-Peat L.A. Laker Dog, hold the onions."

Sunday-Thursday 9:30 a.m.-2 a.m., Friday-Saturday 9:30 a.m.-3 a.m.

WHERE TO STAY

★★★ANDAZ WEST HOLLYWOOD

8401 Sunset Blvd., West Hollywood, 323-656-1234, 800-633-7313; www.andaz.com

The former Hyatt West Hollywood has had such a facelift, it is almost unrecognizable from before. Since the Hyatt's new trendy hotel brand ANdAZ is reaching for a younger audience, the hotel emerged transformed in early 2009. The new hotel attempts to wow with a dramatic glass garden pavilion with a Jacob Hashimoto sculpture and the intimate RH restaurant and bar (which features fresh, seasonal ingredients and a market to table approach), and a private wine room in charcoal and cream with mosaic tiles.

257 rooms. Restaurant, bar. Business center. Fitness center. Pool. $151-250

★★★CHAMBERLAIN WEST HOLLYWOOD

1000 Westmount Drive, West Hollywood, 310-657-7400, 800-201-9652;
www.chamberlainwesthollywood.com

People like the Chamberlain for its English-modern and neo-classical interi-
or with striking and eclectic elements like tropical jade and patina green tiles
and lacquered Asian-style coffee table. The location isn't shabby, either, as
the intimate hotel is centrally set in West Hollywood, but in a lesser-traveled
residential neighborhood. The dusty-blue and gray rooms have luxurious
details such as gas log fireplaces, balconies, velvet chairs and modern conveniences such as iHome docks. Head down to the bistro (like a greenhouse
with olive banquettes, plants lining the patio outside the windows and a lush
outdoor patio), where chef Mark Pierce puts a Cali twist on bistro fare.
114 rooms. Restaurant, bar. Fitness center. Pool. $251-350

★★★CHATEAU MARMONT HOTEL AND BUNGALOWS

8221 Sunset Blvd., West Hollywood, 323-656-1010, 800-242-8328;
www.chateaumarmont.com

If you can't take the scene (amid important Hollywood types and hangers-on
lounging in heavy chairs, sipping wine and making demands), get out of the
Chateau Marmont. Constant updates are not the thing at this elite hilltop retreat (although there are iPod docking stations and cashmere throws), where
every celebrity you could conceive of—plus creative types and socialites—
lingers around the dimly lit lounge's cozy couches and dark wooden décor.
Outside, the pretty garden dining area is like another world: light, airy and
peppered with flowers. Just above one of Hollywood's busiest boulevards
(a two-minute downhill walk), the hotel draws in crowds to the popular Bar
Marmont restaurant and lounge. The restaurant's food wasn't anything special until the arrival in early 2008 of chef Carolynn Spence, formerly of New
York's West Village hot spot, The Spotted Pig. Now diners come out to devour haute snacks like bacon-wrapped prunes and deviled eggs and entrées
such as brown butter roasted halibut. Because of the crowds, privacy and
intimate conversation are at a premium here. Modeled after a royal estate in
France's Loire Valley, the hotel looks as if it could be the setting for a British
farce or starlet-centered murder mystery. In fact, Bungalow No. 3 was the
site of John Belushi's death.
63 rooms. Restaurant, bar. Fitness center. Pool. Pets accepted. $351 and up

★★★THE GRAFTON ON SUNSET

8462 W. Sunset Blvd., West Hollywood, 323-654-4600, 800-821-3660;
www.graftononsunset.com

The Grafton is located right on the Sunset Strip, which offers endless bars
and restaurants ranging from Asia de Cuba to cheesy but star-filled Ketchup.
A rehab gave the hotel some pizzazz, including lively décor such as zebra-
printed Italian bedding, oversized photographic prints and a heated saltwater
pool (which means no need for toxic chlorine). If you're all about the pool,
book a Deluxe Poolside room for immediate access to the pool party. The
Grafton's long, enclosed pool area is a great place to lounge, especially late
at night, when all the Sunset haunts have closed (usually by 2 a.m.).
108 rooms. Restaurant, bar. Business center. Fitness center. Pool. $151-250

★★★LE MONTROSE SUITE HOTEL

900 Hammond St., West Hollywood, 310-855-1115, 800-776-0666; www.lemontrose.com

If you have a suite tooth, Le Montrose Hotel in West Hollywood may be the place for you. Only junior, executive and one-bedroom suites are available at this unassuming, recently refurbished boutique find. The apartment-style spot also offers laundry facilities, a saltwater pool and lighted tennis courts. Nestled on a quiet residential street, you'd never guess that frenetic Sunset Strip is just five minutes away. But the décor isn't quiet at all, and it borders on too-trendy, with wild elements such as oversized cylindrical lamps and mixed-pattern bedding. The private dining room is exclusively for guests, although many don't know about it, and it has plasma screens for your viewing pleasure. Santa Monica and Sunset boulevards are both lined with tons of fabulous restaurants, so hop over to Café La Boheme for Wagyu beef sliders. 133 suites. Restaurant, bar. Business center. Fitness center. Pool. Tennis. $251-350

★★★LE PARC SUITE HOTEL

733 N. W. Knoll Drive, West Hollywood, 310-855-8888, 800-578-4837;
www.leparcsuites.com

Hidden on a picturesque residential street right off Melrose that looks like it belongs in a small-town East Coast neighborhood, Le Parc Suite Hotel is worthwhile, if only for the easy underground parking. This particular part of Melrose offers several lovely breakfast, brunch and lunch spots, from Urth Caffé to Le Pain Quotidien and the new, amazing David Myers brasserie Comme Ça just across La Cienega (try the crème brûlée French toast). The hotel's own restaurant, Knoll, offers Mediterranean/French cuisine. Le Parc itself is low-key, but nice and offers a good value. All suite-style rooms are muted in soft chocolates and purples and offer complimentary wireless Internet. Sporty types will want to volley above West Hollywood—head up to the roof deck for poolside chaises and a tennis court,

154 suites. Restaurant, bar. Business center. Fitness center. Pool. Tennis. Pets accepted. $251-350

★★★THE LONDON WEST HOLLYWOOD

1020 N. San Vicente Blvd., West Hollywood, 866-282-4560;
www.thelondonwesthollywood.com

The London West Hollywood is *Hell's Kitchen* on earth. Fans of the TV show flock to the former Bel Age Hotel to taste the culinary stylings and witness the magic of celebrity chef Gordon Ramsay at his namesake restaurant. The sibling of sister property The London NYC has been revamped with Hollywood glamour in mind. The spectacular views are still there, but now the rich brown-and-cream rooms have Waterworks jet and raindrop shower heads, multiple docking stations and free phone calls for up to eight hours to the city of London each day. But even chef Ramsay adds a California twist to his worldly cuisine, playing on seasonal local produce. The spectacular pool/roof deck has been updated in the vein of an English garden as well, and a spa is expected to open sometime down the road. In plain English, The London is a gem.

200 suites. Restaurant, bar. Fitness center. Pool. Spa. Pets accepted. $351 and up

★★★MONDRIAN

8440 Sunset Blvd., West Hollywood, 323-650-8999; www.mondrianhotel.com

Once, Mondrian's Skybar was the most elite door in all of L.A. Perhaps even more impressive in this ever-changing city, the hip hotel and bar have managed to maintain an A-list clientele even after the initial heat diminished to a simmer. Still, it was time for a refresh and, while excellent Asian-Latin fusion eatery Asia de Cuba (the calamari salad is nothing but crunchy goodness) has remained intact, designer Benjamin Noriega Ortiz revised the rest of the original Philippe Starck masterpiece (although the much-loved original base stayed). The new aesthetic, often described as *Alice in Wonderland* meets old Hollywood glamour, brings a bit more color and eclectic touches to the famously sleek, whitewashed space. You'll also fine more high-tech gadgets, an updated Agua Spa and a new lobby lounge. Meanwhile, although Sunset Boulevard is one big chaotic party, some frat-boy havens have given way to impressive culinary ventures such as the newer BLT Steak; so going out on Sunset is perhaps a bit more palatable than it used to be.

237 rooms. Restaurant, bar. Business center. Pool. Spa. $251-350

★★★THE ORLANDO

8384 W. Third St., West Hollywood, 323-658-6600;www.theorlando.com

Those who claim that L.A. isn't a walking city may eat their words (and everything else in an eight-block radius) after visiting The Orlando. The simple hotel—with nice touches like a dimly lit lobby lounge with cushy armchairs and a 50-inch plasma TV—sits on Third Street, a blossoming stretch of trendy eateries (especially for brunch), including the newly expanded Joan's On Third (think Dean & Deluca, but with more celebrities and better cupcakes). Chic shops also abound, including Modern Sage and Satine, which stock known designers like Alexander Wang and Derek Lam as well as inspired new names from as far as Japan and Austrailia. On the downside, the pool is small, but overall it's a great value. Rooms have flat-screen TVs and warm, muted tones. Don't be surprised to bump into a famous musician or two, as—perhaps for privacy's sake—they tend to gravitate to this quiet, unpretentious best-kept-secret spot within walking distance to just about everything you need.

98 rooms. Restaurant, bar. Fitness center. Pool. Pets accepted. $151-250

★★★PALIHOUSE HOLLOWAY

8465 Holloway Drive, West Hollywood, 323-656-4100;www.palihouse.com

Hordes of actors and bicoastal types who visit L.A. for productions and pilot season are making their reservations now for Palihouse Holloway. The brand-new long-term-stay hotel, hearkening back to old Hollywood days when actors would hole up in hotels, is a welcome luxury alternative to corporate options. As you traipse down the stairs at the hotel's entrance toward The Hall's beautiful brick-lined floors, it's almost like discovering a private club. To the right is an eclectic living-room-style lounge with distressed leather chairs and unusual *Indiana Jones*-type relics, and to the left is French-style espresso bar and the indoor/outdoor eatery, The Hall courtyard brasserie. If you're planning on staying a while (rates drop the longer you do stay), the studios and one- and two-bedroom suites upstairs, where rain showers, C.O. Bigelow products, hardwood floors and Fili d'Oro Egyptian cotton linens recall a luxury hotel, and amenities including a washer and dryer and a cleaning supply kit make it feel more like home. The roof deck is available for private parties. A Palihouse Vine annex will open in the not too distant future, so you can have your pied-à-terre in whichever neighborhood you feel at home.

36 rooms. Restaurant, bar. Pets accepted. $251-350

★★★SUNSET MARQUIS HOTEL AND VILLAS

1200 N. Alta Loma Road, West Hollywood, 310-657-1333, 800-858-9758; www.sunsetmarquishotel.com

The intimate and refined Sunset Marquis Hotel & Villas—just off the Strip from famous music spot the Whisky A Go-Go—has long attracted music's biggest names, from Bette Midler to the Red Hot Chili Peppers to the Wu Tang Clan (and a few actors, including Brad Pitt, Uma Thurman and George Clooney). Having recently completed a $25 million renovation, the beautiful hotel renamed its notoriously elite lounge Bar 1200 (formerly Whisky Bar). Now exclusive Ross Halfin photographs of former hotel and onsite recording studio guests dot the bar's wall. Wander down lushly landscaped stone paths and over a bridge to 42 new villas with beautifully tiled bathrooms, butler service and 400-weave sheets; 12 original (but revamped) villas; and a two-story Presidential Suite, which comes with a Bentley or a chauffeured limo or SUV. The makeover also includes a new restaurant with illustrious executive chef Guillaume Burlion at the helm and a spa with exclusive Erbe products (from the longtime Vatican apothecary). Meanwhile, in case you rock stars need to stow your vehicles, Sunset Marquis also offers underground parking designed to hold (and wash) four tour buses

153 rooms. Restaurant, bar. Fitness center. Pool. Spa. $351 and up

★★★SUNSET TOWER HOTEL

8358 Sunset Blvd., West Hollywood, 323-654-7100; www.sunsettowerhotel.com

You're in good company at the Sunset Tower Hotel (formerly The Argyle, but thehotel returned to its inaugural name), previously the stomping ground for Marilyn Monroe, Frank Sinatra and Howard Hughes. Even now, heavy hitters like Tom Ford, Leonardo DiCaprio and Nicole Kidman are seen cavorting on the casual terrace or at the more upscale Tower Bar. While overlooking all of Los Angeles, you'll sip coffee from in-room cappuccino machines (in some suites), relax on Egyptian cotton sheets, slather yourself in Kiehl's products, park your iPod in docking stations and let your pet indulge in services like mini-beds and an adjoining dog run. The lobby is nothing showy, but just beyond it is the updated Art Deco pool area that affords extraordinary views. Housed in Bugsy Siegel's old apartment, The Tower Bar and Restaurant (greatly praised under new executive chef Janice Alexander) is a welcome nostalgic throwback, as you'll sip martinis and sidecars amid fairly masculine, dark wood appointments (a gentleman's library) and tap your foot to a jazz pianist's tunes. Downstairs, The Argyle Salon and Spa offers traditional men's shaves, private spa treatment rooms, med-spa offerings and, most significantly, some of the industry's most renowned hair stylists, such as stylist Mateo Herreros, whose clientele includes Uma Thurman and Helena Christenson, and colorist Steven Tapp, who works on big names such as Madonna.

74 rooms. Restaurant, bar. Fitness center. Pool. Spa. Pets accepted. $251-350

WHERE TO EAT

★★AGO

8478 Melrose Ave., West Hollywood, 323-655-6333; www.agorestaurant.com

From the street, the façade of Ago is a blank wall of unassuming off-white, but a closer look at the fleet of luxury cars in the parking lot is a tip-off that this restaurant draws a Hollywood crowd—not a surprise considering that Ago is backed by some of the industry's heaviest hitters, including Bob and Harvey Weinstein, directors Tony and Ridley Scott, and Robert De Niro (who co-owns a number of restaurants, including Nobu). But the cuisine, a combination of flavors from the Italian regions of Tuscany, Liguria and Emilia-Romagna, steals the spotlight here, with such dishes as rack of lamb cooked in a wood-burning oven, and spaghetti with clams.

Italian. Lunch (Monday-Friday), dinner. Reservations recommended. Bar $36-85

★★★BLT STEAK

8720 Sunset Blvd., West Hollywood, 310-360-1950; www.bltsteak.com

BLT Steak, part of the Laurent Tourondel empire, occupies a prime spot if ever there was one: the space formerly occupied by the swanky, star-studded Le Dôme on the Sunset Strip. And BLT lives up to the legendary digs, offering expertly prepared steakhouse fare such as the 22-ounce rib eye and the 32-ounce BLT cut bone-in double sirloin for two. Although the steak is the main attraction, we never skip the generously sized popovers or the raw bar selections, such as the picture-perfect shrimp cocktail. And just order the onion rings, which come piled high in a golden-brown tower of deliciousness. If you can, save room for dessert: The lemon-cassis meringue pie is toothsome and fluffy.

Steakhouse. Dinner. Reservations recommended. Bar. $36-85

★★★BOA STEAKHOUSE

9200 Sunset Blvd., West Hollywood, 310-278-2050; www.boasteak.com

Having recently moved from its old location in the Grafton Hotel on the Sunset Strip, BOA has settled into its new digs just a little west on Sunset Boulevard. This installation is a lot bigger—it now features 13,000 square feet of space, including a 4,000-square-foot outdoor patio. As you enter through the patio area to the interior, you'll note the bold colors of the bar, with sleek red leather couches and a red granite bar from India. The bold color carries over into the main dining room with its red felt walls which were hand-crafted in London. BOA offers an à la carte menu of your favorite surf-and-turf classics—think whole Maine lobster, 40-day dry-aged New York strip steak and premium Wagyu. Put yourself in your server's hands; despite its modern setting, the restaurant's staff is attentive, professional and down-to-earth, probably the best elements of an old-school steakhouse experience. Just be sure to try the Caesar salad, which is prepared tableside to your liking, and one of the specialty cocktails. Afterward, the lounge is a great spot for another drink—just flip over your cocktail table for a game of backgammon.

Steak. Lunch, dinner. Reservations recommended. Bar. $36-86

★★★CAFÉ LA BOHEME

8400 Santa Monica Blvd., West Hollywood, 323-848-2360; www.globaldiningca.com

A West Hollywood staple for nearly 20 years, Café La Boheme has long been known as the kind of over-the-top venue where yards and yards of red velvet upholstery go to die (or loom over diners). But at the end of 2007, it underwent a complete transformation. The velvet, the tablecloths and the elaborate trompe l'oeil and mosaic accents are all gone, and the dining room is more stripped down and casual. The red accents and signature chandeliers remain—they were too special to be discarded—but Café La Boheme is no longer just a special-occasion restaurant; it's now a great place for after-work dinner and drinks. The bar is much larger, and the dining room suggests a modern supper club, with lots of private booths, a roaring fireplace and handsome wood-beam ceilings. The menu, which reflects executive chef Christine Banta's classical French training and Japanese-American heritage, has been updated as well, offering comfort foods with an Asian touch, including Japanese pumpkin ravioli and miso glazed salmon.
International. Dinner. Bar. $36-85

★★★COMME ÇA

8479 Melrose Ave., West Hollywood, 323-782-1104; www.commecarestaurant.com

Foodies have been buzzing about Comme Ça, the busy Melrose Avenue bistro opened by chef-owner David Myers (who also brought us nearby Sona). If you're expecting classic bistro décor, however, you might be surprised by the quasi-minimalist design, which features stark white chairs, black wainscoting and a collage-like arrangement of mirrors adorning the walls. Plus, everyone on the waitstaff looks like a member of SAG, the tables (which you'll wait for in an elbow-to-elbow crowd for an infuriatingly long time) are placed a bit too close for comfort, and the noise level isn't conducive to intimate conversation. But you'll have plenty to talk about after your meal, which features well-prepared French bistro fare such as a delightful duck confit with pommes Lyonnaise and cabbage slaw.
French. Breakfast, brunch, lunch, dinner. Reservations recommended. Bar. $16-35

★★★GORDON RAMSAY AT THE LONDON

The London West Hollywood, 1020 N. San Vicente Blvd., West Hollywood,
310-358-7788; www.gordonramsay.com

Thankfully, the inventive cuisine at one of the most eagerly anticipated restaurants in town doesn't come with a side of the celebrity chef's signature vitriol, so frequently dispensed during Fox's reality series *Hell's Kitchen* and *Kitchen Nightmares*. On the contrary, the environment here is a little slice of heaven, with serene pastel shades, lots of gold accents and a courteous staff that expertly explains the menu of delectable small plates. The restaurant's savory offerings, from swordfish carpaccio with heart of palm, grapefruit and yuzu vinaigrette to beef filet and Kobe short rib with cipollini onions and baby beets, prove that Gordon Ramsay really can cook—not just shout at people who can't.
American. Breakfast, lunch, dinner. Reservations recommended. Bar. $36-85

★★★JAR

8225 Beverly Blvd., West Hollywood, 323-655-6566; www.thejar.com

Jar might stand for "just another restaurant," but there's nothing derivative about this fabulous eatery from executive chef/owner Suzanne Tracht, a place that's just right when you can't handle another evening of small plates or you need some classic-but-high-end comfort food. With its excellent chophouse offerings—like the 16 oz. Kansas City steak and the signature pot roast with carrots and caramelized onions—Jar is more like a distillation of everything a fine neighborhood restaurant ought to be: a place that offers reliably great food and service, and a warm atmosphere. Okay, so this space is a little more sleek than your typical neighborhood spot but it's still functional. Designed as a 1940s supper club, the décor is simple yet stylish with warm shades of brown and hints of orange throughout, black and white photography hanging on wood-paneled walls and brown bucket chairs. Cheese lovers would do well to head here on Monday for the Mozzarella menu, which features a number of scrumptious dishes that incorporate burrata and, of course, mozzarella, among other cheeses. And no matter which day you go, have a cocktail—all the mixed drinks, from martinis to Manhattans, are nonpareil, much like the restaurant itself.

American. Dinner, Sunday brunch. Reservations recommended. Bar. $36-85

★★★KATANA

8439 W. Sunset Blvd., West Hollywood, 323-650-8585; www.katanarobata.com

From the same folks who brought you BOA Steakhouse (right down the street), Katana sits above the Sunset Strip in the ornate Piazza del Sol. The place is always packed with scenesters who fill up the heated patio on any given night, but the sushi and robata (Japanese charcoal-grilled) styles are best enjoyed in the superbly lit Dodd Mitchell-designed interior. All the hard surfaces make it a bit loud, but once the food arrives, you'll forget that you're shouting to be heard. The ama ebi (sweet shrimp) sashimi is winsomely succulent and pairs well with one of Katana's numerous premium sakes.

Japanese. Dinner. Reservations recommended. Bar. $36-85

★★★KOI

730 N. La Cienega Blvd., West Hollywood, 310-659-9449; www.koirestaurant.com

Perennial hot spot Koi was recently remodeled, and the result is a predictably lovely, transporting space, what with the calming water elements, bamboo accents and twinkling glowing candles everywhere. It's a fitting backdrop for its equally beautiful clientele—which consists almost entirely of model types, industry bigwigs and their various entourages and, naturally, A-list actors—who have kept this Japanese restaurant and lounge consistently booked for years. An evening at Koi is more about seeing and being seen than about debating the subtle merits of a particular cut of mackerel or hamachi. The sushi here is fairly traditional, and signature dishes include yellowtail carpaccio with grape seed oil, ponzu and wasabi tobiko. For fans of the cooked stuff, there's a flavorful Kobe filet mignon toban-yaki, so tasty it may just have you drooling over dinner instead of the starlets around you.

Japanese. Dinner. Reservations recommended. Bar. $86 and up

★★★LUCQUES

8474 Melrose Ave., West Hollywood, 323-655-6277; www.lucques.com

Like so many buildings in Los Angeles, Lucques might look nondescript on the outside, but it boasts a storied past, having once been the carriage house of silent film-era actor and producer Harold Lloyd. With an interior reimagined by designer Barbara Barry, Lucques retains its brick walls and its sense of history, even as a posh, minimalist space with warm, chocolate leather booths. Reservations are hard to come by, but when you finally score one, you'll be glad you waited for a taste of co-owner and chef Suzanne Goin's simple and absolutely delicious dishes, like Colorado lamb carpaccio with roasted romano beans, Dijon mustard and salsa rustica; followed by braised beef short ribs with sautéed greens, cippolinis and horseradish cream. American. Lunch (Tuesday-Saturday), dinner. Bar. $36-85

★★★RESTAURANT NISHIMURA

8684 Melrose Ave., West Hollywood, 310-659-4770

Los Angeles is a sushi town, and Nishimura, dipped in ivy and tucked into a tiny space across from the Pacific Design Center, has long commanded the respect of the town's critical sushi aficionados, for whom nothing will do but the freshest cuts and the most skilled preparation. (The toro here practically still moves in your mouth.) Chef Hiro Nishimura oversees the offerings that arrive on your plate, which, coincidentally, are not just any plates, but one-of-a-kind pieces fashioned by acclaimed potter Mineo Mizuno. If you've got a fistful of cash to burn, relinquish all control and order the omakase, which starts at $100 a head.

Japanese. Lunch (Monday-Friday), dinner. Closed Sunday. Bar. $86 and up

★★★★SONA

401 N. La Cienega Blvd., West Hollywood, 310-659-7708; www.sonarestaurant.com

If you're looking for a familiar, been-there-done-that meal, then skip chef David Myers's Sona. Adventurous eaters, though, will be rewarded at this temple to culinary creativity, which clocks in as one of the most cutting-edge eateries in the city. Stark and minimalist with a six-ton granite wine bar at the center of the room, Sona is about both innovation and execution, offering two imaginative degustation menus: the six-course Découverte and the nine-course Spontanée. With either menu (which change frequently), your taste buds will fall in love with dishes such as Maine lobster with Vietnamese green curry and beef strip loin with fingerling potatoes and baby carrots. What will keep you coming back are the wild desserts, including the liquid chocolate with smoked foam, sassafras gel and tobacco ice cream or the fried lemon meringue pie with lemon confit, mint and popcorn ice cream. French. Dinner. Closed Sunday-Monday. Bar. $36-85

★URTH CAFFE

8565 Melrose Ave., West Hollywood, 310-659-0628; 267 S. Beverly Drive, Beverly Hills, 310-205-9311; 2327 Main St., Santa Monica, 310-314-7040; 451 S. Hewitt St., Downtown, 213-797-4534; www.urthcaffe.com

Long known for its organic teas and coffees, Urth Caffé is also famous for celeb sightings, especially at the original West Hollywood location. The food here is excellent—in that healthy California way. The menu is chock-full of scrumptious lunchtime options, such as organic soups, hearty sandwiches with springtime-fresh mixed greens, and a pastry case full of gorgeous cakes and cookies. What's more, the place has charm, from the Spanish tile to the quaint jars of coffee beans and loose-leaf teas. Bring a few dollars for the valet, though, because parking is scarce.

American. Breakfast, lunch, dinner. $15 and under

★★★XIV

8117 Sunset Blvd., West Hollywood, 323-656-1414; www.sbe.com/xiv

A powerful trio backs one of the city's most buzzed about restaurants—this is chef Michael Mina's first L.A. restaurant (and his 14th overall), the interior is designed by Philippe Starck, and nightlife powerhouse SBE is also part of the team. Needless to say, the place has been packed since it opened. The outdoor patio draws people who work nearby on Sunset, especially since they introduced 6IX, a happy hour where everything is $6 and includes a menu of champagne, wine and a collection of Mina classics such as black truffle popcorn and lobster corn dogs. Inside, you can order Mina's signature items such as the lobster pot pie and Kobe burger with a trio of French fries and "secret sauce," while taking in the interesting juxtaposition Starck is known for—lots of paintings and bookshelves and photos in frames, chandeliers and a sleek stainless-steel open kitchen. The wine list is substantial and this being an SBE venture, there are plenty of fun cocktails.

Contemporary American. Dinner. Bar. Reservations recommended. $36-85

WESTLAKE VILLAGE

This affluent neighborhood in the western edge of Los Angeles County is close enough to the city but far enough away to escape the hustle and bustle (about 20 miles from Malibu). Many celebrities call it home, and you'll find some nice accommodations.

WHERE TO STAY

★★★★FOUR SEASONS HOTEL WESTLAKE VILLAGE

2 Dole Drive, Westlake Village, 818-575-3000, 800-819-5053; www.fourseasons.com

Set on expansive, landscaped grounds, this hotel in suburban Los Angeles offers a tranquil escape from the city. Connected to the California Longevity and Health Institute, a premier medical spa, the hotel provides serenity-seeking Angelenos a place to rest up and rejuvenate themselves in style. Rooms are traditionally decorated with classic touches like mahogany furniture, chintz-covered sofas and marble bathrooms. The onsite Onyx restaurant serves light, healthful Asian cuisine.

269 rooms. Restaurant, bar. Pool. Spa. $351 and up

★★★HYATT WESTLAKE PLAZA

880 S. Westlake Blvd., Westlake Village, 805-557-1234, 800-633-7313;
www.hyattwestlake.com

Spanish mission-style architecture can be found at this comfortable hotel. Rooms include flat-screen televisions, iHome stereos with iPod docks and large work desks. Many rooms also have a balcony or patio.

262 rooms. Restaurant, bar. Business center. Fitness center. Pool. $151-250

★★★WESTLAKE VILLAGE INN

31943 Agoura Road, Westlake Village, 818-889-0230, 800-535-9978;
www.westlakevillageinn.com

Relax by the Mediterranean-style pool or hit the links. For practice at night, try the area's only lighted driving range. Enjoy live entertainment at Bogies, the hotel's nightclub, or dine at Le Café, the bistro and wine bar onsite. Guest rooms at this charming inn include Italian bedding and flat-screen televisions, among other things.

144 rooms. Restaurant, bar. Complimentary breakfast. Pool. $151-250

SPA
★★★★THE SPA AT FOUR SEASONS WESTLAKE VILLAGE

2 Dole Drive, Westlake Village, 818-575-3000; www.fourseasons.com

A 40,000-square-foot space with Asian-influenced décor, this spa in the Four Seasons Los Angeles, Westlake Village is a peaceful spot for top-notch pampering. Treatments also take their cue from Asian traditions, with everything from shiatsu to reiki making an appearance on the spa menu. Couples can opt for a traditional massage in the outdoor spa cabanas, which include a private plunge pool. Or book a spa suite for your treatment, which features a fireplace and plunge pool.

IRVINE

See also Costa Mesa, Laguna Beach, Newport Beach, Santa Ana

In the heart of Orange County, Irvine is one of the nation's largest planned communities, as well as the home of the University of California, Irvine, and several large corporations.

WHAT TO SEE
WILD RIVERS WATERPARK

8770 Irvine Center Drive, Irvine, 949-788-0808; www.wildrivers.com

One of Southern California's biggest water parks (20 acres), Wild Rivers offers rides designed for children, teens and adults.
Mid-May-late September; hours vary.

WHERE TO STAY
★★★HYATT REGENCY

17900 Jamboree Road, Irvine, 949-975-1234, 800-233-1234; www.irvine.hyatt.com

Centrally located to the business districts of Irvine and Newport, all rooms at this hotel feature luxury bedding and pillow-top mattresses. Opting for the business plan rooms will provide free breakfast and local calls and 24-hour access to copying, printing and business supplies, plus city mountain views and marble baths.

536 rooms. Restaurant, bar. Complimentary breakfast. Fitness center. Pool. $151-250

WHERE TO EAT
★★★RUTH'S CHRIS STEAK HOUSE

2961 Michelson Drive, Irvine, 949-252-8848; www.ruthschris.com

Born from a single New Orleans restaurant that Ruth Fertel bought in 1965

for $22,000, the chain is a favorite among steak lovers. Aged prime Mid-western beef is broiled and served on a heated plate sizzling with butter and with sides like creamed spinach and au gratin potatoes.
Steak. Dinner. $36-86

LAGUNA BEACH

See also Avalon, Costa Mesa, Irvine, Laguna Nigel, Newport Beach, San Clemente, San Juan Capistrano

The beaches are beautiful and artists have contributed to the quaint charm of this seaside town. Lots of art and antique shops make leisurely strolling a pleasure. Few places offer such a breadth of cultural and natural landscapes, from the Pacific-swept beaches to the cliffs and canyons of the San Joaquin Hills, amidst such luxurious accommodations. Like its coastal sisters, Laguna has all the allure of a beachside city but has a distinct personality of its own with its a hilly landscape, artsy twist and decidedly friendly atmosphere.

WHAT TO SEE
LAGUNA ART MUSEUM
307 Cliff Drive, Laguna Beach, 949-494-8971; www.lagunaartmuseum.org

Artists have flocked to Laguna since the 1800s for inspiration, and there remains no better place to see the fruits of their labor than the Laguna Art Museum. With perhaps the largest permanent collection of artwork by Californian artists and ever-changing exhibitions, this museum is a great option for those looking to experience Laguna's early days.
Daily 11 a.m.-5 p.m.

LAGUNA PLAYHOUSE
606 Laguna Canyon Road, Laguna Beach, 949-497-2787; www.lagunaplayhouse.com

The oldest running playhouse on the West Coast, this 1920s-era theater presents every kind of theatrical event imaginable, from dramas and comedies to musicals and children's theater. Make time for a performance before or after dinner and don't forget your swimsuit; the theater is just steps from the beach.
Main stage: Mid-July-June, Tuesday-Sunday.

REDFERN GALLERY AT MONTAGE RESORT
30801 S. Coast Highway, Laguna Beach, 949-715-6193; www.redferngallery.com

In addition to impeccable accommodations and spectacular views, the Montage Resort also houses the Redfern Gallery, which features early California impressionist painting. Here, you'll find the likes of Granville Redmond's *Patch of Poppies*, a lovely painting that is reminiscent of Claude Monet's *The Poppy Field*, near Argenteuil.

SPECIAL EVENTS
FESTIVAL OF ARTS AND PAGEANT OF THE MASTERS
650 Laguna Canyon Road, Laguna Beach, 949-494-1145, 800-487-3378;
www.foapom.com

Exhibits by 160 artists are highlighted in the festival.
Mid-July-August.

SAWDUST FINE ARTS AND CRAFTS FESTIVAL

935 Laguna Canyon Road, Laguna Beach, 949-494-3030; www.sawdustartfestival.org

More than 175 Laguna Beach artists create paintings, photographs, sculptures, jewelry, ceramics, hand-blown glass and other works of art. July-early September.

WHERE TO STAY
★★HOLIDAY INN

25205 La Paz Road, Laguna Hills, 949-586-5000, 800-972-2576; www.holidayinn.com

This newly renovated Holiday Inn is right across from the beach. Rooms face a pretty courtyard with a pool, and the friendly staff will get you anything you need (forgot your sunblock?). The property also includes a fitness center, restaurant and lounge, plus outdoor patio dining.

147 rooms. Restaurant, bar. Complimentary breakfast. Pool. Pets accepted. $151-250

★★★★MONTAGE LAGUNA BEACH

30801 S. Coast Highway, Laguna Beach, 949-715-6000, 877-782-9821;
www.montagelagunabeach.com

Reigning over Laguna Beach from its rugged cliff-top location, this stylish getaway blends arts and crafts style with the luxury of a full-service resort. Rooms, suites and bungalows feature 400-thread-count linens and marble bathrooms with a large shower and tub, and private balconies or patios with ocean views. Dining at Montage takes sophisticated California cuisine to a new level, particularly at the romantically cozy oceanfront bungalow restaurant, Studio. The full-range spa has more than 20 treatment rooms and the poolside cabanas are decked out with flat-screen TVs and DVD/CD players.

262 rooms. Restaurant, bar. Pets accepted. $351 and up

★★★SURF & SAND RESORT

1555 S. Coast Highway, Laguna Beach, 949-497-4477, 877-786-6835;
www.surfandsandresort.com

This resort blends coastal elegance with West Coast cool. Guest rooms feature marble tiled entryways and private balconies with ocean views. The Aquaterra Spa offers a wide variety of treatments and the fitness center and yoga studio will get guests in shape. The restaurant and lounge serve up signature Southern California views with a Mediterranean-inspired menu.

152 rooms. Restaurant, bar. Fitness center. Pool. Spa. $351 and up

WHERE TO EAT
★★CEDAR CREEK INN

384 Forest Ave., Laguna Beach, 949-497-8696; www.cedarcreekinn.com

The Cedar Creek Inn is a cozy spot for sandwiches, salads and hearty dishes such as meatloaf with mashed potatoes or fish and chips. Start off with the grilled artichoke or the goat cheese wontons. The outdoor patio is a great place to dine in the evening next to the roaring fireplace.

American. Lunch, dinner. $16-35

★THE COTTAGE

308 N. Coast Highway, Laguna Beach, 949-494-3023; www.thecottagerestaurant.com

Come her for a Sunday-style brunch, served any day of the week. Dishes include two poached eggs with smoked salmon on an English muffin topped with a dill hollandaise sauce. All brunch items include a glass of California champagne. Lunch includes a variety of sandwiches, while steak, pasta and pork chops are all on the menu for dinner.

American. Breakfast, lunch, dinner. $16-35

★★FIVE FEET RESTAURANT

328 Glenneyre St., Laguna Beach, 949-497-4955; www.fivefeetrestaurants.com

The eclectic decor (modern light fixtures, colorful artwork) matches the diverse menu: crispy Mississippi farmed catfish, hoison bbq short ribs, kung pao chicken, and for dessert, homemade lemon ice cream.

Contemporary Chinese. Dinner. $36-85

★LAGUNA THAI BY THE SEA

31715 S. Coast Highway, Laguna Beach, 949-415-0924; www.lagunathai.com

For fresh, authentic Thai food, this is the place in Laguna. The menu includes everything from drunken noodles to pad thai to thai soup with lemongrass.

Thai. Lunch, dinner. $16-35

★★LAS BRISAS DE LAGUNA

361 Cliff Drive, Laguna Beach, 949-497-5434; www.lasbrisaslagunabeach.com

Overlooking the Pacific, Las Brisas serves the cuisine of the Mexican Riviera. Seafood is the focus with dishes like sea bass marinated in tangy lime-orange juice with mango, bell peppers, chiles, onions and cilantro. Also try the black bean soup with bacon and spices served tableside with condiments.

Mexican. Breakfast, lunch, dinner, Sunday brunch. $36-85

★★★★★STUDIO

30801 S. Coast Highway, Laguna Beach, 949-715-6000; www.studiolagunabeach.com

Housed in a cozy arts and crafts cottage overlooking the ocean, this restaurant at Montage Laguna Beach is a study in understated elegance. The menu is the creation of award-winning chef James Boyce and features contemporary California cuisine made with the freshest local ingredients. Settle in for a supper made up of dishes like pan-seared John Dory with baby fennel, cipollini onions and caramelized cauliflower, or vinegar-braised short ribs with butter-roasted asparagus. The wine cellar features more than 1,800 bottles with plenty of California selections and wines available by the glass.

American. Dinner. Closed Monday. $36-85

★★TI AMO RISTORANTE

31727 South Coast Highway, Laguna Beach, 949-499-5350;
www.tiamolagunabeach.com

This Old World Italian restaurant is lit with candelabras and a fireplace, and includes a heated garden atrium. The food is old school Italian: flavorful pastas, lush salads and a nice selection of chicken, veal and pork second courses.

Italian. Dinner. $36-86

SPA
★★★★★SPA MONTAGE, LAGUNA BEACH
Montage Laguna Beach, 30801 S. Coast Highway, Laguna Beach, 949-715-6000,
866-271-6953; www.spamontage.com

Spa Montage is a stunning facility that takes advantage of its superior beachfront setting. An indoor-outdoor structure and floor-to-ceiling windows framing 160-degree views alleviate any guilt guests may feel for opting to stay in for a bit of pampering on a sunny day. The spa's holistic, get-back-to-nature approach is evident in its design, as well as in the products it uses. Custom-mixed lotions and oils blend natural ingredients, including eucalyptus, lavender, orange blossoms and citrus. Wrap up in one of the spa's plush robes and try any number of therapies, from a California citrus polish to an algae cellulite massage. Hungry spa-goers can find a cozy spot by the lap pool, where healthy snacks and meals are available from the Mosaic Grille.

LONG BEACH
See also Anaheim, Avalon (Catalina Island), Los Angeles, Newport Beach, Santa Ana

Located between Los Angeles and Orange County, a multibillion dollar redevelopment program has finally helped Long Beach become one of Southern California's most diverse waterfront destinations, recapturing the charm it first attained as a premier seaside resort in the early 1900s. A 21½-mile light rail system, the Metro Blue Line, connects Long Beach and Los Angeles.

WHAT TO SEE
AQUARIUM OF THE PACIFIC
100 Aquarium Way, Long Beach, 562-590-3100; www.aquariumofpacific.org

This enormous aquarium houses more than 12,000 animals in 50 exhibits, including a hands-on shark lagoon where you can touch the sharks. Other exhibits feature sea lions and Australian birds. Take a behind-the-scenes tour to learn about the daily operations of the aquarium, see a movie in 3D exploring the deep ocean, take a harbor cruise, and much more.

Admission: adults $23.95, seniors $20.95, children 3-11 $11.95. Daily 9 a.m.-6 p.m.

CATALINA EXPRESS
95 Berth, San Pedro, 800-481-3470; www.catalinaexpress.com

Board one of eight state-of-the-art catamarans and cruise over to Catalina Island in about an hour. The boats include airline-style seating, panoramic viewing windows and on-deck seating. San Pedro and Long Beach Fares

Admission: adults $66.50, seniors $60, children 2-11 $51, children under 3 $4. Schedules vary, check the Web site for more information.

LONG BEACH MUSEUM OF ART
2300 E. Ocean Blvd., Long Beach, 562-439-2119; www.lbma.org

The permanent collection features American art, German expressionists and video art. It also includes a contemporary sculpture garden and an education gallery. The café and gift shop are housed in a 1912 mansion overlooking the Pacific Ocean.

Admission: adults $7, students and seniors $6, children under 13 free. Free Friday. Tuesday-Sunday 11 a.m.-5 p.m.

QUEEN MARY SEAPORT

1126 Queens Highway, Long Beach, 562-435-3511, 800-437-2934;
www.queenmary.com

For 25 years, the rich and famous boarded this 12-deck luxury ocean liner to cross the Atlantic in grand style. Since 1967, the ship has been docked in Long Beach and now people board it for tours, special events, shipboard dining or an overnight hotel stay in one of its 365 staterooms. The price of admission includes a ghosts and legends tour (some say the vessel is haunted), but for $5 extra, a World War II tour is offered, giving insight into the role the ship played in transporting American military personnel from 1940 to 1946. You can also board a Foxtrot submarine Russians used to track enemy forces in the Pacific during the Cold War. Self-guided and Ghosts and Legends tours included with admission.

Admission: adults $24.95, seniors $21.95, children 5-11 $12.95. Daily 10 a.m.-6 p.m.

SHORELINE VILLAGE

429 Shoreline Village Drive, Long Beach, 562-435-2668; www.shorelinevillage.com

This seven-acre shopping, dining and entertainment complex recaptures the look and charm of a turn-of-the-century California seacoast village. It includes a collection of unique shops and galleries, plus a historic carousel and a complete marine center with daily harbor cruises and seasonal whale-watching excursions. Transportation to Shoreline Village is available via the free Promenade Tram from downtown Long Beach, the Runabout Shuttle (also from downtown Long Beach) and the water taxi that transports passengers between Shoreline Village and the downtown marina.

Daily.

SPECIAL EVENTS
LONG BEACH JAZZ FESTIVAL

562-424-0013

Held every year on a grassy knoll, this annual event features top artists, delicious food and fabulous art.

Mid-August.

NAPLES CHRISTMAS BOAT PARADE

562-570-5333; www.longbeach.gov

Festively decorated boats wind through the canals of Naples Island and along the water by Shoreline Village each year.

December.

TOYOTA GRAND PRIX

3000 Pacific Ave., Long Beach, 562-981-2600; www.longbeachgp.com

This international race takes place on downtown streets.

April.

SOUTHERN CALIFORNIA

★ ★★
★ ★★★
★ ★★★
★ ★★

114

WHERE TO STAY

★★★HILTON LONG BEACH
701 W. Ocean Blvd., Long Beach, 562-983-3400, 800-345-6565; www.hilton.com

Conveniently located in downtown Long Beach, this hotel is within walking distance of theaters and shopping, and within four blocks of the convention center and beach. The comfortable guest rooms feature a gray and gold motif, interesting artwork of historic Long Beach, large showers and Crabtree & Evelyn bath amenities.

393 rooms. Restaurant, bar. Business center. Fitness center. Pool. Pets accepted. $251-350

★★★HYATT REGENCY LONG BEACH
200 S. Pine Ave., Long Beach, 562-491-1234; www.hyatt.com

Located next to the convention center and within walking distance of the Pier and the downtown area, this California-style Hyatt is a good choice for both business and leisure travelers. The spacious guest rooms provide plush bedding, work areas and views of the harbor.

528 rooms. Restaurant, bar. Business center. Pool. $151-250

★★★RENAISSANCE LONG BEACH HOTEL
111 E. Ocean Blvd., Long Beach, 562-437-5900, 888-236-2427;
www.renaissancehotels.com

This downtown Long Beach property features is within walking distance to shops, restaurants and sights and includes guest rooms with comfy beds with white linens and marble bathrooms. The new restaurant, Tracht's, serves steaks and seafood in a sleek dining space.

374 rooms. Restaurant, bar. Fitness center. Pool. Pets accepted. $251-250

WHERE TO EAT

★★KING'S FISH HOUSE
100 W. Broadway, Long Beach, 562-432-7463; www.kingsfishhouse.com

This California chain has a variety of daily regional specials and oysters, as well as crab, lobster and other seafood favorites.

Seafood. Lunch, dinner, brunch. $16-35

★★★L'OPERA RISTORANTE
101 Pine Ave., Long Beach, 562-491-0066; www.lopera.com

This local favorite serves up modern Northern Italian cuisine. Sample dishes include ravioli stuffed with duck, and mint pasta filled with fava beans and ricotta cheese. Massive marble columns grace the lovely dining room and the service is warm and attentive.

Italian. Lunch (Monday-Friday), dinner. Bar. $36-85

★★PARKER'S LIGHTHOUSE
435 Shoreline Village Drive, Long Beach, 562-432-6500; www.parkerslighthouse.com

A waterfront location affords views of the Queen Mary, while the menu focuses on the freshest seafood, including sesame crusted red snapper and Santa Barbara white sea bass. You'll also find several meat dishes on the menu, such as a spice rubbed cajun ribeye and filet mignon.

Seafood. Lunch, dinner. $16-35

★★THE YARD HOUSE

401 Shoreline Village Drive, Long Beach, 562-628-0455; www.yardhouse.com

The Yard House claims to have the world's largest selection of draft beers. The menu is also quite extensive, with everything from chicken nachos to a crab cake hoagie to mac and cheese with roasted chicken.

American. Lunch, dinner, late-night. Bar. $36-85

MORRO BAY

See also Cambria, San Luis Obispo

Located halfway between Los Angeles and San Francisco, Morro Bay is a peaceful, slow-paced waterfront retreat. Its most striking feature is a 576-foot volcanic dome discovered by Juan Rodríguez Cabrillo in 1542 at the entrance to the harbor. A number of attractions are found here, including beaches, gardens and whale-and-seal-watching. Enjoy water sports, golfing and winery tours nearby.

WHAT TO SEE
MONTANA DE ORO STATE PARK

350 Pecho Valley Road, Los Osos, 805-528-0513, 800-772-7434; www.parks.ca.gov

There's spectacular scenery along seven miles of shoreline with tide pools, beaches and camping. Hikers enjoy trails up the 1,347-foot Valencia Peak. The park is also popular for whale-watching and viewing harbor seals and sea otters along the shore.

MORRO BAY STATE PARK

Morro Bay, 805-772-2560; www.parks.ca.gov

Approximately 2,400 acres on Morro Bay make up this park. Fishing, boating, an 18-hole golf course, picnicking, hiking, and tent and trailer camping are available.

Daily 10 a.m.-5 p.m.

MORRO ROCK

845 Embarcadero Road and Coleman Drive, Morro Bay, 805-772-4467;
www.morrobay.org

This 576-foot-high volcanic boulder is often called "the Gibraltar of the Pacific," or simply "the Rock." Drive to the base of the rock for optimum viewing.

Daily.

WHERE TO STAY
★★★THE INN AT MORRO BAY HOTEL

60 State Park Road, Morro Bay, 805-772-5651, 800-321-9566;
www.innatmorrobay.com

Located in Morro Bay State Park, this coastal hideaway made up of Cape Cod-style buildings is a destination itself. After a day of sightseeing, golf or bike riding, return to a gourmet meal before sinking into a feather bed. The inn also offers a full range of body treatments in the spa.

98 rooms. Restaurant, bar. Pool. Spa. $151-250

WHERE TO EAT
★HOFBRAU
901 Embarcadero Road, Morro Bay, 805-772-5166; www.hofbraurestaurant.com
If you're going to eat one meal in Morro Bay, make it one of the French dip sandwiches at Hofbrau, with the hot German potato salad on the side. The restaurant has been selling hand-carved beef for more than 35 years. You'll also find burgers, fish sandwiches, soups and salads. Beers are on tap.
American. Lunch, dinner. $15 and under

NEWPORT BEACH
See also Avalon (Catalina Island), Costa Mesa, Huntington Beach, Irvine, Laguna Beach
This seaside community—sometimes referred to as the American Riviera—is famous for elegant waterfront villas, shops, restaurants and beautiful Pacific Coast scenery. There are eight small islands within Newport Harbor. Attractions are clustered around the Newport Pier, a popular fishing spot, and the Balboa Peninsula, a six-mile finger of land running east and west. You'll find some of the best California beaches here.

WHAT TO SEE
BALBOA ISLAND
www.balboaisland.com
This tiny, densely populated man-made island is one of Orange County's most popular attractions. You can drive onto the island via Jamboree Road or hop the ferry from Balboa Peninsula. The pretty island has some of the most expensive real estate in the country and the main street, Marine Avenue, is lined with boutiques, restaurants and ice cream shops selling the popular Balboa Bars, vanilla ice cream dipped in chocolate and then covered with nuts or candy, or the frozen chocolate bananas.

BALBOA FUN ZONE
600 E. Bay Ave., Newport Beach, 949-673-0408; www.thebalboafunzone.com
Go round and round on the Ferris wheel, hop on some rides, play video games or visit the arcade—it's all in a day's worth of fun at this amusement park surrounding the Balboa Pavilion.
Sunday-Thursday 11 a.m.-9 p.m., Friday-Saturday 11 a.m.-10 p.m.

CORONA DEL MAR
www.orangecounty.net
Newport Beach's stretch of Highway 1 is packed with restaurants, bars and boutiques, and also leads to one of the locals' favorite beaches, Corona del Mar, which is made up of two beaches: Little Corona and Big Corona. Colorful reefs make it an ideal spot for snorkelers. You'll also find volleyball courts, fire pits and food stands.

CRYSTAL COVE STATE PARK
www.crystalcovestatepark.com
Crystal Cove State Beach, between Corona del Mar and Laguna, attracts beachgoers who are looking for a more secluded area and is one of the loveliest beaches you'll see. You can access Crystal Cove beach from Highway 1 and parking costs $10 per day.

ORANGE COUNTY MUSEUM OF ARTS

850 San Clemente Drive, Newport Beach, 949-759-1122; www.ocma.net

The OCMA showcases modern and contemporary art, with an emphasis on Californian art since World War II.

Admission: adults $12, seniors and students $10, children under 13 free. Free second Sunday of the month. Wednesday, Friday-Sunday 11 a.m.-5 p.m., Thursday 11 a.m.-8 p.m.

FASHION ISLAND

2647 E. Pacific Coast Highway, Corona del Mar, 949-721-2000;
www.shopfashionisland.com

Though Newport is well known as a beach town, it also has some serious shopping centers. Stop by this outdoor mall for a shopping fix at Neiman Marcus or Bloomingdale's to name a few.

Monday-Friday 10 a.m.-9 p.m., Saturday 10 a.m.-7 p.m., Sunday 11 a.m.-6 p.m.

SPECIAL EVENTS
CHRISTMAS BOAT PARADE

Newport Beach Harbor, Newport Blvd., Newport Beach, 949-729-4400;
www.christmasboatparade.com

Hundreds of yachts, boats, kayaks and canoes sail around the harbor decked out in Christmas lights, and many go all out with holiday scenes, music and costumed carolers.

Mid-December.

TASTE OF NEWPORT

Newport Center Drive, Newport Beach, 949-729-4400; www.tasteofnewport.com

For three days, 75,000 people attend this festival to taste countless culinary creations from some of the area's best-loved restaurants. In addition to pizza, tacos, gyros and ribs, you'll find prime rib, crab cakes and sushi. The Sound Stage features live music throughout the festival. Sample wines from premium California wineries.

Mid-September.

WHERE TO STAY
★★★BALBOA BAY CLUB & RESORT

1221 W. Coast Highway, Newport Beach, 888-445-7153; www.balboabayclub.com

Set on 15 waterfront acres, the rooms at this comfortable and whimsical resort feel like private bungalows with their furnished patios and plantation shutters. Sit back and watch the yachts in the bay, hit the spa or enjoy the numerous attractions nearby. The First Cabin Restaurant offers a seasonal menu of California cuisine in a cozy setting with panoramic views of the bay.

160 rooms. Restaurant, bar. Spa. Pets accepted. $251-350

★BAY SHORES PENINSULA HOTEL

1800 W. Balboa Blvd., Newport Beach, 949-675-3463, 800-222-6675;
www.thebestinn.com

This small, family-owned hotel has a home-away-from-home feel with bright rooms and friendly service. The staff will provide you with what you need for the beach, whether it is a boogie board or chair.

25 rooms. Complimentary breakfast. Business center. $61-150

★★★FAIRMONT NEWPORT BEACH

4500 MacArthur Blvd., Newport Beach, 949-476-2001, 800-810-3039;
www.fairmont.com

This hotel's exterior replicates a Mayan temple with a stacked semi-pyramid design. While an ocean view doesn't come with the room rate here (the ocean is about eight miles away from the hotel), don't let this sway any plans to stay. The hotel recently completed a $32 million renovation and the result is a new high-end spa, a redesigned sky pool and luxurious new rooms with Egyptian cotton sheets and flat-screen TVs. And be sure to visit the pool, located next to the spa on the hotel's third floor, where the cabanas are sheathed in golden curtains the color of egg yolks.

440 rooms. Restaurant, bar. Fitness center. Pool. Spa. Pets accepted. $151-250

★★★HYATT REGENCY NEWPORT BEACH

1107 Jamboree Road, Newport Beach, 949-729-1234, 800-633-7313; www.hyatt.com

This Spanish-style hotel sits on 26 lush acres overlooking Newport Beach. The rooms echo the surroundings with tropical-inspired décor, and there's plenty to do: golf, volleyball, a relaxing spa and three outdoor pools.

403 rooms. Restaurant, bar. Business center. Fitness center. Pool. Spa. $151-250

★★★★THE ISLAND HOTEL, NEWPORT BEACH

690 Newport Center Drive, Newport Beach, 866-554-4620; www.theislandhotel.com

This 20-story tower is angled toward the Pacific Ocean and is only minutes from the beach. Guest rooms are spacious and comfortable with marble bathrooms, luxurious Italian linens and well-appointed workspaces. The private balconies in some suites and furnished patios offer exceptional views of the Pacific Ocean and Newport Harbor. You may never want to leave the pool with its lush landscaping, 17-foot fireplace for chilly evenings and dataports and telephone jacks to stay in touch. Overlooking the nearby islands of Balboa, Lido and Catalina, this Newport Beach gem is only minutes from upscale shopping and golf facilities.

383 rooms. Restaurant, bar. Business center. Pool. Spa. Golf. Pets accepted. $251-350

★★★NEWPORT BEACH MARRIOTT BAYVIEW

500 Bayview Circle, Newport Beach, 949-854-4500, 800-228-9290; www.marriott.com

This all-suite hotel features separate bedrooms and living areas, balconies and oversized marble bathrooms. Some rooms have views of Upper Back Bay, so be sure to ask when making a reservation.

254 suites. Restaurant, bar. Pool. $151-250

★★★NEWPORT BEACH MARRIOTT HOTEL AND SPA

900 Newport Center Drive, Newport Beach, 949-640-4000, 800-228-9290;
www.newportstay.com

A $70 million renovation turned this into a sleek and modern hotel. Nautical-inspired rooms have feather beds, Egyptian cotton sheets, flat-screen televisions and glass enclosed showers. The hotel is just blocks from Newport Harbor and next door to the high-end Fashion Island mall. Onsite Pure Blue Spa is a haven for relaxation.

532 rooms. Restaurant, bar. Fitness center. Spa. Pets accepted. $151-250

★★★★THE RESORT AT PELICAN HILL

22701 Pelican Hill Road South, Newport Coast, 949-467-6800, 800-315-8214;
www.pelicanhill.com

The area's newest place to stay is located in the small enclave of Newport Coast. The Resort at Pelican Hill resembles a beautiful (and very large) Tuscan villa. The property has 204 hillside bungalows and private villas that overlook the world class Tom Fazio-designed golf courses. Each bungalow has its own patio (a perfect spot for your morning cup of coffee from the well-sourced beans in your room), large bathroom and plush bedding. The pool is supposedly the largest circular pool in the world—it certainly looks as if it could be the largest—and you will likely want to spend all day there as the staff delivers fruit-scented water and food from the Coliseum Restaurant. If you prefer the beach, the friendly staff will send you off with your own tote bag full of everything you need for a day under the sun. (Shuttles take you back and forth to Crystal Cove Beach.) End the day with a visit to the luxurious Spa at Pelican Hill and a meal at Andrea, which serves delicate, homemade pasta in an elegant setting (try to get a seat on the terrace while the sun is setting). Throughout your stay, indulge is creamy scoops of the housemade gelato in the café.

332 rooms. Restaurant, bar. Spa. Pool. Fitness Center. $351 and up

WHERE TO EAT

★★21 OCEANFRONT

2100 W. Oceanfront, Newport Beach, 949-673-2100; www.21oceanfront.com

Known for its steaks and seafood, 21 Oceanfront is an elegant, beachfront spot. If you're in town on a Monday, the surf and turf special includes a Caesar salad, lobster tail, filet mignon, garlic mashed potatoes and homemade chocolate cake for $49 a person.

Seafood, steak. Dinner. $36-85

★★★★ANDREA

The Resort at Pelican Hill, 22701 Pelican Hill Road South, Newport Coast,
949-467-6800, 800-315-8214; www.pelicanhill.com

With an elegant interior of natural colors, lush potted trees and a covered terrace providing unparalleled views of the ocean and golf greens, you may think you are in Tuscany, and that's before the fresh northern Italian dishes and unique pastas made in the restaurant's own temperature controlled pasta rooms even hit your table. The friendly service will lead you to believe this is a more casual restaurant than it is, but make no mistake, the food served here is carefully executed and well-sourced. The typical prosciutto, for example, is elevated with a Zibbibo wine-marinated melon. This kind of simple yet

SOUTHERN CALIFORNIA
★ ★
★★
★★
★★
★

refreshing bite provides the perfect lead in to the delicate hand-rolled pasta. Standout pasta selections when we visited included the ravioli di ricotta, a simple ravioli filled with fresh spinach and ricotta and finished in a heavenly sage butter sauce. Pasta is not the only item that gets special billing here, however, as all meals should end with a scoop of the artisan gelato.

Italian. Dinner. Bar. Reservations recommended. $36-85

★★EL TORITO GRILL

951 Newport Center Drive, Newport Beach, 949-640-2875; www.eltorito.com

El Torito serves up authentic Mexican. Salsas are made fresh, guacamole is prepared tableside and the tamales are hand made. There's also a kid's menu and ice cream sundaes are free for dessert.

Mexican. Lunch, dinner, Sunday brunch. $16-35

★★★THE RITZ

880 Newport Center Drive, Newport Beach, 949-720-1800; www.ritzrestaurant.com

The moment you step inside this epicurean eatery, you'll feel transported. Dim lighting is not a bother but a fine comfort; its mellow but rich light is ideal for a romantic dinner or drink. The restaurant's ambience achieves European charm through its dark wood walls, black leather booths and giant bottles of Moët & Chandon champagne that stand behind one particular booth. Yellow chandeliers with light bulbs shaped as bunches of grapes contribute to the golden lighting while potted palms add to the elegance and no fewer than six distinctive, richly appointed indoor and outdoor dining spaces grace the premises. The Escoffier Room (a pavilion-style space that exudes rosy light and with Georgian accents and portraits of the renowned Paris Ritz Hotel chef Auguste Escoffier) is in contrast to the darker, more subdued and private Wine Cellar (a vaulted brick chamber accessed through an oval tunnel that seats large parties of up to 32 people) and the outstanding cuisine encompasses French, Italian and American styles. For lunch, try the wild mushroom "cappuccino," along with the enormous Ritz salad, and leave room for the Harlequin soufflé, made with Belgian chocolate and Grand Marnier served with a Marnier crème anglaise sauce.

American, French. Lunch, dinner. Reservations recommended. Bar. $36-85

★★★TRADITION BY PASCAL

1000 N. Bristol St., Newport Beach, 949-263-9400; www.pascalnewportbeach.com

Much-lauded chef/restaurateur Pascal Olhats showcases his French countryside cuisine in this rose-filled, farmhouse-style space. The light French food includes beet salad with lemon flavored goat cheese and roasted hazelnuts, and dijon crusted lamb with celery root purée. A three-course prix fixe menu is available, as well as two lavish four-course meals.

French. Lunch (Monday-Friday), dinner (Tuesday-Sunday). $36-85

★★SAPORI

1080 Bayside Drive, Newport Beach, 949-644-4220; www.saporinb.com

The heated outdoor patio is the perfect spot for indulging in the rich pasta and meat dishes. Tasty antipasti, including mozzarella caprese, and an extensive wine list round out the experience.

Italian. Lunch, dinner. $36-85

SPA
★★★★THE SPA AT THE ISLAND HOTEL
690 Newport Center Drive, Newport Beach, 949-759-0808, 866-554-4620;
www.theislandhotel.com

Slip away to the Spa at the Island Hotel for a muscle-relieving massage or detoxifying volcanic clay treatment that is said to reenergize the body from head to toe. Spacious and modern, the spa's elegant touches—granite floors, silver tea pitchers and a calming water wall—instantly set a tranquil and tasteful tone. The spa's signature rituals use rejuvenating elements from India, Bali and the Hawaiian Islands to smooth, soften and invigorate skin. The Island Tropical Splendor is a full-body scrub blending fresh coconut, rice and vetiver—a perennial grass native to India known for its medicinal and aromatic properties.

★★★★★THE SPA AT THE RESORT AT PELICAN HILL
The Resort at Pelican Hill, 22701 Pelican Hill Road South, Newport Coast,
949-467-6800, 800-315-8214; www.pelicanhill.com

If you think the Pelican Hill Resort is transporting, wait until you arrive at the Spa at Pelican Hill where they will easily address one of three goals: replenishment, invigoration or relaxation. Prior to your treatments, spend your time in the Aqua Colonnade, the epitome of Tuscan-inspired relaxation complete with an herbal steam room and sauna. Your needs are so tended to that the therapist is offering you lunch from the delectable spa menu while you have your nails carefully polished. Just as in Italy, gelato is everywhere, so give in to the Body Gelato, which is a seasonally-inspired treatment incorporating luxurious herbs and fruit that will leave your skin feeling refreshed and nourished. If a full day is in your future, indulge in The Master's Palette, a nearly six hour affair of the spa's most decadent treatments.

OJAI
See also Santa Barbara Ventura

Located 15 miles inland from the Pacific Coast, Ojai is a small, tranquil community surrounded by 500,000 acres of picturesque mountains, green valleys and streams, which have been the backdrop for many Hollywood productions. It's also known for its adorable downtown, which has world-class art galleries, boutiques, cafés, restaurants, bookstores, a small park and a movie theater, and a handful of luxury spas.

WHAT TO SEE
LAKE CASITAS RECREATION AREA
11311 Santa Ana Road, Ojai, 805-649-2233; www.lakecasitas.info

At this recreation area, you can do some fishing, boating, picnicking and camping (for reservations, call 805-649-1122). Beaches, golf courses and tennis courts are all nearby. Pets must be on a leash.
Daily.

OJAI CENTER FOR THE ARTS
113 S. Montgomery, Ojai, 805-646-0117; www.ojaiact.org

The center hosts rotating exhibitions of local artists and live theater productions. Check Web site for performance information.

OJAI VALLEY MUSEUM

130 W. Ojai Ave., Ojai, 805-640-1390; www.ojaivalleymuseum.org

Permanent and changing exhibits at this museum explore environmental, cultural and historical factors that shaped the Ojai Valley. There's also a research library.

Admission: adults $4, children 6-18 $1, children under 6 free. Thursday-Friday 1-4 p.m., Saturday 10 a.m.-4 p.m., Sunday noon-4 p.m. Guided tours Wednesday.

SPECIAL EVENTS
OJAI MUSIC FESTIVAL

Libbe Bowl, 201 S. Signal St., Ojai, 805-646-2094; www.ojaifestival.org

For four days in June, the Libby Bowl hosts talented classical musicians performing pieces from composers such as Mozart, Stravinsky and Beethoven. Early June.

OJAI SHAKESPEARE FESTIVAL

Matilija JHS Auditorium, 703 El Paseo St., Ojai, 805-646-9455;
www.ojaishakespeare.org

See outdoor evening and matinee performances of Shakespeare plays. July-August.

OJAI STUDIO ARTISTS TOUR

Ojai Art Center, 113 S. Montgomery St., Ojai, 805-646-8126;
www.ojaistudioartists.com

Recognized artists open their studios to the public. Mid-October.

OJAI VALLEY TENNIS TOURNAMENT

Ojai, 805-646-7241; www.ojaitourney.org

Held since 1895, this is the oldest amateur tennis tournament in the nation. Games take place at a variety of venues, including Libby Park, the Ojai Valley Athletic Club and area high schools and colleges. Late April.

WHERE TO STAY
★★★OJAI VALLEY INN & SPA

905 Country Club Road, Ojai, 805-646-1111; www.ojairesort.com

This gorgeous resort sits on 220 acres and includes championship golf and tennis, lavish rooms with plus beds, fireplaces and extra-large bathrooms, and a spectacular spa. Guests are shuttled around the grounds on golf carts by the friendly and attentive staff, and the SoCal cuisine served at the resort is outstanding.

308 rooms. Restaurant, bar. Business center. Spa. Pets accepted. Golf. $251-350

WHERE TO EAT
★★★THE RANCH HOUSE
102 Besant Road, Ojai, 805-646-2360; www.theranchhouse.com

One of the forerunners of California cuisine, The Ranch House made a name for itself many decades ago by offering simple, made-from-scratch dishes—many of them vegetarian—that burst with fresh flavors. The years have seen some changes, but many things remain the same here. Fresh herbs from the garden are still used in all the recipes, and the loaves of bread that are served to patrons (and sold to locals) are still made fresh daily. Dishes like wild mushroom strudel and grilled diver scallops with sweet corn sauce have been keeping guests coming back, and its garden setting with quiet streams and lush foliage make it a perfect spot for a relaxing lunch.

American. Dinner, Sunday brunch. Closed Monday. $36-85

SPA
★★★★SPA OJAI
905 Country Club Road, Ojai, 805-646-1111, 888-697-8780; www.ojairesort.com

Golfers, hikers and couples on romantic getaways all come to this sophisticated 31,000-square-foot sanctuary of health and well-being for a spa experience like no other. Spa Ojai features signature services such as Kuyam—a treatment that combines the therapeutic effects of cleansing mud, dry heat, inhalation therapy and guided meditation. This communal experience (kuyam means "a place to rest together") accommodates up to eight men or women. There's also an extensive array of facial, skin and body treatments, as well as a variety of art classes in the adjacent studio.

PALM DESERT
See also Indio, Palm Springs

This city is located approximately 10 miles from Palm Springs. Many people come to live here in the winter, and of course, scores of people visit to play golf.

WHAT TO SEE
CLASSIC CLUB
75200 Classic Club Blvd., Palm Desert, 760-601-3601; www.classicclubgolf.com

Gaining fame in 2006 and 2007 by hosting the PGA's Bob Hope Chrysler Classic, this semiprivate club presents a challenging course of rolling terrain, wide landing areas, and 30 acres of water elements. Five sets of tees makes Classic Club playable for golfers of all levels.

DESERT WILLOW GOLF RESORT
38-995 Desert Willow Drive, Palm Desert, 760-346-7060; www.desertwillow.com

The resort, one of the best public access facilities in Southern California, has two championship courses: The tougher of the two, Firecliff, has more than 100 bunkers and numerous water hazards. Mountain View has wider fairways, sloping greens and less sand. Both have environmentally smart designs and construction.

LIVING DESERT

47-900 S. Portola Ave., Palm Desert, 760-346-5694, www.livingdesert.org

This 1,200-acre wildlife and botanical park contains interpretive exhibits from the world's deserts. The park also has Native American exhibits, picnic areas, nature trails, a gift shop, a café and a nursery. Check out the special weekend programs.

September-mid-June, daily 9 a.m.-5 p.m.; mid-June-August, daily 8 a.m.-1:30 p.m.

SPECIAL EVENT
BOB HOPE CHRYSLER CLASSIC

39000 Bob Hope Drive, Rancho Mirage, 760-346-8184; www.bhcc.com

Golf pros and celebrities play at four country clubs: Bermuda Dunes, La Quinta, Palm Desert and Indian Wells.

Mid-January.

WHERE TO STAY
★★★DESERT SPRINGS JW MARRIOTT RESORT & SPA

74855 Country Club Drive, Palm Desert, 760-341-2211, 800-255-0848;
www.desertspringsresort.com

The policy here is the bigger the better, as the largest resort and convention complex in the southwestern United States. The guest rooms and suites are located in wings surrounding swimming pools, lakes, verdant fairways, lush English gardens and manicured lawns. Spacious guest rooms have luxury beds, and granite, limestone and Italian marble bathrooms with separate tubs and showers. Two Ted Robinson championship golf courses provide a total of 36 rounds of golf, plus there are tennis courts (hard, clay and grass), basketball courts, a European spa, and lawn croquet. It's almost too much to take in at once. Did we mention the gondola rides from the lobby?

884 rooms. Restaurant, bars. Business center. Fitness center. Spa. $251-350

WHERE TO EAT
★★★CUISTOT

72-595 El Paseo, Palm Desert, 760-340-1000; www.cuistotrestaurant.com

Chef/owner Bernard Dervieux serves up inventive dishes inspired by his upbringing in France. Look for quail stuffed with sweetbreads with black rice and Chablis sauce, or skillet-roasted veal chop with mushrooms, roasted garlic and fresh thyme. The restaurant is reminiscent of a French farmhouse, with beamed cathedral ceilings, a large stone fireplace and candlelight.

French. Lunch, dinner. Closed Monday. $36-85

★★★JILLIAN'S

74-155 El Paseo, Palm Desert, 760-776-8242; www.jilliansfinedining.com

Housed in a 1948 hacienda, this restaurant features a beautiful garden through which guests pass to reach the dining area, where tables are set with fresh flowers and candles. Selections from the lengthy and impressive wine list perfectly accompany the eclectic menu, which includes creations like prime boneless short ribs braised in California cabernet and rack of Colorado lamb with a Dijon herb crust. Featured desserts, like chocolate brioche pudding and blueberry cheesecake, are made daily.

International. Dinner. Closed Sunday and mid-October-mid-June. Reservations recommended. $36-85

★★LG'S PRIME STEAKHOUSE
74-225 Highway 111, Palm Desert, 760-779-9799; www.lgsprimesteakhouse.com
LG's serves USDA Prime steaks, including a 30-ounce Porterhouse. Other specialties include the rack of lamb, thick-cut prime rib and Ceasar salad, prepared tableside. There's also an extensive wine list.
Steak. Dinner. $36-86

★★★RISTORANTE MAMMA GINA
73-705 El Paseo, Palm Desert, 760-568-9898; www.mammagina.com
This sister restaurant to one in Florence carries on the decades-old tradition of serving freshly prepared, traditional Tuscan fare. Pappa al pomodoro (authentic Florentine-style thick tomato bread soup), spaghetti alla Bolognese and risotto Mamma Gina (arborio rice with imported wild porcini mushroom sauce) are a few dishes on the menu that keep customers coming back. An award-winning wine list and a number of decadent desserts add to the authentic Tuscan experience.
Italian. Dinner. $36-86

★★★RUTH'S CHRIS STEAK HOUSE
74-740 Highway 111, Palm Desert, 760-779-1998; www.ruthschris.com
Born from a single New Orleans restaurant that Ruth Fertel bought in 1965 for $22,000, the chain is a favorite among steak lovers. Aged prime Midwestern beef is broiled at 1,800 degrees and served on a heated plate sizzling with butter and with sides like creamed spinach and au gratin potatoes.
Steak. Dinner. $36-86

★★★TUSCANY
74855 Country Club Drive, Palm Desert, 760-341-2211; www.desertspringsresort.com
One of the many restaurants in the JW Marriott Desert Springs Resort and Spa, this eatery has a seasonal menu that features dishes like ravioli stuffed with fresh Maine lobster, minestrone with pesto and house-made tiramisu. The mile-long wine list is comprehensive and has bottles from around the world. Soft music and frescoes add to the authentic vibe.
Italian. Dinner. $36-86

PALM SPRINGS
See also Palm Desert, Indio
Located 120 miles east of Los Angeles and 135 miles north of San Diego, Palm Springs has long been the vacation getaway for Southern California's elite. The desert oasis is complete with spectacular resorts, fine dining and unique mid-century modern desert architecture. Recently, the town's resorts have been undergoing a renovation revival, with star designers such as Jonathan Adler and Kelly Wearstler called in to dream up funky, colorful and stylish interiors. There are nearly 90 golf courses within a 15-mile radius of the city. Originally the domain of the Cahuilla, the city has been laid out in a checkerboard pattern, with nearly every other square mile still owned by the tribe.

WHAT TO SEE
INDIAN CANYONS

38520 S. Palm Canyon Drive, Palm Springs, 760-325-1862; www.indian-canyons.com
The remains of the ancient Cahuilla people include rock art, mortars ground into bedrock, pictographs and shelters built atop high cliff walls. Spot bighorn sleep and wind ponies along the hiking trails. Rangers give interpretive walks.
Daily 8 a.m.-5 p.m.

KNOTT'S SOAK CITY WATER PARK PALM SPRINGS

1500 Gene Autry Trail, Palm Springs, 760-327-0499; www.knotts.com
This 22-acre water park has 13 water slides, an inner tube ride and a wave pool.
Admission: adult $29.99, seniors $19.99, children under 48" $19.99.
Late March-August, daily; hours vary.

MOORTEN'S BOTANICAL GARDEN

1701 S. Palm Canyon Drive, Palm Springs, 760-327-6555;
www.palmsprings.com/moorten
Approximately 3,000 varieties of desert plants reside in this botanical garden. It also features the world's first "cactarium," which contains several hundred species of cactus and desert plants from around the world.
Admission: adults $3, children $1.50. Monday-Tuesday, Thursday-Saturday 9 a.m.-4:30 p.m., Sunday 10 a.m.-4 p.m.

OUTDOOR ROCK-CLIMBING

Joshua Tree, 760-366-3799, 888-254-6266; www.uprising.com
Uprising Adventure Guides is an outdoor rock-climbing gym that offers training and climbing for all ages. There's also night climbing available.

PALM SPRINGS AERIAL TRAMWAY

1 Tramway Road, Palm Springs, 760-325-1449, 760-325-1391; www.pstramway.com
Take a ride along the world's longest double-reversible, single-span aerial tramway. Two 80-passenger revolving cars make the 2½-mile trip (ascending to 8,516 feet) to the top of Mount San Jacinto. There are also opportunities for picnicking, camping in the summer and a bite to eat at the cafeteria at the summit.
Admission: adults $22.95, seniors $20.95, children 3-12 $15.95. Monday-Friday every half-hour from 10 a.m., Saturday-Sunday from 8 a.m.

PALM SPRINGS AIR MUSEUM

745 N. Gene Autry Trail, Palm Springs, 760-778-6262; www.air-museum.org
Vintage World War II aircraft are on display at this museum. And you'll also see period photographs and video documentaries.
Admission: adults $12, seniors and children13-17 $10, children 6-12 $5, children under 7 free. Daily 10 a.m.-5 p.m.

PALM SPRINGS DESERT MUSEUM

101 Museum Drive, Palm Springs, 760-325-4490; www.psmuseum.org

Enjoy diverse art collections of world-renowned artists, science exhibitions with interactive elements and educational programs for the whole family. The Annenberg Performing Arts Theater features jazz, classical, dance and Broadway performances.

Admission: adults $12.50, seniors $10.50, children free. Free every Thursday 4-8 p.m. Tuesday-Wednesday, Friday-Sunday 10 a.m.-5 p.m., Thursday noon-8 p.m.

PALM SPRINGS HISTORICAL SOCIETY ON VILLAGE GREEN

221 S. Palm Canyon Drive, Palm Springs, 760-323-8297; www.palmsprings.com/history

The historical society is composed of two 19th-century buildings that exhibit artifacts from early Palm Springs. McCallum Adobe (circa 1885) is the oldest building in the city and it houses an extensive collection of photographs, paintings, clothes, tools, books and Native American wares. The Cornelia White House (circa 1893) was partially constructed of rail ties from the defunct Palmdale Railway and is furnished with authentic antiques.

Mid-October-late May, Wednesday, Sunday noon-3 p.m., Thursday-Saturday 10 a.m.-4 p.m.

TAHQUITZ CREEK GOLF RESORT

1885 Golf Club Drive, Palm Springs, 760-328-1005; www.tahquitzgolfresort.com

The club features two 18-hole courses: the Legend course and the Resort course. The Legend course has a traditional layout, with tree-lined fairways and 40 bunkers, but was designed with severely sloped greens from back to front. The Resort course is a desert links-style layout, with rolling terrain, strategically placed sand and eye-catching mountain views.

WHERE TO STAY

★★★COLONY PALMS HOTEL

572 N. Indian Canyon Drive, Palm Springs, 800-557-2187; www.colonypalmshotel.com

Some hotels rely on marketing to conjure up images of good times and suave guests, but the Colony Palms Hotel only needs to look to its history. Open since the 1930s, the Colony Palms has enjoyed several lifetimes of good, but not always clean, fun (it once included a brothel). Today's guests can expect laid-back luxury in this newly renovated hotel where Turkish suzani headboards and a Morocco-inspired spa provide a sexy international vibe. The poolside Purple Palm Restaurant & Bar is the place to be if you're into delicious Mediterranean fare. Beds feature Italian linens and down duvets, to ensure that the nap that'll inevitably follow the food coma is a good one.

71 rooms. Restaurant, bar. Fitness center. Pool. Spa. $351 and up

★★★DORAL DESERT PRINCESS RESORT

67-967 Vista Chino, Cathedral City, 760-322-7000, 888-386-4677; www.doralpalmsprings.com

The panoramic mountain views from this sprawling resort set the mood for a true California golf weekend. All of the comfortable guest rooms are spacious enough, but should you choose to bunk with your golf buddies, suites have an extra bedroom, dining room, wet bar and wraparound balconies to take in the above-mentioned view. You can also squeeze in games of golf right here on the resort's PGA-rated 27-hole golf course. Work out knots afterward at the spa—or if you're not already sore enough, squeeze in a game of tennis. Feast on hearty portions of herb roasted chicken or "carb friendly" pasta alfredo at the Fairway Café, which specializes in California cuisine and also offers lovely views of the San Jacinto Mountains.

285 rooms. Restaurant, bar. Fitness center. Spa. Pets accepted. Golf. $61-150

★★★HILTON PALM SPRINGS RESORT

400 E. Tahquitz Canyon Way, Palm Springs, 760-320-6868, 800-522-6900;
www.hiltonpalmsprings.com

From its dramatic setting at the foot of the steeply rising San Jacinto Mountains to the grand rooms with Italian travertine flooring, contemporary furnishings and cozy sitting areas, this is a popular resort for business travelers and vacationing families. It's less than two miles from the airport and within walking distance of cafés, galleries, boutiques, a casino and the Palm Springs Desert Museum.

261 rooms. Restaurant, bar. Business center. Fitness center. Pool. Spa. Pets accepted. $61-150

★★★HYATT REGENCY SUITES PALM SPRINGS

285 N. Palm Canyon Drive, Palm Springs, 760-322-9000, 800-223-1234;
www.palmsprings.hyatt.com

This Hyatt hotel is set in a prime downtown location overlooking the San Jacinto Mountains. Guest rooms feature separate sitting areas with pull-out sofas and dining tables, and furnished balconies give way to views of the mountains, pool or city. There are plenty of onsite activities, including jogging paths, bicycle trails, a heated pool and putting green. The hotel's restaurant, the Palm Court Café, is in the center of the six-story atrium and serves eclectic California cuisine in a casual setting.

194 suites. Restaurant, bar. Business center. Fitness center. Pool. Spa. $151-250

★★★INGLESIDE INN

200 W. Ramon Road, Palm Springs, 760-325-0046, 800-772-6655;
www.inglesideinn.com

Everyone from Rita Hayworth to Arnold Schwarzenegger has stayed at this quiet inn fashioned from an early-1900s estate. Today it's a throwback to 1920s Hollywood with individually-decorated suites and villas with old world décor and modern amenities like steam baths and whirlpool tubs. Melvyn's Restaurant is perfect for those who don't like to fuss: For a flat $70 a day, you can eat all your meals in the restaurant or in your room. The Casablanca Room is an intimate piano bar.

30 rooms. Restaurant, bar. Pool. $151-250

★★★RANCHO LAS PALMAS RESORT AND SPA

41-000 Bob Hope Drive, Rancho Mirage, 760-568-2727, 866-423-1195;
www.rancholaspalmas.com

This family-friendly hotel is in the heart of Rancho Mirage on 240 acres surrounded by mountains, lakes and gardens. Activities include a Ted Robinson-designed golf course, a 25-court tennis center, a 100-foot water slide and a 20,000-square-foot European spa. The warm and bright Spanish-style guest rooms feature plush bedding and French doors that open up to furnished patios or balconies overlooking the breezy flower-filled grounds.
466 rooms. Restaurant, bar. Fitness center. Pool. Spa. $151-250

★★★SPA RESORT CASINO

401 E. Amado Road, Palm Springs, 888-999-1995, 800-854-1279;
www.sparesortcasino.com

The rooms here are less luxurious than those found in other hotels in the area. But if your idea of the perfect vacation is golf by day and blackjack by night, you've found a place to rest your head. This is the only full-service resort/casino in Palm Springs, and has more than 1,000 slots and 30 tables (plus a private room for serious betters) to try your luck. The resort also has all the dining options of a typical casino: two Asian restaurants, a New York-style deli, a large buffet-style restaurant and several bars. Plus, you are just a block from Palm Canyon Drive where there are numerous shopping and dining options.
228 rooms. Restaurant, bar. Spa. Casino. $61-150

★★★VICEROY PALM SPRINGS

415 S. Belardo Road, Palm Springs, 760-320-4117, 800-670-6184;
www.viceroypalmsprings.com

Built in 1929 and updated by designer Kelly Wearstler to reflect the Hollywood Regency style popular during the city's original glamour era, this boutique hotel located in the historic district is a great way to spoil yourself on a golf weekend with your spouse. Luxurious rooms, suites and villas, which look like they jumped out of the pages of a magazine, are surrounded by gorgeous gardens and are outfitted with Italian linens, custom beds and all the fun accessories: speaker phones, LCD televisions and mini-refrigerators stocked with gourmet snacks. Villas have private patios and full kitchens. The full-service spa will you feel pampered with its specialty outdoor treatments. Mani/pedis and massages are delivered poolside in cabanas. Gourmet restaurant Citron dishes up delicious California cuisine in a bright, outdoorsy setting with lemon yellow walls and white, marble-tiled floors.
68 rooms. Restaurant, bar. Pets accepted. $151-250

★★★THE VILLA ROYALE INN

1620 S. Indian Trail, Palm Springs, 760-327-2314, 800-245-2314; www.villaroyale.com

Just a mile from downtown, this hotel combines the pampered privacy of a bed and breakfast with the amenities of a full-service hotel. Individually appointed Mediterranean-style suites and villas nestled amid tranquil, lushly landscaped courtyards and two heated pools are decorated with European antiques and feature down duvets, luxurious robes and herbal bath products. Larger rooms also have fireplaces, open-beam ceilings, kitchens and private patios. The intimate restaurant, Europa, serves award-winning continental cuisine under the stars.

30 rooms. Restaurant, bar. Complimentary breakfast. Pool. $151-250

★★★THE WESTIN MISSION HILLS RESORT AND SPA

71333 Dinah Shore Drive, Rancho Mirage; www.westin.com/missionhills

Set on 360 acres surrounded by mountains, palm trees and lush landscaping, there's almost no need to leave the resort. Activities are plentiful, with two championship golf courses, three swimming pools—one with a 60-foot water slide—a 14,000-square-foot spa with a state-of-the-art fitness center and seven lighted tennis courts. Handsome guest rooms have private patios and sitting areas with a couch and coffee table.

472 rooms. Restaurant, bar. Fitness center. Pool. Pets accepted. $251-350

★★★THE WILLOWS HISTORIC PALM SPRINGS INN

412 W. Tahquitz Canyon Way, Palm Springs, 760-320-0771;
www.thewillowspalmsprings.com

Built in 1924, this legendary Mediterranean villa in the heart of Old Palm Springs has hosted everyone from Marion Davies to Albert Einstein, and is a great choice if you're looking for something small and intimate. The inn has only eight guest rooms, each with its own style, from the slate flooring in the Rock Room to the coffered ceiling in the Library, where Clark Gable and Carole Lombard spent their honeymoon.

8 rooms. Pool. $251-350

★★WYNDHAM PALM SPRINGS HOTEL

888 Tahquitz Canyon Way, Palm Springs, 760-322-6000, 800-996-3426;
www.wyndham-palmsprings.com

Just eight blocks from the airport and adjacent to the convention center, the Wyndham anchors a 40-acre commercial development, making it a good choice for business travelers. The hotel's Spanish-colonial exterior gives way to a more contemporary décor inside the guest rooms, which feature oversized desks, high-speed Internet access and scenic mountain views. Amenities include a staffed health club, complete body spa and a large pool with an adjacent bar and barbecue.

410 rooms. Restaurant, bar. Fitness center. Pool. Spa. Pets accepted. $151-250

WHERE TO EAT

★★BLUE COYOTE BAR & GRILL

445 N. Palm Canyon Drive, Palm Springs, 760-327-1196; www.bluecoyote-grill.com

After a day on the links, this lively Mexican spot may be just the ticket. You have to love a restaurant that calls itself "the home of the Wild Coyote margarita." Gold tequila, orange curacoa and fresh lime juice are used to create the potent concoction. Just be sure to fill up on the tantalizing Mexican food at the same time, including Yucatan mahi-mahi, pollo cilantro, quesadillas and flan.

Southwestern. Lunch, dinner. Closed August. Bar. $16-35

★★EUROPA

1620 Indian Trail, Palm Springs, 760-327-2314; www.villaroyale.com

Housed in the Villa Royale Inn, this restaurant is beloved by locals for its delightful continental cuisine, inspired by the sun-basked countries of Southern Europe, and strong wine list. Dine on duck confit or osso bucco poolside by the fountains or enjoy a bottle of wine fireside in the cozy dining room. Continental. Dinner. Closed Monday. Bar. $36-85

★★KAISER GRILL

205 S. Palm Canyon Drive, Palm Springs, 760-323-1003; www.kaisergrille.com

You don't have to break the bank to get great food in Palm Springs. From a classic Caesar salad to wood oven-fired pizzas to house specialties like Greek steak and shrimp Pancetta, the vast menu satisfies every craving. The lively atmosphere is also a draw, and the large tables are perfect for large groups.
California, Mediterranean. Lunch, dinner. Reservations recommended. Bar. $16-35

★★★LE VALLAURIS

385 W. Tahquitz Canyon Way, Palm Springs, 760-325-5059; www.levallauris.com

Housed in a 1924 home with Louis XV furniture, rich tapestries and an enchanting tree-shaded garden surrounded by flowers, Le Vallauris transports you to the French countryside. Daily selections—from rack of lamb to Grand Marnier soufflé—are written on a board brought to the table. The impressive wine list includes bottles from France and California as well as Italy, New Zealand and Spain.
French. Lunch, dinner. Closed July-August. Bar. $36-85

★★★MELVYN'S

200 W. Ramon Road, Palm Springs, 760-325-0046; www.inglesideinn.com

Located in the Ingleside Inn, this classic steakhouse is a long-standing Palm Springs tradition. Start with drinks at the fully restored carved oak and mahogany bar before sitting down to select from the extensive American menu that features a variety of beef, seafood, pasta and poultry dishes. Wine aficionados will especially appreciate Melvyn's two well-stocked wine cellars.
Continental. Lunch (Monday-Friday), dinner, Saturday-Sunday brunch. Reservations recommended. Bar. $36-85

★★★SAMMY G'S TUSCAN GRILL

265 S. Palm Canyon Drive, Palm Springs, 760-320-8041; www.sammygsrestaurant.com

Located in the heart of downtown Palm Springs, Sammy G's features a variety of Italian dishes from pastas to chicken, seafood and meats. They feature housemade pastas and risottos such as gnocchi with either a tomato basil sauce, a four-cheese sauce or pesto; lasagna Bolognese; and risotto with shrimp and a tomato-cream sauce. Enjoy ive music Thursday through Saturday evenings.
Italian. Dinner. Closed Monday. Bar. $36-85

PASADENA

See also Arcadia, Glendale, Los Angeles

Home of the world-famous Tournament of Roses, Pasadena was first chosen as a health refuge for wintering Midwesterners, and later as a retreat for Eastern millionaires. Today, it is a cultural and scientific center with many research, development and engineering companies centered in Pasadena.

WHAT TO SEE

KIDSPACE CHILDREN'S MUSEUM

480 N. Arroyo Blvd., Pasadena, 626-449-9144; www.kidspacemuseum.org

Kids can climb aboard raindrops as they travel through the water cycle or dig up -fossils and dinosaur eggs at this interactive museum.

Admission: adults and children $10. September-May, Tuesday-Friday 9:30 a.m.-5 p.m., Saturday-Sunday 10 a.m.-5 p.m.; June-August, Monday-Friday 9:30 a.m.-5 p.m., Saturday-Sunday 10 a.m.-5 p.m.

NORTON SIMON MUSEUM OF ART

411 W. Colorado Blvd., Pasadena, 626-449-6840; www.nortonsimon.org

The Norton Simon may not be as large as Los Angeles County Museum of Art, but it boasts an impressive collection that's worth seeing. The museum opened to the public in the mid-1970s, and Frank Gehry updated the interior in the late 1990s, adding skylights and limestone floors to create a sense of light. The Norton Simon houses sculpture and paintings originating from all over Asia, and showcases works by Picasso, Rembrandt, Goya, Degas, Van Gogh and Kandinsky. Stop by the museum's garden, which features a number of sculptures by Henry Moore and is reminiscent of Monet's garden in Giverny, France.

Admission: adults $8, seniors $4, students and children 18 and under free. Monday, Wednesday-Thursday, Saturday-Sunday noon-6 p.m., Friday noon-9 p.m. Free first Friday 6-9 p.m. of every month.

PACIFIC ASIA MUSEUM

46 N. Los Robles Ave., Pasadena, 626-449-2742; www.pacificasiamuseum.org

Inside this Chinese Imperial Palace-style building, you'll see changing exhibits of traditional and contemporary Asian and Pacific Basin art. The grounds also include a Chinese courtyard garden, a research library and a bookstore. Docent tours are available.

Admission: adults $9, seniors and students $7, children under 11 free. Wednesday-Sunday 10 a.m.-6 p.m.

PASADENA MUSEUM OF HISTORY

470 W. Walnut St., Pasadena, 626-577-1660; www.pasadenahistory.org

Housed in the 18-room Fenyes Estate since 1970, the museum includes original furnishings, antiques, paintings and accessories, giving a glimpse of the elegant lifestyle that existed on Orange Grove Boulevard at the turn of the century.

Mansion tours: Wednesday-Friday 1 p.m., Saturday-Sunday 1:30 p.m. and 3 p.m. Exhibit hours: Wednesday-Sunday noon-5 p.m.

ROSE BOWL

1001 Rose Bowl Drive, Pasadena, 626-577-3101; www.rosebowlstadium.com

Although no longer the home of the annual big game between the winners of the Pac-10 and the Big Ten conferences, the Rose Bowl still hosts the Bowl Championship Series games every year. During the regular season, UCLA's Bruins football team plays at the venue.

SPECIAL EVENT
TOURNAMENT OF ROSES

391 S. Orange Grove Blvd., Pasadena, 626-449-4100; www.tournamentofroses.com

Millions turn out each New Year's Day to watch the gorgeous floral floats, high-stepping marching bands and beautiful equestrian units. After the parade, get an up-close look at the Showcase of Floats.
January 1.

WHERE TO STAY
★★★HILTON PASADENA

168 S. Los Robles Ave., Pasadena, 626-577-1000, 800-445-8667; www.hilton.com

Located just steps from the Pasadena Convention Center and Old Town Pasadena and its hundreds of dining, shopping and entertainment options, the spacious guest rooms at this hotel are equipped with data ports, wireless Internet access and comfortable ergonomic chairs for business travelers. The lively bar has a pool table and multiple video screens.

296 rooms. Restaurant, bar. Business center. Fitness center. Pool. Pets accepted. $151-250

★★★THE LANGHAM, HUNTINGTON HOTEL & SPA, PASADENA

1401 S. Oak Knoll Ave., Pasadena, 626-568-3900; www.langhamhotels.com

People have been escaping to the quiet beauty of Pasadena for decades and, since 1907, they've often been heading straight for The Huntington Hotel & Spa. This landmark hotel, set on 23 acres at the foothills of the San Gabriel Mountains, is a destination unto itself. The 11,000-square-foot award-winning spa is reason alone to visit, as are the elegant European-style rooms fitted with Italian marble baths and Frette linens. Fine dining and top-notch service complete the first-class experience.

380 rooms. Restaurant, bar. Business center. Fitness center. Pool. Spa. $251-350

★★★SHERATON PASADENA HOTEL

303 E. Cordova St., Pasadena, 626-449-4000, 800-457-7940;
www.starwoodhotels.com

Within walking distance of many of the city's attractions, this hotel is a nice spot for business and leisure travelers. Guest rooms include pillow-top mattresses and large desks. A complimentary shuttle will take you to places within a three-mile radius.

317 rooms. Restaurant, bar. Business center. Fitness center. Pool. $151-250

★★★WESTIN PASADENA

191 N. Los Robles Ave., Pasadena, 626-792-2727; www.westin.com/pasadena

This beautifully appointed hotel in the heart of downtown appeals to families and those traveling on business. An in-house kids' club supplies coloring books, bath toys and a phone line dedicated to bedtime stories. Office rooms come with a fax and printer, and all accommodations feature signature Heavenly Beds with pillow-top mattresses.

350 rooms. Restaurant, bar. Business center. Fitness center. Pool. $151-250

WHERE TO EAT

★BECKHAM GRILL

77 W. Walnut St., Pasadena, 626-796-3399; www.beckhamgrill.com

Head to this cozy British pub for a pint and fish and chips. You'll spot it by the old London taxicab out front.

American. Lunch (Monday-Friday), dinner. Bar. $16-35

★★★BISTRO 45

45 S. Mentor Ave., Pasadena, 626-795-2478; www.bistro45.com

Located in an Art Deco building on a quiet Old Pasadena street, this top-ranked restaurant features a French-influenced California menu focused on fresh ingredients. Notable specialties include pan seared bluefin crab cake, roasted wild brook trout with caramelized shallot and marble potatoes, and beef tenderloin with sautéed mushrooms.. All dishes are presented with refined service and a wine list that should impress even the most discerning connoisseur.

California. Lunch (Tuesday-Thursday), dinner. Closed Monday. Bar. $36-86

★★CAFE SANTORINI

64 W. Union St., Pasadena, 626-564-4200; www.cafesantorini.com

Dine outside on the lively roofdeck. Start off with a tasty mezze, which includes grape leaves, olives, feta cheese, tabouleh and hummus, before digging into one of the flavorful entrees, including chicken kebobs or lamb souvlaki.

Mediterranean. Lunch, dinner. $16-35

★CROCODILE CAFE

140 S. Lake Ave., Pasadena, 626-449-9900; www.crocodilecafe.com

Everything at this cozy cafe is made more delicious thanks to an oakwood grill. The cafe is known for its juicy burgers, housemade pastas, wood fired pizzas, and a delicious blue corn tostada salad with grilled chicken, fresh corn, black beans and guacamole.

American. Lunch, dinner. $16-35

★★★THE DINING ROOM

1401 S. Oak Knoll Ave., Pasadena, 626-568-3900; www.langhamhotels.com

Dine on perfectly prepared grilled meats and seafood at this clubby dining room located within the elegant Langham hotel. The service is top-notch, and the waitstaff and kitchen will gladly accommodate any special request. The dimly lit dining room surrounds guests with warm, neutral tones and tables topped with crisp white linens and candles. It's a perfect spot for either a romantic dinner or for entertaining clients.

American. Dinner. Closed Sunday-Monday. $36-85

★★MAISON AKIRA
713 E. Green St., Pasadena, 626-796-9501; www.maisonakira.com

Chef Akira Hirose blends French and Japanese cuisine to create dishes such as miso marinated grilled Chilean sea bass with grilled ratatouille in a honey lemon jus, and pan roasted rack of lamb in a rosemary sauce with potato mousseline. Several tasting menus are also available, including a nine-course chef's tasting menu.

French, Japanese. Lunch, dinner. Closed Monday. $36-85

★★MI PIACE
25 E. Colorado Blvd., Pasadena, 626-795-3131; www.mipiace.com

Mi Place is an Italian restaurant, bakery and lounge all rolled into one. The trendy and upbeat restaurant is perfect for breakfast, lunch, dinner or drinks. For breakfast, just try deciding between the Italian-style Eggs Benedict with polenta, prosciutto and sun-dried tomatoes, or the blueberry buttermilk pancakes with fresh orange zest. Do yourself a favor and order both.

Italian. Breakfast, lunch, dinner. $36-85

PASO ROBLES
See also Morro Bay

Paso Robles is booming with vineyards; there are nearly 100 wineries here.

SPECIAL EVENT
WINE FESTIVAL
805-239-8463; www.pasowine.com

The fest includes a wine tasting, concerts and open houses.
Third Saturday in May.

WHERE TO STAY
★ADELAIDE INN

1215 Ysabel Ave., Paso Robles, 805-238-2770, 800-549-7276; www.adelaideinn.com

108 rooms. Complimentary breakfast. Fitness center. Pool. Spa. $66-150

★★BEST WESTERN BLACK OAK MOTOR LODGE
1135 24th St., Paso Robles, 805-238-4740, 800-780-7234; www.bestwestern.com

110 rooms. Restaurant, bar. Pool. $66-150

WHERE TO EAT
★F. MCCLINTOCK'S SALOON
1234 Park St., Paso Robles, 805-238-2233; www.mclintocks.com

Steak. Breakfast, lunch, dinner. $16-35

PISMO BEACH
See also Morro Bay, San Luis Obispo

Pismo Beach is famous for its 23 miles of scenic beaches. Ocean fishing, dunes, swimming, surfing, diving, golf, horseback riding and camping make the area popular with vacationers. Pismo Beach is also in a growing wine region. It is the last Pacific oceanfront community where autos can still be driven on the beach (access ramps are at two locations along the sand). A more dramatic and rugged coastline is found at Shell Beach to the north, which has been incorporated into Pismo Beach.

WHERE TO STAY
★★★THE CLIFFS RESORT
2757 Shell Beach Road, Pismo Beach, 805-773-5000, 800-826-7827;
www.cliffsresort.com
The cliff-top location overlooking the Pacific, inn-style hospitality and proximity to the local airport make this resort a good choice. Guest rooms feature work desks, Italian marble baths, and private balconies or patios with coastal or mountain views. Activities such as surfing, kayaking, hiking and golf are available onsite or nearby, and dozens of wineries are within driving distance.
160 rooms. Restaurant, bar. Business center. Pool. Pets accepted. $151-250

★OXFORD SUITES RESORT—PISMO BEACH
651 Five Cities Drive, Pismo Beach, 805-773-3773, 800-982-7848;
www.oxfordsuites.com
The Oxford is a good choice if you're on a budget. Each suite includes a living room and sleeper sofa; and breakfast, an evening reception (excluding Sunday) and Internet are all free.
132 suites. Complimentary breakfast. Business center. Pool. Pets accepted. $61-150

★SANDCASTLE INN
100 Stimson Ave., Pismo Beach, 805-773-2422, 800-822-6606;
www.sandcastleinn.com
The Sandcastle Inn is a family-friendly getaway right on the beach. The bright and cheerful guest rooms have a beach decor, there's a fireplace to gather around in the lounge, and you can rent bikes onsite.
75 rooms. Complimentary breakfast. Pets accepted. $151-250

★★SPYGLASS INN
2705 Spyglass Drive, Pismo Beach, 805-773-4855, 800-824-2612;
www.spyglassinn.com
Designed to resemble a cozy lodge, this inn is right on the beach and most rooms have balconies or patios with views. The lounge is a nice spot for a nightcap.
82 rooms. Pool. Spa. Pets accepted. $61-150

WHERE TO EAT
★★F. MCLINTOCK'S
750 Mattie Road, Pismo Beach, 805-773-1892; www.mclintocks.com
F. McLintock's is a Pismo Beach favorite, so be prepared to wait. And definitely come hungry. Steaks and ribs are cooked over an oat-pit barbeque, and dinners come with so many sides (onion rings, beans, garlic bread, sherbet for dessert), you'll be stuffed for days.
Steak. Dinner. $16-35

RANCHO SANTA FE

See also Del Mar

This idyllic town (you'll often see people riding their horses on trails) is modeled after a Spanish village. The Inn at Rancho Sante Fe was once a destination for Hollywood stars, including Bette Davis and Bing Crosby. Today, many people visit to play the Rancho Santa Fe Golf Course, which is considered one of the best courses in Southern California, while the Rancho Valencia is a well-known tennis resort.

WHERE TO STAY

★★★INN AT RANCHO SANTA FE

5951 Linea Del Cielo, Rancho Santa Fe, 858-756-1131, 800-843-4661;
www.theinnatranchosantafe.com

With several small cottages dotting the 20-acre property, guest accommodations are available in three varieties: deluxe rooms, suites and private cottages. The deluxe rooms have patios or decks, and many have fireplaces, wet bars, kitchenettes or sitting areas (some of the older rooms have hardwood floors). Suites are one- or two-bedroom cottages, each with a living room, kitchen and fireplace, plus a patio or deck. The one-, two- and three-bedroom private cottages have a full-sized kitchen and guest bath. A full-service spa, a fitness program (offering guided runs and walks, swimming lessons, water aerobics and weight training classes), tennis courts, a croquet lawn and walking and jogging trails provide plenty of recreation.

87 rooms. Restaurant. Fitness center. Pool. Spa. Pets accepted. $151-250

★★★MORGAN RUN RESORT & CLUB

5690 Cancha de Golf, Rancho Santa Fe, 858-756-2471, 800-378-4653;
www.morganrun.com

The Morgan Run Resort & Club is both a club for area residents and a resort for guests. Travelers can take full advantage of the club and its facilities, including a 27-hole championship golf course, tennis courts and a fitness center offering Pilates and yoga classes. The guest rooms are traditional and elegant, and each has its own private patio or balcony. The resort is only five miles from the beach community of Del Mar with its sandy shores, boutiques and Del Mar Race Track, where's there's plenty of horse-racing action.

90 rooms. Restaurant, bar. Fitness center. Spa. $151-250

★★★★RANCHO VALENCIA RESORT & SPA

5921 Valencia Circle, Rancho Santa Fe, 858-756-1123, 800-548-3664;
www.ranchovalencia.com

Located in the canyon of Rancho Santa Fe on 40 manicured acres of rolling hills, this relaxing retreat is just minutes from the charming boutiques and cafés of La Jolla. If you're looking for something secluded, this is it. The resort is made up of 20 pink casitas, which house only 49 suites, each featuring fireplaces with hand-painted tiles, beamed ceilings and private garden patios and large bathrooms, some with bathtubs and steam showers. There's also an award-winning tennis program, spa and privileges at local golf courses. An outstanding restaurant makes for a perfect stay.

49 suites. Restaurant, bar. Fitness center. Spa. Pets accepted. $251 and up

WHERE TO EAT
★★DELICIAS
6106 Paseo Delicias, Rancho Santa Fe, 858-756-8000; www.deliciasrestaurant.com

This elegant yet casual Rancho Santa Fe restaurant offers a menu of up-scale comfort food with French and California influences. Smoked salmon pizza with crème fraiche, Bermuda onions and a trio of caviars; grilled bistro steak with parmesan-truffle fries and balsamic-honey butter; and a jazzed-up macaroni and cheese that includes proscuitto, peas and black truffles are a few menu standouts. The food, along with a warm, romantic atmosphere with indoor and outdoor fireplaces and stunning flower arrangements, makes Delicias a favorite with local residents. "Gourmet hamburger night" each Thursday is also a draw.

American. Lunch (Tuesday-Friday), dinner. Closed Sunday. Reservations recommended. Bar. $36-85

★★★MILLE FLEURS
6009 Paseo Delicias, Rancho Santa Fe, 858-756-3085; www.millefleurs.com

This elegant restaurant serves such unforgettable dishes as vegetable ravioli with cave-aged Gruyère and venison loin from New Zealand. Many of the fruits and vegetables come from a farm just down the road, which the chef visits every morning. An outdoor patio, seasonal music and a piano bar make for a perfect evening.

French. Lunch (Tuesday-Friday), dinner. Bar. $36-85

★★★THE RESTAURANT RACHO VALENCIA
Rancho Valencia, 5921 Valencia Circle, Rancho Santa Fe, 858-759-6216;
www.ranchovalencia.com

Just off the mission-style courtyard of the Rancho Valencia resort, you'll find Valencia, a romantic dining experience reminiscent of the French countryside, with whitewashed walls, beamed ceilings, live palms and a tiered patio. The menu features seafood, fresh vegetables and aged beef. Highlights include the Diver scallops; a Colorado lamb rib eye with escargots, garlic, and shallots; and the Valencia veal picatta with olive oil mashed potatoes and broccoli rabe. Save room for one of the decadent desserts or the artisan cheese plate. The restaurant also offers an outstanding Sunday brunch.

Seafood. Breakfast, lunch, dinner, Sunday brunch. $86 and up

SPA
★★★THE SPA AT RANCHO VALENCIA
Rancho Valencia, 5921 Valencia Circle, Rancho Santa Fe, 858-756-1123;
www.ranchovalencia.com

This spa's mosaic-tiled décor echoes the Spanish mission-style look of the Rancho Valencia Resort. The 10 treatment rooms, outfitted with showers and private patios, are luxurious retreats where the staff delivers massages, exfoliations, masks and wraps that make full use of the area's natural bounty, from Pacific sea salt to seaweed, sweet citrus fruits and cypress.

REDLANDS

See also Big Bear Lake, Lake Arrowhead, Riverside

Named for the color of the earth in the area and known as the place where naval orange were grown, Redlands still handles a large volume of citrus fruits. The charming downtown area is filled with shops (including some where you can buy antiques) and restaurants.

WHAT TO SEE

KIMBERLY CREST HOUSE AND GARDENS

1325 Prospect Drive, Redlands, 909-792-2111; www.kimberlycrest.org

This is the former estate of John Kimberly, founder of the Kimberly-Clark Corporation. The 1897 French château-style structure and accompanying carriage house on 6½ acres is representative of the "Mansion Era" of Southern California. Guided tours are available.

September-July, Thursday-Sunday 1-4 p.m. Closed August.

LINCOLN MEMORIAL SHRINE

125 W. Vine St., Redlands, 909-798-7632; www.lincolnshrine.org

Learn about the former president and the Civil War at this shrine featuring George Grey Barnard's Carrara marble bust of Lincoln, murals by Dean Cornwell and a painting by Norman Rockwell.

Tuesday-Sunday 1-5 p.m.

PHARAOH'S LOST KINGDOM

1101 California St., Redlands, 909-335-7275; www.pharaohslostkingdom.com

This family theme park features a race car complex with Indy, Grand Prix and kiddie cars; a water park with wave pools; miniature golf; and 16 amusement rides. There is also an Arcade, indoor playground and amphitheater. Daily; hours vary.

REDLANDS BOWL

25 Grant St., Redlands, 909-793-7316; www.redlandsbowl.org

Locals call this amphitheater the "Little Hollywood Bowl" because of the free concerts held every Tuesday and Friday in the summer.

SAN BERNARDINO COUNTY MUSEUM

2024 Orange Tree Lane, Redlands, 909-307-2669; www.co.san-bernardino.ca.us

Check out the mounted collection of birds and bird eggs of Southern California, reptiles, mammals, rocks and more.

Admission: adults $8, seniors $6, students $5, children 5-12 $4, children under 5 free. Tuesday-Sunday 9 a.m.-5 p.m., Sunday noon-5 p.m.

SPECIAL EVENT

CHERRY FESTIVAL

Stewart Park, Ninth St. and Orange Ave., Beaumont, 951-845-9541;
www.ci.beaumont.ca.us

This annual festival celebrates the area's cherry harvest. Activities include a parade, entertainment and carnival rides.

Early June.

WHERE TO EAT

★★★JOE GREENSLEEVES

220 N. Orange St., Redlands, 909-792-6969; www.joegreensleevesrestaurant.com

This charming restaurant, housed in a historic 19th-century red brick building, is a favorite special-occasion destination in the Inland Empire. Its rustic-themed dining room is inviting and features a stone fireplace and back booths that are perfect for private, romantic dinners. Although the menu is dominated by a number of tempting steak and seafood dishes, long-standing favorites include roasted Anaheim chile stuffed with venison, and Sonoma goat cheese with smoked corn sauce and diced tomatoes. The wine list has been nationally recognized for its excellence, and housemade desserts are the perfect ending to a meal.

Seafood, steak. Lunch, dinner. $36-85

RIVERSIDE

See also Big Bear Lake, Redlands

Riverside is known for the navel orange, which was introduced to America from -Brazil by the first settlers in this area. It's home to the Parent Navel Orange Tree, from which all North American navel oranges are descended. Vast navel orange groves make Riverside the center of the "Orange Empire."

WHAT TO SEE

CALIFORNIA MUSEUM OF PHOTOGRAPHY

3824 Main St., Riverside, 951-827-4787; www.cmp.ucr.edu

The photography museum has a large collection of photographic equipment, prints and stereographs. There's an interactive gallery, a walk-in camera and a library.

Admission: adults $3, seniors and children under 13 free. Tuesday-Saturday noon-5 p.m.

CASTLE AMUSEMENT PARK

3500 Polk St., Riverside, 951-785-3000; www.castlepark.com

This amusement park offers 30 rides and attractions, including an 80-year-old Dentzel carousel with hand-carved animals. Four 18-hole miniature golf courses and a video arcade also can be found at the park.

Monday-Friday 10 a.m.-11 p.m., Saturday-Sunday 11 a.m.-11 p.m.

MARCH FIELD AIR MUSEUM

22550 Van Buren Blvd., Riverside, 951-697-6602; www.marchfield.org

Adjacent to the March Air Reserve Base, this museum houses more than 60 historic aircraft, including the first operational jet used by the U.S. Air Force and the speed record-breaking SR-71 Blackbird. Take a spin in the G-force flight simulator or explore the collection of 2,000 artifacts dating back to 1918.

Admission: adults $8, children 5-11 $5, children under 6 free. Tuesday-Sunday 9 a.m.-4 p.m.

PARENT WASHINGTON NAVEL ORANGE TREE

Magnolia and Arlington Avenues, Riverside

Planted in 1873, this tree is propagated from one of the two original trees from Bahia, Brazil. All navel orange trees stem from this tree or from its offspring.

RIVERSIDE ART MUSEUM

3425 Mission Inn Ave., Riverside, 951-684-7111; www.riversideartmuseum.org

Housed in a 1929 Mediterranean-style YWCA building designed by Julia Morgan, this museum features changing exhibits of historical and contemporary sculpture, painting and graphics.

Admission: adults $5, seniors and students $2, children 12 and under free. Monday-Saturday 10 a.m.-4 p.m.

RUBIDOUX DRIVE-IN

3770 Opal St., Riverside, 951-683-4455; www.rubidoux.icyspicy.com

The Rubidoux opened in 1948 and has three screens, each showing double features year-round.

WHERE TO STAY

★★COURTYARD RIVERSIDE

1510 University Ave., Riverside, 951-276-1200, 800-321-2211; www.marriott.com

Convenient to area shopping, dining, and the University of California-Riverside campus, visitors will appreciate this hotel's location and amenities, including new Marriott bedding, free Internet and large work desks.

163 rooms. Restaurant, bar. Pool. $61-150

★★★RIVERSIDE MARRIOTT

3400 Market St., Riverside, 951-784-8000, 800-228-9290; www.marriott.com

Adjacent to the Riverside Convention Center and close to Ontario International Airport, this hotel attracts business and leisure travelers looking for a range of amenities. Spacious, elegant rooms offer comfort and practical business features, including work desks, speaker phones and complimentary coffee. Olio Ristorante specializes in Italian food, while Martini's Lounge serves an eclectic menu. Antique stores, museums, shops and other attractions are within walking distance.

292 rooms. Restaurant, bar. Business center. Pool. $151-250

★★★MISSION INN HOTEL AND SPA

3649 Mission Inn Ave., Riverside, 951-784-0300; www.missioninn.com

A National Historic Landmark, the Mission Inn hosted both Theodore Roosevelt and Andrew Carnegie in the early 20th century. After a period of decline in the mid-20th century, it was restored and reopened in the 1990s. Today, this stunning hotel has an ornately decorated lobby with dark wood floors, columns and ceramic tile. No two guest rooms are alike. The hotel features two chapels, perfect for weddings and other occasions (Tiffany stained-glass windows adorn the larger of the two).

239 rooms. Restaurant, bar. Fitness center. Pool. Spa. $151-250

WHERE TO EAT
★★CIAO BELLA
1630 Spruce St., Riverside, 951-781-8840; www.ciaobellariverside.com
With understated décor and warm, mellow colors, this airy restaurant serves a variety of Italian dishes such as lobster ravioli and veal osso bucco, as well as wood-fired pizzas. Afterward, you can adjourn to the wine and martini lounge.
Italian. Lunch, dinner. Closed Sunday. $36-85

★★GERARD'S
9814 Magnolia Ave., Riverside, 951-687-4882; www.gerardsevebistro.com
Set in a renovated house just outside of Riverside, Gerard's serves classic French cuisine in a relaxed, cozy setting. Diners here are encouraged to take their time, savor their meals, and sample from a menu featuring traditional French mainstays like bouillabaisse and tournedos of beef.
French. Dinner, Sunday brunch. Closed Monday-Tuesday. Reservations recommended. Bar. $16-35

★MARKET BROILER
3525 Merrill Ave., Riverside, 951-276-9007; www.marketbroiler.com
For fresh fish and a fun atmosphere, locals come to this California mini-chain to choose from 18 varieties of fish and shellfish. All of the fish is mesquite-broiled and served in pretty much any form and flavoring you could imagine. The menu also includes wood-fired pizzas and a "dishes without fishes" section, featuring chicken, pasta, and steak entrees.
Seafood. Lunch, dinner. $16-35

REDONDO BEACH
See also Los Angeles
This recreation and vacation center just south of LAX features a two-mile beach and the popular King Harbor, which houses hundreds of watercraft. Once a commercial port, the historic beach town's pier now features shops, restaurants and marinas. Biking, fishing, surfing and all sorts of water sports are popular here.

WHAT TO SEE
GALLERIA AT SOUTH BAY
1815 Hawthorne Blvd., Redondo Beach, 310-371-7546; www.southbaygalleria.com
The Galleria at South Bay includes Nordstrom and Robinsons-May department stores, as well as perennial favorites such as Banana Republic and Gap. Restaurants include California Pizza Kitchen.
Monday-Friday 10 a.m.-9 p.m., Saturday 10 a.m.-8 p.m., Sunday 11 a.m.-7 p.m.

REDONDO BEACH PIER
Torrance Blvd., Redondo Beach, 310-318-0631, 800-280-0333; www.redondopier.com
With its laid-back atmosphere and white sandy beaches, Redondo is a beach bum's paradise. Surfing and volleyball are popular and there are many funky beach restaurants and bars. Daily.

WHERE TO STAY
★★★CROWNE PLAZA
300 N. Harbor Drive, Redondo Beach, 310-318-8888, 800-368-9760;
www.crowneplaza.com

This oceanfront Crowne Plaza is seven miles from LAX and close to attractions and activitics. Many rcstaurants arc within walking distance and a free shuttle is offered to area shopping malls. Guests also get access to the adjacent Gold's Gym. Comfortable guest rooms feature a separate living room, work desks and refrigerators. Some guest rooms offer balconies with a water view.

339 rooms. Restaurant, bar. Fitness center. Pool. Pets accepted $61-150

★★PORTOFINO HOTEL & YACHT CLUB
260 Portofino Way, Redondo Beach, 310-379-8481, 800-468-4292;
www.hotelportofino.com

Located on a private peninsula on King Harbor near the Rodando Beach Pier, the Portofino is a quiet escape. Guests can relax around the oceanfront pool, or walk to nearby restaurants and shopping. The recently renovated guest rooms feature a nautical decor and flat-screen televisions.

160 rooms. Restaurant, bar. Fitness center. Pool. $251-350

WHERE TO EAT
★★★CHEZ MELANGE
1611 S. Catalina Ave., Redondo Beach, 310-540-1222; www.chezmelange.com

Chez Melange raised the bar for fine California cuisine in the beach cities years ago, and the upscale clientele is still fiercely loyal. The décor may scream 1985 with its peach walls, but the menu is up-to-the-minute, offering a full sushi list as well as modern twists on classics like rabbit three ways, spicy fried oysters and steak tartare.

American. Lunch (Monday-Friday), dinner, Sunday brunch. $36-86

★★KINCAID'S BAY HOUSE
500 Fisherman's Wharf, 310-318-6080; www.kincaids.com

This fish, chop and steak house chain specializes in classic favorites such as prime rib, baby back ribs and crab legs. Sides include molasses baked beans and mac n' cheese with bacon. There's also an extensive wine list, which includes wine flights and several good options by the glass.

Seafood, steak. Lunch, dinner, Sunday brunch. Bar. $36-86

SAN DIEGO
See also Carlsbad, Del Mar, La Jolla

Can't decide between the city and the beach? You don't have to. In San Diego, there is plenty of culture, great shopping and wonderful restaurants—plus beaches with top-notch surfing, snorkeling and sea lions that crawl to the shore to sun themselves. Weathermen here have it easy: every day is 70 degrees and sunny.

It wasn't too long ago that San Diego was a sleepy little town, a place where -movie stars came to get away from it all. In the past 10 to 15 years, however, the city has grown by leaps and bounds. It now has a population of 1.3 million (2.8 million countywide) and is the seventh-largest city in the

United States. Much of the growth has come from people who want to shop in shorts all year. Other growth has come from companies that have relocated here because of the ease of recruiting workers. The area is also filled with Navy and Marine personnel from bases nearby.

San Diego is where California began. In 1542, explorer Juan Rodriguez Cabrillo was commissioned by the governor of Guatemala to take a voyage up the California coast under the flag of Spain. He reached "a very good enclosed port," now known as San Diego Bay (a Cabrillo statue stands at the edge of Cabrillo Park on the spot where he is believed to have anchored). In the mid-18th century, when it was feared that Russian interest in Alaska was a prelude to Southern expansion, Spanish missionaries came to California, and Father Junipera Serra built the first of his 31 famous California missions in San Diego.

San Diego is a city in which the arts flourish. Balboa Park, the largest urban cultural park in the country, features 15 museums, numerous art galleries, free outdoor concerts, the Tony Award-winning Old Globe theater and the world-famous San Diego Zoo. (The upscale community of La Jolla, a few miles up the coast, is the site of the La Jolla Playhouse, another Tony Award-winning theater.) There are quirky museums, like the Museum of Making Music. And kids won't know what to do first: swim in the ocean, visit SeaWorld, pan for gold in an old hard-rock gold mine, go to Legoland, explore the tide pools or visit the Aerospace Museum and Hall of Fame, where they can go on a motion-simulator ride that takes them on different planes throughout time.

WHAT TO SEE
AEROSPACE MUSEUM AND HALL OF FAME
2001 Pan American Plaza, San Diego, 619-234-8291; www.aerospacemuseum.org
Learn about the extraordinary accomplishments of the world's leading aviation pioneers, including the Wright brothers, Amelia Earhart, Neil Armstrong, Yuri Gagarin and Benjamin O. Davis, Jr., a Tuskegee airman and the first African-American graduate of West Point. Don't miss Wings, a motion-simulator ride that takes you on different planes through time.
June-August, daily 10 a.m.-5:30 p.m.; September-May, daily 10 a.m.-4:30 p.m.

BALBOA PARK
1549 El Prado, San Diego, 619-239-0512; www.balboapark.org
Located in the heart of the city, this 1,200-acre park includes galleries, museums, theaters, restaurants, recreational facilities and miles of garden walks. It's also the site of the world-famous zoo.

BALBOA PARK GOLF COURSE
2600 Golf Course Drive, San Diego, 619-239-1660; www.sannet.gov
These municipal courses have 18 and nine holes. A pro shop, a driving range, three putting greens and a restaurant are also on the grounds.

BELMONT PARK

3146 Mission Blvd., San Diego, 858-488-1549; www.belmontpark.com

The seaside amusement park has a vintage wooden roller coaster and other rides, as well as the largest indoor swimming pool in Southern California. Hours vary by season.

CABRILLO NATIONAL MONUMENT

1800 Cabrillo Memorial Drive, San Diego, 619-557-5450; www.nps.gov/cabr

In late autumn of 1542, explorer Juan Rodriguez Cabrillo and his crew arrived at what he called a very good enclosed port, the San Diego Harbor. Today, his statue looks out over one of the most beautiful views in all of San Diego. The grounds of this national park include a historic lighthouse. From late December to mid-March, natives come to this site to watch the annual migration of Pacific gray whales. Don't miss the coastal tide pools, particularly exciting during winter's low tides, when the sea pushes back to reveal a unique world of marine plants and animals in little pockets of the earth.

CASA DE ESTUDILLO

4002 Wallace St., San Diego, 619-220-5422; www.sandiegohistory.org

The Casa is a restored example of a one-story adobe townhouse with period furnishings (1820-1829).

Daily 10 a.m.-5 p.m.

CORONADO ISLAND

619-435-8788, 866-599-7242; www.coronadovisitorcenter.com

Coronado is a place for walkers. Once across the bridge, park your car and stroll past homes with gardens of flowers native only to this part of the country, and through the quaint stores of Orange Street, which includes San Diego's largest independent bookstore (Bay Books). Hop the ferry to Ferry Landing Marketplace, a center of fine dining, specialty shops, art galleries and bike rentals. There's also a waterfront park, fishing pier, beach, bike path, family amusement center and farmers' market every Tuesday 2:30-6 p.m.

GASLAMP QUARTER

Downtown San Diego; www.gaslamp.org

A 16½-block national historic district bordered by Broadway on the north, Sixth Avenue on the east, Harbor Drive on the south and Fourth Avenue on the west. This area formed the city's business center at the turn of the century, and many Victorian buildings are under restoration. Now the revitalized area is a hot spot for fine dining, bars and shops.

HORTON PLAZA

324 Horton Plaza, San Diego, 619-239-8180; www.westfield.com

Horton Plaza has reinvigorated downtown San Diego, and it's not difficult to see why. Sixteen years of research went into the design of this whimsical, multilevel shopping mall with more than 140 specialty shops, department stores and restaurants. The black concrete and narrow walkways were patterned after those found in European marketplaces, and many merchants display their goods on carts.

Monday-Friday 10 a.m.-9 p.m., Saturday 10 a.m.-8 p.m., Sunday 11 a.m.-6 p.m.

HUMPHREY'S CONCERTS BY THE BAY

2241 Shelter Island Drive, San Diego, 619-220-8497; www.humphreysconcerts.com
The 1,295-seat venue, with palm tress on one side and the harbor on the other, has staged acts such as Smokey Robinson and Jay Leno.

KEN CINEMA

4061 Adams Ave., San Diego, 619-819-0236; www.landmarktheatres.com
Seeing a film at the Ken means hard seats and subtitles. But for movie buffs, that's an invitation, not a deterrent. This San Diego landmark has long been the local place for art films, foreign cinema and revivals.

KOBEY'S SWAP MEET

3500 Sports Arena Blvd., San Diego, 619-226-0650; www.kobeyswap.com
This is San Diego's largest and most popular open-air market, featuring furniture, fashion, electronics and fresh produce. The faithful come frequently and are usually in place when the doors open at 7 a.m. The back section, with its secondhand goods, is a bargain hunter's delight. Vendors sell food and beverages, and live entertainment gets shoppers ready to spend.
Friday-Sunday 7 a.m.-3 p.m.

MINGEI INTERNATIONAL MUSEUM OF WORLD FOLK ART

1439 El Prado, San Diego, 619-239-0003; www.mingei.org
Six galleries here contain art exhibits of people from cultures around world. Many art forms—such as costumes, jewelry, dolls, utensils, painting and sculpture—are shown in different collections and changing exhibitions. Also residing at the museum are a theater, a library, a research center and educational facilities.
Admission: adults $7, seniors $5, children 6-17 $4, children under 7 free.
Tuesday-Sunday 10 a.m.-4 p.m.

MISSION BAY PARK

2688 E. Mission Bay Drive, San Diego, 619-276-8200; www.sandiego.gov
This aquatic park on 4,600 acres provides swimming, waterskiing, fishing, boating, sailing (rentals, ramps, landings, marinas), golf, camping and more. It is also the home of SeaWorld San Diego.
Daily.

MISSION SAN DIEGO DE ALCALA

10818 San Diego Mission Road, San Diego, 619-281-8449; www.missionsandiego.com
San Diego de Alcala marks the birthplace of Christianity in the Far West. It was California's first church and the first of the 21 great California missions. This remarkable shrine, still an active Catholic parish, provides an interesting look into San Diego's Spanish heritage, as well as an understanding of the beginning of Catholicism in this corner of the world. The San Diego Trolley makes a stop just half a block from the mission, which is a National Historic Landmark. There is also a gift shop and a visitors' center.

Daily 9 a.m.-4:45 p.m.

MOUNT WOODSON ROCK CLIMBING

Highway 67, between towns of Poway and Ramona

Mount Woodson may be the best place for rock climbing in Southern California. There are super-thin cracks, super-wide ones, mantles, edging, low-angle climbs and friction climbing. You can bring your own equipment and practice leading cracks or climb walls with problems ranging in difficulty levels. For simpler climbs, bring a chalk bag and you're off. To explore, make sure you're with someone who knows these routes. To get here, park about three miles north of the Highway 67/Poway Road junction in the vicinity of the state forestry fire station. A short dirt trail passes through the trees until it hits a paved road, which winds all the way to the top of Mount Woodson.

MUSEUM OF CONTEMPORARY ART SAN DIEGO

1001 Kettner Blvd., San Diego, 619-234-1001, 858-454-3541; www.mcasd.org

The permanent and changing exhibits feature contemporary painting, sculpture, design, photography and architecture. Get a souvenir at the bookstore. Monday-Tuesday, Thursday-Sunday 11 a.m.-5 p.m.

MUSEUM OF MAN

1350 El Prado, San Diego, 619-239-2001; www.museumofman.org

See anthropological exhibits about people and places around the world. One exhibit to check out is "Footsteps Through Time," which takes visitors through four million years of human evolution. Don't miss the Children's Discovery Center, where kids can experience aspects of royal and ordinary Egyptian life in the 18th Dynasty by bartering in an Egyptian market, navigating a small boat on the Nile and dressing in costume. Daily 10 a.m.-4:30 p.m.

MUSEUM OF PHOTOGRAPHIC ARTS

1649 El Prado, San Diego, 619-238-7559; www.mopa.org

Changing exhibitions spotlight works by world-renowned photographers from the early 19th century to today. The collection includes more than 9,000 images. Tuesday-Sunday 10 a.m.-5 p.m. Free guided tours Sunday.

OCEAN BEACH FARMERS' MARKET

1868 Bacon St., San Diego, 619-224-4906; www.oceanbeachsandiego.com

Ride a llama around this farmers' market in Ocean Beach, or shop for fresh produce and flowers, and sample delicious treats well into the early evening. November-March, Wednesday 4-7 p.m.; April-October, Wednesday 4-8 p.m.

OLD GLOBE

1363 Old Globe Way, San Diego, 619-231-1941; www.theoldglobe.org

This 581-seat venue, a replica of Shakespeare's theater in London, is frequently used for pre-Broadway tryouts. Many new works are also produced

here. The Old Globe is one of three associated theaters on a grassy complex in Balboa Park, the other two being the Cassius Carter Center, an intimate, 225-seat theater, and the 612-seat Lowell Davies Festival Theater, used in the summer primarily for Shakespeare.
Tours: Saturday-Sunday 10:30 a.m.

OLD TOWN
Mason St. and San Diego Ave., San Diego
The historic section of city has many restored or reconstructed buildings, including old adobe structures. You'll find restaurants and shops here. Old Town includes Old Town San Diego State Historical Park, Presidio Park, the Serra Museum and The Whaley House.

OLD TOWN SAN DIEGO STATE HISTORIC PARK
San Diego Ave. at Twiggs St., San Diego, 619-220-5422; www.parks.ca.gov
This area within Old Town is bounded by Congress, Wallace, Twigg and Juan Streets. The park includes Casa de Estudillo, the San Diego Union Museum and Seely Stable.
Admission: Free. Daily 10 a.m.-5 p.m.

PRESIDIO PARK
2811 Jackson St., San Diego
Inside the park is the site of the first mission in California. Mounds mark the original presidio and fort.
Daily 6 a.m.-10 p.m.

REUBEN H. FLEET SCIENCE CENTER
1875 El Prado, San Diego, 619-238-1233; www.rhfleet.org
This science museum offers the latest in interactive and virtual reality exhibits. Check out planetarium shows and a collection of astronomical photography. The Explorazone 3 area offers a hands-on experience with such concepts as wind, illusion and turbulence.
Monday-Thursday 9:30 a.m.-5 p.m., Friday 9:30 a.m.-9 p.m., Saturday 9:30 a.m.-8 p.m., Sunday 9:30 a.m.-6 p.m.

SAN DIEGO BAY AND THE EMBARCADERO
1300 N. Harbor Drive, San Diego
The port is used for active Navy ships, cruise ships, commercial shipping and tuna fleet. Sailing, powerboating, waterskiing and sport fishing are available at Shelter Island, Harbor Island, the Yacht Harbor and America's Cup Harbor.

SAN DIEGO-CORONADO FERRY
1050 N. Harbor Drive, San Diego, 619-234-4111; www.sdhe.com
There are hourly departures from the San Diego Harbor Excursion dock to Ferry Landing Marketplace in Coronado.
Daily.

SAN DIEGO EARLY MUSIC SOCIETY

3510 Dove Court, San Diego, 619-291-8246; www.sdems.org

The San Diego Early Music Society, a group dedicated to preserving Europe-an medieval, Renaissance and baroque music, brings musicians from all over the world to play six times a year at the lovely St. James by-the-Sea Church. Performers frequently play on authentic instruments such as a harpsichord or a baroque guitar. The group also holds concerts featuring local musicians six Sundays each year at the San Diego Museum of Art in Balboa Park.

SAN DIEGO HALL OF CHAMPIONS SPORTS MUSEUM

2131 Pan American Plaza, San Diego, 619-234-2544; www.sdhoc.com

Sports fans will appreciate the exhibits on more than 40 sports in the area at this museum located in Balboa Park. Check out the exhibit on legends (and San Diegans) Tony Hawk, Andy MacDonald and Bike Sherlock, all the Sports Illustrated covers featuring San Diego natives, the Breitbard Hall of Fame and more.

Admission: adults $8, seniors $6, children 7–17 $4, children under 7 free. Daily 10 a.m.-4:30 p.m.

SAN DIEGO HARBOR EXCURSION

1050 N. Harbor Drive, San Diego, 619-234-4111, 800-442-7847; www.sdhe.com

A one-hour (12-mile) narrated tour highlights Harbor Island, Coronado and the Navy terminals at North Island and 32nd St. The two-hour (25-mile) narrated tour also includes Shelter Island, Ballast Point (where Cabrillo is believed to have first landed in 1542), the harbor entrance, the ship yards and the Navy's submarine base.

Daily.

SAN DIEGO JUNIOR THEATRE AT THE CASA DEL PRADO THEATER

1650 El Prado, San Diego, 619-239-1311; www.juniortheatre.com

Few children's theater groups have entertained one million people or boast alums like Raquel Welch. This San Diego institution, founded in 1947, has put on Broadway standards like Guys and Dolls and Oliver! The company has also adapted kids' literature like Nancy Drew and James and the Giant Peach. Children not only perform but also work on costumes and lighting, serve as the stage crew and even staff the ticket windows.

Days and times vary.

SAN DIEGO MARITIME MUSEUM AND STAR OF INDIA

1492 N. Harbor Drive, San Diego, 619-234-9153; www.sdmaritime.com

The Maritime Museum of San Diego has one of the finest collections of historic ships, including the world's oldest active ship, Star of India, which hosts movies in the summer on its deck. The maritime museum uses a state-of-the art digital projector to display the films on a special sail rigged to the main mast. Fridays are date nights, while Saturdays are family nights with popular children's movies.

Admission: adults $14, seniors $11, children 6-17 $8, children under 6 free. Daily 9 a.m.-8 p.m.; movies start after sundown.

SAN DIEGO MUSEUM OF ART

1450 El Prado, San Diego, 619-232-7931; www.sdmart.orq

See collections of art from all over the world. The museum includes European and American paintings and decorative arts; Japanese, Chinese and other Asian art; and contemporary sculpture.

Admission: adults $12, seniors $9, children 6-17 $4.50, children 5 and under free. Tuesday-Saturday 10 a.m.-5 p.m., Sunday noon-5 p.m.

SAN DIEGO NATURAL HISTORY MUSEUM

1788 El Prado, San Diego, 619-232-3821; www.sdnhm.org

The natural history museum exhibits flora, fauna and mineralogy of the southwestern United States and Baja California.

Admission: adults $13, seniors $11, children 13-17 $8, children 3-12, $7, children 2 and under free. Sunday-Thursday 10 a.m.-7 p.m., Friday-Saturday 10 a.m.-9:30 p.m.

SAN DIEGO OPERA

Civic Center Plaza, 1200 Third Ave., San Diego, 619-533-7000; www.sdopera.com

The San Diego Opera Company was born in 1965 and has grown to become one of the most respected opera companies in America. Between January and May, the company presents five productions and several concerts. Brief English translations of the opera lyrics are projected onto the stage.

SAN DIEGO SCENIC TOURS

2255 Garnet Ave., San Diego, 858-273-8687; www.sandiegoscenictours.com

Take a narrated bus and harbor tour of the city. One of the tours explores nearby Tijuana, Mexico.

Daily.

SAN DIEGO TROLLEY

707 F St., San Diego, 619-233-3004; www.sdcommute.com

The 47-mile light rail system goes east to Santee and north through Old Town from downtown, serving many major shopping centers in Mission Valley and Qualcomm Stadium for easy access to Chargers games.

Daily.

SAN DIEGO ZOO

2920 Zoo Drive, San Diego, 619-231-1515; www.sandiegozoo.org

Widely considered the nation's top zoo, this zoo located in Balboa Park houses more than 4,200 rare and exotic animals representing 800 species, many of which are displayed in natural habitats. The children's zoo features a petting paddock and an animal nursery. There are also walk-through aviaries. Check out the animal shows that take place daily. Take a 40-minute guided tour aboard double-deck bus or go on the aerial tramway for a nice view of the zoo.

Daily; hours vary.

SEAPORT VILLAGE

849 W. Harbor Drive, San Diego, 619-235-4014; www.spvillage.com

Designed to look like a 100-year-old fishing village, this area provides a place to sit at the water's edge and sip a glass of wine or wander through the 75 specialty stores. Four restaurants are on the premises. Don't miss the Broadway Flying Horses Carousel, originally built at Coney Island in 1890. Daily 10 a.m.-10 p.m.

SEAWORLD SAN DIEGO

500 SeaWorld Drive, San Diego, 800-257-4268; www.seaworld.com

Check out the more than 400 penguins or sit and watch in amazement as orca whales Shamu, Baby Shamu and Namu entertain. Open since 1964, SeaWorld has continued to add attractions and animals and has even ventured beyond the sea: its newest section Pets Rule! is devoted to dogs and cats. The park has ten different shows, eight rides and more than 20 exhibits and attractions. In summer, don't miss Cirque de la Mer, an on-the-water acrobatic performance.

Admission: adults $65, children 3-9 $55, children 2 and under free. Daily; hours vary by season.

SERRA MUSEUM

2727 Presidio Drive, San Diego, 619-232-6203; www.sandiegohistory.org

This museum, which interprets the Spanish and Mexican periods of the city's history, stands on top of the hill recognized as the site where California's first mission and presidio were established in 1769.

Daily 10 a.m.-4:30 p.m.

SPANISH VILLAGE CENTER

1770 Village Place, San Diego, 619-233-9050; www.spanishvillageart.com

Observe artists and craftspeople working.

Daily 11 a.m.-4 p.m.

SPRECKELS ORGAN CONCERTS

Spreckels Organ Society, 1549 El Prado, San Diego, 619-702-8138;
www.sosorgan.com

The magnificent Spreckels organ, nestled in an ornate pavilion in the heart of Balboa Park, is a sight to see and hear with its 4,446 individual pipes ranging from less than a half inch to more than 32 feet in length. The organ has been in almost continuous use since brothers John and Adolph Spreckels gave it to the city in 1914. Free hour-long concerts are held on Sundays at 2 p.m., with seating for 2,400. In summer, a 12-week Organ Festival takes place on Monday evenings.

STARLIGHT BOWL/STARLIGHT THEATRE

2005 Pan American Drive, San Diego, 619-232-7827; www.starlighttheatre.org

Since the first strands of The Naughty Marietta played in 1946, the San Diego Civic Light Opera Association has staged 120 musicals in this open-air theater. The company employs union actors, musicians and stagehands, but also hires local actors and technicians who are able to get a start in Starlight's apprentice and internship programs. The season runs from mid-June to September. If you attend a performance, be sure to look for the legendary red box: on opening night in 1946, a costume designer took her red sewing box, tied it with a gold tassel and gave it to the stage manager as something regal for the bride to carry when she ran off to get married in a performance of The Mikado. The show was so successful the red box has been on stage ever since.

Box office: Monday-Friday 10 a.m.-5 p.m., Saturday-Sunday noon-4 p.m.

TAVERN BRICK BY BRICK

1130 Buenos Ave., San Diego, 619-275-5483; www.brickbybrick.com
This neighborhood music club features everything from techno, rock and pop to heavy metal (buy tickets in advance). There's also a relaxing lounge in the back with round, white cocktail tables and matching swivel stools and a small bar.

Daily 8 p.m.-2 a.m.

TIMKEN MUSEUM OF ART

1500 El Prado, San Diego, 619-239-5548; www.timkenmuseum.org
Located in Balboa Park, the Timken has a collection of European Old Masters, 18th- and 19th-century American paintings, and Russian icons.
Admission: Free. Tuesday-Saturday 10 a.m.-4:30 p.m., Sunday 1:30 p.m.-4:30 p.m.

VETERANS MEMORIAL CENTER MUSEUM

2115 Park Blvd., San Diego, 619-239-2300; www.veteranmuseum.org
The memorial/museum is housed in a building in Balboa Park that was once the chapel of the U.S. Naval Hospital. It almost became a parking lot extension for the San Diego Zoo, but is now on the National Register of Historic Places. Go there to see historical objects, artifacts, documents and memorabilia dating to the Civil War.

Tuesday-Sunday 10 a.m.-4 p.m.

VILLA MONTEZUMA/JESSE SHEPARD HOUSE

1925 K St., San Diego, 619-239-2211; www.sandiegohistory.org
This lavish Victorian mansion was built for Jesse Shepard, a musician and an author, during the city's Great Boom (1886-1888). More than 20 stained-glass windows reflect Shepard's interest in art, music and literature. The abode includes a restored kitchen and antiques.

Friday-Sunday 10 a.m.-4:30 p.m.

WHALE-WATCHING TRIPS

San Diego
For three months each year (mid-December to mid-February), California gray whales make their way from Alaska's Bering Sea to the warm bays and lagoons of Baja, passing only a mile or so off the San Diego shoreline. As many as 200 whales a day have been counted during the peak of the migration period. Trips to local waters and Baja lagoons are scheduled by the San Diego Natural History Museum. For information on other whale-watching

trips, inquire at local sport-fishing companies (try San Diego Harbor Excursion, 619-234-4111; www.sdhe.com), or at the International Visitors Information Center.

THE WHALEY HOUSE

2476 San Diego Ave., San Diego, 619-297-7511; www.whaleyhouse.org

In the mid-19th century, New Yorker Thomas Whaley came to San Diego via San Francisco, where gold beckoned. This home, which was constructed for him in 1856, was the first brick building in San Diego County. The bricks were made in his own kiln, while the walls were finished with plaster made from ground seashells. The inside of the house has an illustrious heritage as well. Not only have five generations of the Whaley family lived here, but apparently so have a few spirits. This is one of two authenticated haunted houses in California.

Daytime Admission: adults $6, seniors $5, children 3-12 $4, children 2 and under free. Evening Admission: adults $10, children 3-12 $5, children 2 and under free. Early September-late May, Sunday-Tuesday 10 a.m.-5 p.m., Thursday-Saturday 10 a.m.-10 p.m.; late May-early September, daily 10 a.m.-10 p.m.

WILD ANIMAL PARK

★ ★ ★
★ ★

15500 San Pasqual Valley, Escondido, 760-747-8702; www.sandiegozoo.org/wap

More than 3,500 exotic animals wander in herds and packs through this 1,800-acre wild animal preserve, which was opened to the public in 1972 and still operates as a preservation area for endangered species. Go on the Kilimanjaro Safari Walk or journey through the Heart of Africa. Several different tours are conducted daily, such as the highly popular Photo Caravan Tours, which travel right into the field exhibits, where visitors can feed the animals. Special events are also held all summer, including sleepovers. Mid-June-early September, daily 9 a.m.-8 p.m.; early September-mid-June, daily 9 a.m.-5 p.m.

WILLIAM HEATH DAVIS HOME

410 Island Ave., San Diego, 619-233-4692; www.gaslampquarter.org

The William Heath Davis House, the oldest structure in the Gaslamp Quarter, was shipped from Portland, Maine, in 1850. The structure of the house has remained unchanged for 120 years and is an excellent example of a prefabricated saltbox family home—a small, square structure with two stories in front and one in back. A museum occupies the first and second floors. The house is also home to the Gaslamp Quarter Historical Foundation, which gives daily walking tours of the historic area. Call ahead for tour times.

Admission: adults $5, seniors $4. Tuesday-Saturday 10 a.m.-6 p.m., Sunday 9 a.m.-3 p.m.

SPECIAL EVENTS
MISSION FEDERAL ARTWALK

734 W. Beech St., San Diego, 619-615-1090; www.missionfederalartwalk.org

Those in town during April should check out this lively event that fills the streets of Little Italy with all art, music and dance, and delicious food. The

event has been taking place in San Diego for 25 years and attracts more than 100,00 visitors. The festival is free.
Last weekend in April.

BALBOA PARK DECEMBER NIGHTS-THE ANNUAL CELEBRATION OF CHRISTMAS ON THE PRADO

Balboa Park, 1549 El Prado, San Diego, 619-239-0512;
www.balboapark.org/decembernights
On the first Friday or Saturday of December, Balboa Park is transformed into a winter wonderland with walkways and buildings adorned with beautiful lights and decorations, including a 50-foot-tall tree and Nativity scenes. All the museums are open until 9 p.m. and are free. Entertainment includes an eclectic mix of bell choirs, Renaissance and baroque music, African drums and barbershop quartets.
Early December.

CORPUS CHRISTI FIESTA

Mission San Antonio de Pala, San Diego
Held annually since 1816, this festival includes an open-air mass and procession, games, dances and entertainment, plus a Spanish-style pit barbecue.
First Sunday in June.

ETHNIC FOOD FAIR

10410 Corporal Way, San Diego, 619-234-0739; www.sdhpr.org/events.html
In the mood to sample something different? Perhaps Hungarian, Austrian or Lithuanian cuisine? Head for the International Cottages at Balboa Park's House of Pacific Relations during Memorial Day weekend. Each of these 32 tiny cottages representing a different nation is decorated and laid out with the traditional foods of that country. Every cottage is staffed with at least two people, one inside to explain customs and the other outside to talk about food and hand out recipes.
Memorial Day weekend.

FESTIVAL OF BELLS

Mission Basilica San Diego de Alcala, 10818 San Diego Mission Road, San Diego,
619-283-7319; www.festivalofthebells.com
The weekend-long festival commemorates the July 16, 1769, founding of the mission.
Mid-July.

SAN DIEGO BAY PARADE OF LIGHTS

1220 Rosecrans St. San Diego, 619-224-2240; www.sdparadeoflights.org
For two Sunday evenings each December, the San Diego Bay is flooded with color when at least 100 boats adorned with lights and other decorations follow one another on a semicircular path through the calm waters of the bay.
Early December.

WHERE TO STAY
★★★BRISTOL HOTEL
1055 First Ave., San Diego, 619-232-6141, 800-662-4477; www.thebristolsandiego.com
This downtown boutique hotel lures young professionals and couples who are drawn to the funky, contemporary vibe. A pop art collection includes works by Andy Warhol, Roy Lichtenstein and Keith Haring. Rooms are decorated with black and white and pops of colors, and include free Internet access, salon-style hair dryers, honor bars and CD players. The top-floor ballroom features a retractable roof, and the bistro is a favorite among locals who come here for the signature martini, the Craizi Daizi.
102 rooms. Restaurant, bar. Fitness center. Pets accepted. $151-250

★★DOUBLETREE CLUB HOTEL
1515 Hotel Circle South, San Diego, 619-881-6900, 800-222-8733;
www.doubletreeclubsd.com
Providing the closest accommodations to SeaWorld, this stylish and value-priced hotel boasts a private marina on Mission Bay and is popular with families seeking convenience (and a free shuttle) to the park. Local attractions are nearby, and the airport is a short drive away. Guest rooms feature a neutral, modern décor and are equipped with refrigerators, dataports and video games. Shuffleboard, Ping-Pong and bike rentals are among the activities offered on-site; beaches, playgrounds, shops, and restaurants are within walking distance.
219 rooms. Restaurant, bar. Fitness center. Pool. Pets accepted. $61-150

★★★DOUBLETREE HOTEL MISSION VALLEY
7450 Hazard Center Drive, San Diego, 619-297-5466, 800-222-8733;
www.doubletree.com
This comfortable hotel is close to many major attractions, including SeaWorld and the San Diego Zoo, and offers an indoor and outdoor pool as well as tennis and exercise facilities. The oversized guest rooms feature Sweet Dreams beds.
300 rooms. Restaurant, bar. Fitness center. Pool. Pets accepted. $151-250

★★★★THE GRAND DEL MAR
5300 Grand Del Mar Court, San Diego, 858-314-2000; www.thegranddelmar.com
This palatial Mediterranean-style resort has a mind-boggling array of amenities, including world-class golf at the Tom Fazio-designed course and a five-star spa. Foodies can indulge in everything from afternoon tea to gourmet dining at six different venues, and there are four beautiful pools to lounge by, complete with underwater speakers and luxurious cabanas. Even the kids can relax in style; the Explorer's Club keeps them busy with crafts and educational activities. The turn-of-the-century style rooms (dark wood furnishing, crown moldings) have European-style soaking tubs, feather beds and LCD televisions.
280 rooms. Restaurant, bar. Business center. Fitness center. Pool. Spa. $351 and up

★★★HILTON AIRPORT/HARBOR ISLAND
1960 Harbor Island Drive, San Diego, 619-291-6700, 800-774-1500;
www.sandiegoairport.hilton.com

With its waterfront setting on Harbor Island, the hotel has rooms with views of Big Bay, Harbor Island marina and Point Loma. Sailboat and bicycle rentals are available nearby, as are golf courses and the beach. There's a fully equipped fitness center with sauna and outdoor heated pool.

211 rooms. Restaurant, bar. Fitness center. Pool. $151-250

★★★HILTON SAN DIEGO GASLAMP QUARTER

401 K St., San Diego, 619-231-4040, 800-774-1500; www.hilton.com

This modern hotel is in the heart of the historic Gaslamp Quarter, where you'll find shopping, restaurants and nightclubs, and across the street from the San Diego Convention Center. Opting to stay at the hotel's Lofts on Fifth Avenue will get you a residential space with 14-foot ceilings, Frette linens and robes, a whirlpool tub and a private entrance. Amenities include a spa and Fitness center, outdoor heated pool and hot tub, and adjacent walking trails that border Big Bay. The outdoor fire pit is a nice spot for cocktails and appetizers or dessert.

282 rooms. Restaurant, bar. Fitness center. Pool. Spa. $251-350

★★★HILTON SAN DIEGO MISSION VALLEY

901 Camino del Rio South, San Diego, 619-543-9000;
www.sandiegomissionvalley.hilton.com

This family-friendly hotel is set on the hillside of Mission Valley's business district, surrounded by trees and gardens. Popular Southern California tourist destinations are nearby, including SeaWorld, the historic Gaslamp Quarter and Balboa Park. Relax in spacious, modern rooms that feature Serta luxury mattresses and Crabtree & Evelyn bath products.

51 rooms. Restaurant, bar. Business center. Fitness center. Pool. $151-250

★★★HILTON SAN DIEGO RESORT

1775 E. Mission Bay Drive, San Diego, 619-276-4010, 800-345-6565;
www.sandiegohilton.com

The family-friendly Hilton San Diego Resort is on Mission Bay, just steps from the beach and only one mile from SeaWorld. The hotel was recently remodeled, and the result is an airy, beachy feel. There is also a new spa and state-of-the-art Fitness center. Enjoy concerts while relaxing on the lawns of the garden by the bay in summer.

357 rooms. Restaurant, bar. Fitness center. Spa. $251-350

★★★HYATT REGENCY MISSION BAY SPA AND MARINA

1441 Quivira Road, San Diego, 619-224-1234; www.missionbay.hyatt.com

This towering fixture in the heart of Mission Bay Park is the closest hotel to SeaWorld and offers panoramic views of the marina. A recent renovation resulted in a spa, a water playground with multiple slides and new restaurants. Downtown San Diego and the airport are six miles away.

430 rooms. Restaurant, bar. Business center. Fitness center. Pool. Spa. $151-250

★★★THE IVY HOTEL

600 F St., San Diego, 619-814-1000; www.ivyhotel.com

A boutique hotel in San Diego's Gaslamp Quarter, the Ivy has rooms decorated with contemporary furniture and outfitted with plasma TVs, luxury linens and iPod -docking stations. The Quarter Kitchen serves dressed-up comfort food like caviar tacos and mini Kobe hot dogs, while the rooftop Eden bar and pool is a prime spot for after-dinner drinks. For those who want to zoom around town in style, the hotel offers chauffeured Escalade service. 159 rooms. Restaurant. Fitness center. Pool. Pets accepted. $251-350

★★★THE KEATING

432 F St., San Diego, 619-814-5700; www.thekeating.com

Housed in a historic building in San Diego's Gaslamp Quarter, this boutique hotel is completely of-the-moment. Italian design firm Pinanfarina, the force behind Ferrari and Maserati, dreamed up the look of this property from the stylish lobby to the luxe guest rooms. Plasma TVs, cutting-edge sound systems, Frette linens and espresso machines are some of the in-room amenities. The lounge, with its Saarinen-inspired chairs and cozy couches, is a good spot for cocktails, which are poured by personal hosts (a shade more attentive than your standard waiter).

35 rooms. Restaurant, bar. Spa. Pets accepted. $251-350

★★★KONA KAI HOTEL & SPA

1551 Shelter Island Drive, San Diego, 619-221-8000, 800-566-2524;
www.shelterpointe.com

Just five minutes from SeaWorld and downtown, this hotel on the tip of Shelter Island strikes a balance between offering convenience and being a quiet retreat for travelers of all types. Rooms feature elegant, contemporary décor with amenities such as data ports and coffeemakers as well as patios or balconies with bay or coastal views.

206 rooms. Restaurant, bar. Fitness center. Pool. Spa. Pets accepted. $151-250

★★★MANCHESTER GRAND HYATT SAN DIEGO

1 Market Place, San Diego, 619-232-1234, 800-223-1234;
www.manchestergrand.hyatt.com

Combining a resort-like atmosphere with the convenience of a downtown location, this luxury property on San Diego Bay is adjacent to the convention center and -Seaport Village. Each room offers at least a partial view of the city or bay with windows that open up to enjoy the fresh air. The full-service Regency Spa and Salon staffs skilled therapists, aestheticians and stylists.

1,625 rooms. Restaurant, bar. Fitness center. Pool. Spa. $251-350

★★★MARRIOTT SAN DIEGO HOTEL & MARINA

333 W. Harbor Drive, San Diego, 619-234-1500, 800-228-9290; www.marriott.com

Adjacent to the convention center and the Seaport Village, this waterfront hotel is in a convenient spot. Rooms are spread between two, 25-story towers and offer bay and marina views.

1,362 rooms. Restaurant, bar. Fitness center. Pool. Spa. Pets accepted.

$251-350

★★★MARRIOTT SAN DIEGO MISSION VALLEY
8757 Rio San Diego Drive, San Diego, 619-692-3800, 800-842-5329;
www.sandiegomarriottmissionvalley.com

This resort-style hotel with Spanish accents is about seven miles northwest of downtown and less than two miles from Qualcomm Stadium. It features a host of amenities for both business travelers and vacationers. Many of the modern and whimsical guest rooms overlook the hotel's beautiful courtyard pool and tropical landscaping, and include conveniences like high-speed Internet access. Concierge, secretarial and childcare services are available. The downtown trolley stop is just steps way.

350 rooms. Restaurant, bar. Fitness center. Pool. $151-250

★★★PACIFIC TERRACE HOTEL
610 Diamond St., San Diego, 858-581-3500, 800-344-3370; www.pacificterrace.com

This seaside hotel in northern San Diego is the perfect place to revel in the Southern California beach atmosphere. Old Spanish style characterizes the exterior and the common areas. The upscale guest rooms feature cheery prints and rattan furnishings with private patios or balconies and fully stocked minibars. Some rooms have fully equipped kitchenettes, and most have fabulous views of the ocean.

73 rooms. Complimentary breakfast. Business center. Fitness center. $251-350

★★★PARADISE POINT RESORT & SPA
1404 W. Vacation Road, San Diego, 858-274-4630, 800-344-2626;
www.paradisepoint.com

This 44-acre private island on Mission Bay offers cabana-style accommodations, making it the perfect spot for those looking for a little relaxation. The light-filled rooms have bright color, comfortable beds and beautiful views of the gardens or bay. The spa incorporates gentle Indonesian body treatments, while those looking for some recreation can enjoy tennis, volleyball and basketball courts; marina rentals; an 18-hole putting green; and bike trails.

460 rooms. Restaurant, bar. Fitness center. Pool. Spa. $251-350

★★★RANCHO BERNARDO INN
17550 Bernardo Oaks Drive, San Diego, 858-675-8500; www.ranchobernardoinn.com

The guest rooms at this inn are warm and inviting, with antiques, original artwork and private patios or balconies. Suites also have wood-burning fireplaces. The hotel offers two excellent options for dining: the Veranda Grill, an outdoor restaurant that overlooks the onsite golf course, and El Bizcocho, known by locals for its French cuisine.

287 rooms. Restaurant, bar. Business center. Spa. Pets accepted. Golf. $151-250

★★★SE SAN DIEGO
1047 5th Ave., San Diego, 619-515-3000; www.sesandiego.com

Located in the trendy Gaslamp district, this newer hotel furthers the area's reputation for swanky surroundings. Guest rooms here look more like fancy design store showrooms with dark exotic wood floors, sleek furniture and luxurious bone finished restrooms. The infinity-edged Siren pool located on the fourth floor is where your days are best spent before retreating to your luxurious room and preparing for dinner or drinks at the sophisticated on-site Suite & Tender restaurant, which features the freshest seasonal ingredients with a seafood focus. Of course, you could always head back up to the pool where the party in the luxurious open-air setting lasts into the night. Spend the next day relaxing in the Asian-inspired spa.

161 rooms. Restaurant, bar. Business center. Fitness center. Pool. Spa. $251-350

★★★SHERATON SAN DIEGO HOTEL AND MARINA

1380 Harbor Island Drive, San Diego, 619-291-2900, 877-734-2726;
www.sheraton.com

This dual-tower waterfront landmark offers panoramic views and fresh, contemporary furnishings. Rooms have custom-designed beds with pillow-top mattresses, oversized desks and private patios or balconies. The East Tower has four restaurants and lounges, including Tapatinis, which serves a tapas menu and martinis. The West Tower features an outdoor heated pool and the restaurant Alfiere's, which specializes in Mediterranean cuisine.

1,053 rooms. Restaurant, bar. Fitness center. Spa. $151-250

★★★SHERATON SUITES SAN DIEGO AT SYMPHONY HALL

701 A St., San Diego, 619-696-9800, 800-962-1367; www.sheraton.com/sandiego

Sharing a roof with Symphony Hall, this downtown all-suite hotel offers rapid access to the convention center, baseball stadium and the historic Gaslamp District. The spacious and contemporary rooms feature living rooms, minibars and custom-designed beds with pillow-top mattresses. The Sky Lobby lounge, with views of the skyline, is a nice place for a cocktail.

264 suites. Restaurant, bar. Business center. Pool. Pets accepted. $151-250

★★★TOWER 23

4551 Ocean Blvd., San Diego, 858-270-2323; www.tower23hotel.com

Perched on Pacific Beach just north of San Diego, this boutique hotel makes the most of its waterfront location with rooms (here, dubbed pads) that open to the surf and sand below. Decorated in cool tones of blue and green, guest rooms have beds swathed in Anichini linens and flat-screen TVs and Xbox gaming systems. Suites are spacious and feature Kohler whirlpool tubs with chromatherapy lighting (which means you can turn your bath bubbles violet, aqua and other colors according to your mood). Jordan restaurant serves breakfast, lunch and dinner in a chic setting, while Eight sushi bar is a perfect spot for a post-surf nosh.

44 rooms. Restaurant, bar. $251-350

★★★★U.S. GRANT HOTEL

326 Broadway, San Diego, 866-837-4270, 800-237-5029; www.usgrant.net

This 100-year-old hotel (opened in 1910 by Ulysses S. Grant Jr. and his wife, Fannie, and now part of Starwood's Luxury Collection) recently underwent a multimillion-dollar renovation that restored the polish to this historic, grand building. The opulent new interiors, from the lobby to the Grant Grill, blend updated Art Deco furniture and decorative objects seamlessly with the belle époque bones of the hotel. Rooms feature original French art, custom imported wool carpets and marble bathrooms. The staff tends to guests' desires with Old World aplomb. Spa treatments, from hot-stone to deep-tissue massage, are available in-room through a local spa.

270 rooms. Restaurant, bar. Business center. Fitness center. $351 and up

★★★W SAN DIEGO

421 W. B St., San Diego, 619-398-3100; www.whotels.com

Taking its cues from the city's beachfront location, this downtown W hotel is lighter and brighter in design than others in the chain. The rooftop Beach bar (though located far from the sand) has a pool and cabanas ideal for lounging and sipping cocktails, while the hotel's living room is filled with rattan arm chairs and board games. Rooms have sea-blue walls and down duvets, flat-screen TVs with CD/DVD players and Bliss bath products. The onsite Rice restaurant is a favorite with locals for its sultry look and spicy Asian-influenced food.

258 rooms. Restaurant, bar. Fitness center. Pool. Spa. Pets accepted. $251-350

★★★WESTGATE HOTEL

1055 Second Ave., San Diego, 619-238-1818, 800-221-3802; www.westgatehotel.com

Located downtown in the Gaslamp District, this sumptuous hotel is a treasure trove of antiques, French tapestries, crystal chandeliers and Persian carpets. The accommodations have Richelieu furniture, distinctive artwork and a bounty of fresh flowers. The dining is top-notch, particularly at Le Fontainebleau, a favorite choice for special occasions where afternoon tea is a tradition.

223 rooms. Restaurant, bar. Complimentary breakfast. Fitness center. Spa. Pets accepted. $251-350

★★★WESTIN HORTON PLAZA

910 Broadway Circle, San Diego, 619-239-2200; www.westin.com/hortonplaza

This Westin hotel is next to the Horton Plaza shopping mall, which features 182 stores and restaurants. It's also within minutes of the historic Gaslamp Quarter, the San Diego Convention Center, Balboa Park, SeaWorld and the San Diego Zoo. Spacious guest rooms are decorated in neutral tones and feature mahogany furnishings, pillow-top mattresses with all-white bedding, sitting areas and minibars.

450 rooms. Restaurant, bar. Business center. Fitness center. Pool. Pets accepted. $151-250

★★★WESTIN SAN DIEGO

400 W. Broadway, San Diego, 619-239-4500; www.starwoodhotels.com/westin

Designed with an urban flair, the Westin San Diego offers a retreat to business and leisure travelers in the heart of downtown. The location means this hotel is minutes away from just about everything: SeaWorld, the zoo, conventions, Old Town, the Padres. The contemporary guest rooms are warm and inviting, with buttery tones and the signature fluffy Westin beds.

436 rooms. Restaurant, bar. Fitness center. Pool. Spa. $151-250

WHERE TO EAT

★★3RD CORNER WINE SHOP & BISTRO

2265 Bacon St., San Diego, 619-223-2700; www.the3rdcorner.com

This wine shop and bistro is a nice choice if wine is the main event. You'll find a wine store on-site with more than 1000 bottles; buy a bottle and uncork it at your table for $5. Meanwhile, choose a variety of nibbles from the menu, anything from a selection of cheeses to a sample of olives to bigger plates like short ribs or mussels.

Continental, French. Lunch, dinner. Closed Monday. $151-250

★★★★★ADDISON

5200 Grand Del Mar Way, San Diego, 858-314-1900; www.addisondelmar.com

Gourmands and style seekers alike will delight in Addison, The Grand Del Mar's signature restaurant. The atmosphere is sophisticated with European-style furnishings, brick-covered floors and grand arched windows overlooking the golf course, but it goes far beyond looks at this award-winning restaurant. Chef William Bradley takes diners on a culinary adventure, offering seasonal and ever-changing four-course menus highlighting his contemporary French cooking style. The impressive, exhaustive wine list carries everything from little-known finds to well-known favorites.

Contemporary French. Dinner. Closed Sunday-Monday. Reservations recommended. Bar. $86 and up

★ATHENS MARKET TAVERNA

109 W. F St., San Diego, 619-234-1955; www.athensmarkettaverna.com

The whole family will enjoy a meal here, where traditional Greek music plays in the background, waiters scream "Opa!" as they light the saganaki, and dishes like moussaka, dolmathes and gyros provide an authentic taste of Greece.

Greek. Lunch, dinner. Closed Sunday. $36-85

★★★BACI

1955 W. Morena Blvd., San Diego, 619-275-2094; www.sandiegobaci.com

This local favorite, which serves classic Northern Italian fare, has lots of Old World charm, from the tuxedo-clad waiters to the romantic dining room and elegant patio. The hearty Italian menu includes dishes like scampi lobster over angel hair pasta, grilled calamari and penne arrabbiata.

Italian. Lunch (Monday-Friday), dinner. Closed Sunday. $36-85

★★★BERTRAND AT MISTER A'S

2550 Fifth Ave., San Diego, 619-239-1377; www.bertrandatmisteras.com

The sophisticated interior and stunning views of the San Diego skyline set the stage for the creative assortment of modern American dishes with French and Mediterranean influences, which includes appetizers like the wedge of iceberg lettuce with housemade blue cheese and blue crab fritters and main courses such as braised prime beef short ribs with foratini gratin and root vegetables. Try the famous truffle fries as a side and the housemade ice cream for dessert.

American. Lunch, dinner. $36-85

★★★BLUE POINT COASTAL CUISINE

565 Fifth Ave., San Diego, 619-233-6623; www.cohnrestaurants.com

Lounge on the black banquettes inside this oyster bar and seafood restaurant, or enjoy dinner—and people-watching—at one of the intimate sidewalk tables. The fresh and flavorful cuisine includes a superb blue point lobster pot pie, spicy calamari and crab and pancetta stuffed whole trout.
Seafood. Dinner. $36-85

★★★BUSALACCHI'S ON FIFTH

3683 Fifth Ave., San Diego, 619-298-0119; www.busalacchis.com

Enjoy the authentic Southern Italian cuisine in one of the gems in the Busalacchi family-owned group of Italian eateries in the area. This site occupies a Victorian-style home and features steaks, seafood and pasta.
Italian. Dinner. $36-85

★CAFE COYOTE

2461 San Diego Ave., San Diego, 619-291-4695; www.cafecoyoteoldtown.com

Café Coyote has earned a reputation for having some of the best traditional Mexican food in the city. This Old Town restaurant creates its flavorful dishes using only the freshest ingredients, including flour tortillas that are hand-made daily on the premises and their very own signature salsa. You'll find casual, rustic decor inside and numerous tables outside on the colorful outdoor patio—perfect for watching the busy shoppers coming in and out of the nearby shops.
Mexican. Breakfast, lunch, dinner. $16-35

★★CAFE PACIFICA

2414 San Diego Ave., San Diego, 619-291-6666; www.cafepacifica.com

An intimate setting with contemporary décor that includes warm, twinkling lights, dark wood furnishings, a neutral color palette, and tables topped with crisp, white linens outlines Café Pacifica. The seafood-focused menu features choices such as Hawaiian ahi tuna, herb-crusted king salmon, and Alaskan halibut, but steak, pasta, and poultry dishes are also offered. Museums, theaters, and shops are all nearby, so it's a perfect spot to enjoy a meal before or after sightseeing.
Seafood. Lunch, dinner. $36-86

★★★CALIFORNIA CUISINE

1027 University Ave., San Diego, 619-543-0790; www.californiacuisine.cc

The chefs here mine the local markets daily to find the freshest ingredients. Dine on dishes like Niman Ranch pork chops with sweet potato gratin, or filet mignon with roasted-garlic smashed Yukon potatoes and Gorgonzola-pinot noir glaze. This elegant restaurant showcases new artwork each season from local artists.
Californian. Dinner. $36-86

★★CHATEAU ORLEANS

926 Turquoise St., Pacific Beach, 858-488-6744; www.chateauorleans.com

Celebrate Mardi Gras any time of the year at Chateau Orleans, where dishes of down home Southern cooking are served atop tables decorated with confetti and colorful carnival masks. Go for the Sunday jazz brunch from 11 a.m.-3 p.m.

Cajun, Creole. Dinner. Closed Monday-Tuesday. $16-35

★★★EL BIZCOCHO

17550 Bernardo Oaks Drive, San Diego, 858-675-8550, 800-770-7637; www.ranchobernardoinn.com

Prepare for an unforgettable experience at this elegant restaurant that's been earning raves in San Diego for three decades. The place is full of Old World charm, but the menu is definitely new, with lots of locally grown produce and handcrafted artisan products. A tasting menu might begin with scallop carpaccio, move on to baby octopus and then a duo of ribeye and 36-hour slow rib, and conclude with pomegranate cheesecake.

French. Dinner, Sunday brunch. $36-85

★★JACK AND GIULIO'S

2391 San Diego Ave., San Diego, 619-294-2074; www.jackandgiulios.com

An intimate, candlelit-filled dining room with rich, red leather chairs makes Jack and Giulio's the perfect destination for a romantic dinner. But in addition to the elegant atmosphere, it's the delicious Italian cuisine that has brought repeat visitors back to this family owned and operated restaurant since it opened in 1961. Homemade pastas, pizzas, and specialties like filet mignon in vermouth and veal scaloppini picatta are lovingly prepared with fresh ingredients, and all choices can be perfectly paired with a selection from the interesting wine list.

Italian. Lunch, dinner. $36-86

★★★THE OCEANAIRE SEAFOOD ROOM

400 J St., San Diego, 619-858-2277; www.theoceanaire.com

The stuffed fish on the walls and blackboards marked with daily specials set the stage for a delicious, super-fresh (delivered daily) seafood dinner prepared every way imaginable. The lounge is a nice locale for a pre- or post-dinner drink and a few oysters.

Seafood. Dinner. $36-85

★★★THE PRADO AT BALBOA PARK

1549 El Prado Way, San Diego, 619-557-9441; www.balboapark.org

This lively, eclectic restaurant is in the historic 1915 Spanish Colonial House of Hospitality building. The attractive interior features colorful glass-blown sculptures, mosaic-tiled tables and beautiful chandeliers. Chef Jeff Thurston offers a delicious menu focusing on Italian-American and Latin American cuisine. The outdoor patio is lovely for kicking back and enjoying the surrounding views and a mojito.

Italian-American, Latin American. Lunch, dinner. $36-85

★★★PREGO

1370 Frazee Road, San Diego, 619-294-4700; www.pregoristoranti.com

Prego brings a piece of the Italian countryside to San Diego with its Tuscan-inspired dining room with arches and columns. The bustling open kitchen turns out authentic pizzas baked in a brick-fired oven, and fresh pasta and seafood.

Italian. Lunch, dinner. $36-85

★★★RAINWATER'S
1202 Kettner Blvd., San Diego, 619-233-5757; www.rainwaters.com

Prime Midwestern beef and fresh seafood are among the specialties at this clubby chophouse with cherry wood accents, leather seating and crisp white linens. The superb wine list, with selections from around the world, and the professional, personalized service make this the perfect spot for a power lunch or an elegant dinner.

American, steak. Lunch, dinner. $86 and up

★★★RUTH'S CHRIS STEAK HOUSE
1355 N. Harbor Drive, San Diego, 619-233-1422; www.ruthschris.com

Born from a single New Orleans restaurant that Ruth Fertel bought in 1965 for $22,000, the chain is a favorite among steak lovers. Aged prime Midwestern beef is broiled at 1,800 degrees and served on a heated plate sizzling with butter and with sides like creamed spinach and au gratin potatoes.

Steak. Dinner. $36-85

★★★SALLY'S
1 Market Place, San Diego, 619-358-6740; www.sallyssandiego.com

Although it's on the Boardwalk adjacent to the Manchester Grand Hyatt, this is no tourist trap. Lots of locals come here to enjoy the beautiful waterfront views and ultra-fresh seafood, which includes pan-fried diver scallops with lychee relish and ahi tuna with miso-mustard. The crab cakes, which are grilled (not fried), are said to be some of the best in the city. For those looking for something besides seafood, dishes like Asian-style tofu lasagna and Colorado lamb loin marinated in Chinese black beans are a sure bet.

American. Lunch, dinner. $36-85

★★★SALVATORE'S
750 Front St., San Diego, 619-544-1865; www.salvatoresdowntown.com

A longtime favorite for locals, Salvatore's has been serving consistently good Italian food since 1987. Perfectly prepared plates of homemade lasagna or eggplant-and-mushroom-filled ravioli are delivered to tables swathed in crisp white linens and set with fine china by a friendly and efficient staff.

Italian. Dinner. $36-85

★★★TAKA
555 Fifth Ave., San Diego, 619-338-0555; www.takasushi.com

This gem in San Diego's Gaslamp District is popular for its traditional, no-frills sushi and delicious seafood that's brought in fresh everyday.

Japanese. Dinner. $16-35

★★★THEE BUNGALOW
4996 W. Point Loma Blvd., San Diego, 619-224-2884; www.theebungalow.com

Chef/owner Ed Moore continually strives to please his loyal following with his famous crispy roasted duck (served with a choice of sauces), sampler platter featuring housemade pâtes and swoon-worthy dessert soufflés. American, French. Dinner. $36-85

★★★TOP OF THE MARKET

750 N. Harbor Drive, San Diego, 619-232-3474; www.thefishmarket.com
The seafood is indeed fresh at this fish market/restaurant, which operates its own fishery and has a partnership with an oyster farm. The elegant, wood-paneled dining room, with large windows offering views of the bay, is the perfect place to indulge.
Seafood. Lunch, dinner. $36-85

★★★WINESELLAR AND BRASSERIE

9550 Waples St., San Diego, 858-450-9557; www.winesellar.com
With crisp white linens and a candlelit atmosphere, this is the perfect destination for a romantic dinner of fine French cuisine. Don't forgot to stop at the lower-level wine shop to browse the large selection of fine wines.
French. Dinner. Closed Sunday. $36-85

★★ZOCALO GRILL

2444 San Diego Ave., San Diego, 619-298-9840; www.brigantine.com
The casually rustic and upbeat atmosphere of Zocalo Grill makes it a great spot for group get-togethers in the heart of San Diego's Old Town. The menu is Latin-focused, but influences from Mexico, the Caribbean and California can be seen in dishes like honey-porter braised carnitas with warm flatbreads, mango salsa and avocado salad; and cornmeal-crusted calamari, with lemon-cilantro aioli and spicy tomato dipping sauce. Live Brazilian guitar music is featured nightly, and a harpist plays during Sunday brunch. A quaint outdoor dining area features a lovely and inviting fireplace.
American. Lunch, dinner, Sunday brunch. $36-85

SPA

★★★★THE SPA AT THE GRAND DEL MAR

5300 Grand Del Mar Court, San Diego, 858-314-2020; www.thegranddelmar.com
With its gleaming Carrera marble and crystal glass tiles, The Spa at The Grand Del Mar is elegance personified. Unwind with the signature Renaissance treatment, which blends a mineral-rich mud wrap, rosemary-infused shower and relaxing massage. From rosemary and sage herbal salt scrubs and herbal reflexology to renewal facials using pomegranate and pumpkin, the focus is on nature-based ingredients. Triad treatments, combining a series of three treatments, are an indulgent way to experience this opulent spa.

★★★SPA SE

Se San Diego, 1047 5th Ave., San Diego, 619-515-3000; www.sesandiego.com
You know this isn't your typical spa from the moment you walk in and you're offered a choice between a traditional blooming flower hot tea or a shot of the hotel's signature vodka with honey and pomegranate. Once you down your treat, try one of the signature treatments, such as the Vibe Swedish massage, which uses unusual and unexpected sound vibrations to soothe your muscles. Or if you prefer a more traditional massage, why not double

the effectiveness with the four-hand massage. Afterward, retreat to one of the nine private treatment rooms and indulge in your own personal steam shower. Although San Diego's weather is second to none, this is one place that makes staying indoors rival the sunniest of days.

SAN DIEGO AREA CITIES AND TOWNS
BORREGO SPRINGS
Although prospectors and cattle ranchers had driven through this desert area in the late 19th century, it wasn't until 1906 that the first permanent settler arrived. In the winter and spring, wildflowers transform the desert's valleys, canyons and washes into a rainbow of colors, creating an oasis in the midst of the desert.

WHAT TO SEE
ANZA-BORREGO DESERT STATE PARK
200 Palm Canyon Drive, Borrego Springs, 760-767-5311; www.parks.ca.gov
The largest state park in California has 600,000 acres of desert wilderness. The best time to visit is November to mid-May, when 600 species of flowering plants are in bloom. Elephant trees reach the northernmost limits of their range and rare smoke trees and fan palms grow here around natural seeps and springs. The park also provides a refuge for wildlife, including roadrunners, rare bighorn sheep and kit foxes. There are miles of hiking trails and campsites scattered throughout the park. Naturalist programs, tours and campfire programs are offered on weekends.
Sunrise-sunset.

WHERE TO STAY
★★★LA CASA DEL ZORRO
3845 Yaqui Pass Road, Borrego Springs, 760-767-5323, 800-824-1884;
www.lacasadelzorro.com
This historic resort dates back to 1937 and is in the heart of San Diego County's majestic Anza Borrego Desert. The region's Spanish history inspires the décor at this serene resort. The 44 deluxe poolside rooms include marble baths and sitting areas with fireplaces and patios or balconies. The private casitas, each with its own pool or spa, range from one to four bedrooms.
63 rooms. Restaurant, bar. Business center. Fitness center. Pool. Spa. $251-350

★★★THE PALMS AT INDIAN HEAD
2220 Hoberg Road, Borrego Springs, 760-767-7788, 800-519-2624;
www.thepalmsatindianhead.com
This historic hotel was built in classic mid-century style with Mondrian influences. The lobby features floor-to-ceiling windows, terrazzo floors and historical photos of the property and its famous former guests, including Marilyn Monroe, Bing Crosby and Cary Grant. The cozy guest rooms are minimalist—no phones, no TVs. Warm cookies are delivered around sunset. Enjoy the Zen garden or go for an invigorating hike.
12 rooms. Restaurant. Complimentary breakfast. Pool. $61-150

WHERE TO EAT
★★★BUTTERFIELD ROOM
3845 Yaqui Pass Road, Borrego Springs, 760-767-5323; www.lacasadelzorro.com

Beautiful oil paintings of the Old West Butterfield Stageline adorn the white-washed adobe walls of this elegant restaurant. Candlelight and sparkling table settings create a romantic atmosphere in which to enjoy creative California cuisine. The menu changes throughout the year, taking advantage of the freshest seasonal ingredients. Previous offerings include a grilled ahi tuna sandwich with cucumber-cilantro salad or Colorado rack of lamb glazed with Dijon mustard, wildflower honey and Provencal herbs.

American. Breakfast, lunch, dinner. $35-85

CARLSBAD

Named for a famous European spa in Karlsbad, Bohemia (now in the Czech Republic), this beach-oriented community is a playground for golfers, tennis players, water-skiers and fishing enthusiasts.

WHAT TO SEE
LEGOLAND
1 Legoland Drive, Carlsbad, 760-918-5346; www.legoland.com

Visitors are greeted by a 9-foot dinosaur of bright red blocks at the entrance to Legoland, and that's just the start. Everything here is made of Legos, from the characters along Fairy Tale Brook to the horses that kids ride through an enchanted forest. Designed for children ages 2-12, the 128-acre park has 60 family rides, hands-on attractions and shows, plus a special area designed for toddlers. The park's centerpiece is Miniland, which replicates areas of New York; Washington, D.C.; the California coastline; New Orleans; and an interactive New England harbor scene using 20 million Lego bricks.

Daily; hours vary.

SPECIAL EVENTS
FLOWER FIELDS AT CARLSBAD RANCH
5704 Paseo Del Norte, Carlsbad, 760-431-0352; www.theflowerfields.com

From its roots as a family-owned flower operation, the annual Flower Fields at Carlsbad Ranch has bloomed into a local phenomenon, thanks to the beautiful tecolote giant ranunculus. A British immigrant and horticulturist brought this Asian relative of the buttercup to California, where it now grows on 50 acres. Locals consider the March flowering to be a harbinger of spring, and more than 150,000 visitors come to check it out every year.

March-May, daily.

WHERE TO STAY
★★★★FOUR SEASONS RESORT AVIARA
7100 Four Seasons Point, Carlsbad, 760-603-6800, 800-819-5053;
www.fourseasons.com/aviara

Avid golfers come to play the 18-hole golf course designed by Arnold Palmer. But that's just one reason to come to this splendid resort on 200 lush acres overlooking the Batiquitos Lagoon, the Pacific Ocean and a nature preserve that's home to a variety of wildlife. The architecture pays homage to the region's history with its Spanish colonial design, and guest rooms feel luxurious and homey, with sumptuous sitting areas, sliding French doors opening up to private patios or balconies and marble bathrooms with deep soaking tubs. Dining choices range from Italian to California cuisine and the lively wine bar, with dramatic floor-to-ceiling windows offering views of the Pacific.

329 rooms. Restaurant, bar. Business center. Fitness center. Pool. Spa. Pets accepted. $351 and up

★★★LA COSTA RESORT AND SPA

2100 Costa Del Mar Road, Carlsbad, 760-438-9111, 800-854-5000; www.lacosta.com

Guests come to La Costa Resort and Spa to hit the links, relax in the spa, feast on mouthwatering meals and lounge by the pool. Designed to resemble a Spanish Colonial village, La Costa has a warm, inviting spirit. Golfers love the two PGA 18-hole courses, while the 21-court tennis center is a favorite of players. The resort is also home to the renowned Chopra Center, which helps guests achieve well-being through Ayurvedic principles. The dazzling spa with a Roman waterfall offers a variety of pampering treatments.

480 rooms. Restaurant, bar. Business center. Fitness center. Pool. Spa. $251-350

WHERE TO EAT
★★★VIVACE

7100 Four Seasons Point, Carlsbad, 760-603-6800; www.fourseasons.com/aviara

Chef Bruce Logue puts his own twist on Central Italian cuisine, with dishes such as black spaghetti with rock shrimp and calabrese sausage, and hand-made orecchiette with braised capon. A large light stone fireplace fills the dining room with warmth while the floor-to-ceiling windows allow breath-taking views of the ocean and lagoon.

Italian. Dinner. $36-85

SPA
★★★★SPA AT FOUR SEASONS RESORT AVIARA

7100 Four Seasons Point, Carlsbad, 760-603-6800, 800-819-5053;
www.fourseasons.com/aviara

The newly renovated 15,000-square-foot spa has both indoor and outdoor treatment rooms and a solarium lounge. Pamper your skin with an avocado body wrap and customized facials. Water shiatsu (watsu) treatments involve massage and stretching while you float in a heated pool. The onsite JoséEber Salon provides hair, nail and makeup services.

CORONADO

Known as the Crown City, Coronado lies across the bay from San Diego and is connected to the mainland by a long, narrow sandbar called the Silver Strand and by the beautiful Coronado Bridge. It is the site of the famous Hotel del Coronado.

WHERE TO STAY
★★★HOTEL DEL CORONADO

1500 Orange Ave., Coronado, 619-435-6611, 800-468-3533; www.hoteldel.com

Few hotels have earned a place in American history like the Hotel del Coronado. Charles Lindbergh was honored here after his first transatlantic flight, and it was at the Del that Marilyn Monroe romped on the beach in Some Like It Hot. It's even rumored that the Duke of Windsor met his future wife, Wallis Simpson, here. Set on 31 acres on the island of Coronado just off San Diego, this beachfront, Victorian-style hotel is the ultimate sand and surf getaway. The lovely rooms are housed in three different areas: the Victorian Building, the Ocean Towers and the California Cabanas.

679 rooms. Restaurant, bar. Business center. Spa. $251-350

★★★LOEWS CORONADO BAY RESORT

4000 Coronado Bay Road, Coronado, 619-424-4000, 800-235-6397; www.loewshotels.com

Situated on a 15-acre peninsula overlooking San Diego Bay, this romantic yet family-friendly resort's lush tropical landscaping is freshened by ocean breezes that sweep through its private marina. Casual, Mediterranean-style elegance and expansive water views define the décor, from the sunny lobby to the luxe accommodations, where pillow-top mattresses, oversized tubs and spacious balconies are featured. Year-round activities include gondola rides, complimentary sailing lessons and dive-in movies, which play poolside on a large screen.

450 rooms. Restaurant. Spa. Pets accepted. $151-250

★★★THE MANSION AT GLORIETTA BAY

1630 Glorietta Blvd., Coronado, 619-435-3101, 800-283-9383; www.gloriettabayinn.com

Built in 1908 by one of San Diego's earliest developers, the mansion was converted to a hotel in the mid-1970s. You can choose to stay in the mansion itself, which offers more luxurious accommodations, or in the surrounding inn buildings, which have more modern rooms perfect for families or business travelers. While there's no restaurant, the hotel is close to dining, shopping and the beach.

183 rooms. Complimentary breakfast. Business center. Pool. $151-250

★★★MARRIOTT CORONADO ISLAND RESORT

2000 Second St., Coronado, 619-435-3000; www.marriott.com

This waterfront resort, just across the bay from downtown San Diego, sits on 16 tropical acres dotted with waterfalls, koi ponds and strolling flamingos. For a special getaway, reserve a villa with a private entrance and pool.

300 rooms. Restaurant. Pets accepted. $151-250

WHERE TO EAT

★★★AZZURA POINT

4000 Coronado Bay Road, Coronado, 619-424-4000; www.loewshotels.com

The Mediterranean menu features a fusion of Northern Italian and French cuisines and uses locally caught seafood and fresh herbs from the resort's private herb garden. The huge curved windows, dressed in leopard print, frame the bay.

California. Dinner. Closed Monday. $36-85

DEL MAR

This village by the sea offers beautiful white beaches and brilliant sunsets. It's also an attractive area for year-round ballooning.

SPECIAL EVENT

DEL MAR THOROUGHBRED CLUB

County Fairgrounds, 2260 Jimmy Durante Blvd., Del Mar, 858-755-1141; www.dmtc.com

Put your bets in and enjoy an afternoon of thoroughbred horse racing. July-mid-September.

WHERE TO STAY

★★★HILTON SAN DIEGO/DEL MAR

15575 Jimmy Durante Blvd., Del Mar, 858-792-5200; www.hilton.com

This comfortable hotel is next to the Del Mar Thoroughbred Club and just minutes from the beach, though the pool may tempt guests to skip the sand. The rooms include Internet access, new Serenity beds and Web TV.

256 rooms. Restaurant, bar. Business center. Fitness center. Pool. Pets accepted. $151-250

★★★L'AUBERGE DEL MAR RESORT AND SPA

1540 Camino del Mar, Del Mar, 858-259-1515, 800-245-9757; www.laubergedelmar.com

This hideaway occupies more than five lush acres on the coast. Play a round of golf on the celebrated Tom Fazio-designed course, go up in a hot-air balloon or take a long walk on the beach. The cheery cottage-style rooms blend Art Deco with antique pieces and feature marble bathrooms. The spa is a destination in its own right.

120 rooms. Restaurant, bar. Fitness center. Pool. Spa. $351 and up

LA JOLLA

Said to be named for the word "jewel" in Spanish, the small, affluent oceanside neighborhood of La Jolla is home to the University of California, San Diego, the legendary Salk Institute, the Birch Aquarium and the renowned Torrey Pines Golf Course. But the crown jewel here is certainly downtown La Jolla, bordering the town's expansive beach. North Torrey Pines Road will take you downtown by way of winding roads and a slow, downhill approach of the beach. To get there, take La Jolla Shores Drive and turn on Camino del Oro. Downtown La Jolla's best street to browse is Girard Avenue, where there are high-end boutiques, including Ralph Lauren. Park anywhere you can find a spot and begin walking. This portion of La Jolla is packed with art galleries, restaurants and hotels. On Girard, you'll spot a small passage with the sign "Arcade Building," which mimics Parisian-style passage shopping. From Girard, you can walk to La Jolla Cove, where the avenue grows narrow and winds slightly downhill until you see an expanse of sapphire-blue ocean and a large, brightly manicured lawn. Grab a coffee from one of La Jolla's cafés and head down to the sea.

WHAT TO SEE
BIRCH AQUARIUM AT SCRIPPS

2300 Expedition Way, La Jolla, 858-534-3474; www.aquarium.ucsd.edu
At the Scripps Institution of Oceanography, see undersea creatures in realistic habitats at this aquarium situated on a hill with spectacular ocean views. Check out the tide pool exhibit. Beach and picnic areas are nearby. Admission: adults $11, seniors $9, children 3-17 $7.50, children 2 and under free. Daily 9 a.m.-5 p.m.

LA JOLLA COVE

1100 Coast Blvd., La Jolla, 619-221-8901; www.sannet.gov
An ideal place for picnicking, the La Jolla Cove provides a marvelous backdrop of the Pacific Ocean and sandy cliffs, and is an ideal place to see the water crash against the craggy rocks at the cove's point. The churning sea perfumes the air with the scent of seaweed. After taking a walk along the sidewalk, relax on the lawn and drink in the sun. Located at the southern edge of the San Diego-La Jolla Underwater Park, the cove is an ecologically protected area. The tiny beach is a great place to sunbathe, snorkel or scuba dive and check out the seals, which are often seen sunbathing on the Cove's rocky edge. Divers can enjoy visibility of more than 30 feet and the waters are ideal for photography.
Daily.

LA JOLLA PLAYHOUSE

2910 La Jolla Village Drive, La Jolla, 858-550-1010; www.lajollaplayhouse.com
This Tony Award-winning venue has long been one of America's premier regional theaters. Gregory Peck, Dorothy McGuire and Mel Ferrer founded it in 1947. Located on the campus of the University of California, San Diego, the playhouse puts on six shows per season. Although Thoroughly Modern Millie and Rent played here, the playhouse is best known for taking chances on new work.
Days and times vary.

LA JOLLA SHORES

8200 Camino del Oro, La Jolla
This beach is a favorite among locals for its tame shore. The sand is silky with glints of false gold and is distinctly darker than the sands of beaches farther north in Orange County and Los Angeles. The beach has several barbeque pits for evening bonfires.

MUSEUM OF CONTEMPORARY ART

700 Prospect St., La Jolla, 858-454-3541; www.mcasd.org
Exhibits focus on contemporary paintings, sculptures, design, photography and architecture. The museum also offers a sculpture garden, a bookstore, films and lecture programs.
Admission: adults $10, seniors $5, ages 25 and under free. Thursday-Tuesday 11 a.m.-5 p.m.; third Thursday of the month 11 a.m.-7 p.m..

TORREY PINES GLIDERPORT

2800 Torrey Pines Scenic Drive, La Jolla, 858-452-9858; www.flytorrey.com

Soar 50 to 150 feet above the pines. Instructors give 20 minutes of paragliding lessons on the ground before sending guests up in tandem with their teachers. Hang gliding is offered as well, but eight lessons are needed to earn a beginner rating before taking flight.

Daily.

TORREY PINES STATE RESERVE

12000 N. Torrey Pines Road, La Jolla, 858-755-2063; www.torreypine.org

The 1,750-acre Torrey Pines State Reserve was established to protect the world's rarest pine tree, the gnarly, malformed Torrey pine, which hundreds of years ago covered Southern California. Today, they are found only on Santa Rosa Island off the coast of Santa Barbara and in the La Jolla reserve. There are miles of unspoiled beaches and eight miles of hiking trails here. The visitors' center and museum are open daily 9 a.m. to sunset. Go on a guided nature walk, weekends and holidays, 10 a.m. and 2 p.m.

Daily 8 a.m.-sunset.

WINDANSEA BEACH

6800 Neptune Place, La Jolla, 619-221-8874; www.beachcalifornia.com

Windansea Beach is best known for surfing, as its intense breaks created by underwater reefs. The only drawback: everyone knows about it. On the best days, Windansea's concentrated surf breaks get crowded very quickly and even ambitious amateurs are advised to stay out of the way.

WHERE TO STAY

★★★HILTON LA JOLLA TORREY PINES

10950 N. Torrey Pines Road, La Jolla, 858-558-1500, 800-762-6160; www.hilton.com

This full-service resort overlooks the famed oceanfront links of the Torrey Pines Golf Course in the heart of La Jolla. Advance reservations at the coveted course are available to guests. Rooms boast a private balcony or deck overlooking the links, ocean or garden. The Torreyana Grille serves up steaks and seafood prepared Pacific -Rim-style.

394 rooms. Restaurant, bar. Business center. Fitness center. $151-250

★★★HOTEL PARISI

1111 Prospect St., La Jolla, 858-454-1511, 877-454-1511; www.hotelparisi.com

This hotel goes above and beyond to help visitors relax, from the award-winning feng shui design to the wide range of Eastern-inspired bodywork in the spa—there's even an on-call psychologist. The elegant rooms have goose-down comforters, Egyptian cotton sheets and gourmet coffee makers. Luxury apartments with full-size kitchens are also available for extended stays.

20 rooms. Complimentary breakfast. $251-350

★★★HYATT REGENCY LA JOLLA AT AVERTINE

3777 La Jolla Village Drive, San Diego, 858-552-1234; www.lajolla.hyatt.com

Situated on 11 acres, this elegant hotel is minutes away from beaches, golf and museums. The rooms have been recently remodeled and include down comforters and Portico bath products. The biggest draw may be the Sporting Club and the Spa, a 32,000-square-foot fitness center that includes a full-size basketball court, two lighted tennis courts and a variety of classes, in addition to pampering treatments.

419 rooms. Restaurant, bar. Business center. Fitness center. Pool. $251-350

★★★★LODGE AT TORREY PINES

11480 N. Torrey Pines Road, La Jolla, 858-453-4420; www.lodgetorreypines.com

The Lodge sits on a rocky cliff overlooking the Pacific Ocean and is surrounded by protected forest and unspoiled beaches. The view is gorgeous, but many are drawn by another aspect of the location: the lodge neighbors the 18th hole of the Torrey Pines Golf Course, one of the most acclaimed courses in the world. Tee times are guaranteed for guests who want to try their hand at the championship course. The resort itself is a celebration of the American Craftsman period, from its stained glass and handcrafted woodwork to its Stickley-style furnishings. The warm guest rooms boast custom-designed furniture, modern amenities and spectacular views of the golf course or courtyard.

171 rooms. Restaurant, bar. Fitness center. Spa. Golf. $251-350

WHERE TO EAT

★★★★A.R. VALENTIEN

The Lodge at Torrey Pines, 11480 N. Torrey Pines Road, La Jolla, 858-453-4220; www.arvalentien.com

La Jolla's Lodge at Torrey Pines may be best known for its golf, but its much-lauded restaurant, A.R. Valentien, is a show-stopper. Named after an impressionist California artist, the dining room is a showcase of stained glass lighting and Mission-style furnishings with large windows overlooking the 18th hole. Chef Jeff Jackson delivers stand-out traditional American cooking focusing on the quality of the ingredients. Settle in and sample dishes like chicken and dumplings, spaghetti and meatballs or the drugstore style hamburger. The outstanding creations of West Coast producers dot the superlative cheese list, so be sure to save room for a taste.

American. Dinner. Reservations recommended. $36-85

★★★THE STEAKHOUSE AT AZUL LA JOLLA

1250 Prospect St., La Jolla, 858-454-9616; www.azul-lajolla.com

Settle into this warm and welcoming restaurant overlooking the Pacific and dig into the all-dressed up burger with crisp bacon, caramelized onions and aged white cheddar cheese or the prime aged beef with any of the outstanding sides, including crispy artichoke hearts or Parmesan risotto, while taking in the sweeping views of the Pacific. The menu also features a milk-fed veal chop, Colorado rack of lamb, free-range chicken and fresh seafood.

American. Lunch (Saturday), dinner, Sunday brunch. $36-86

★★FLEMING'S PRIME STEAKHOUSE & WINE BAR

8970 University Center Lane, La Jolla, 858-535-0078; www.flemingssteakhouse.com

In addition to the usual steaks, you'll find some delicious surprises on the menu, such as tuna mignon and the Australian lamb chops with a champagne meat sauce. The potatoes with cream, jalapeños and cheddar are as good as they sound.

American, steak. Dinner. $36-85

★★★MARINE ROOM
2000 Spindrift Drive, La Jolla, 858-459-7222, 866-644-2351; www.marineroom.com
In operation since 1941, this restaurant owned by the La Jolla Beach & Tennis Club has been a favorite among locals who come here for the fresh global cuisine that's rooted in the French classics, superb wine list, spectacular ocean views and professional service. The menu features such delights as spinach-wrapped oysters and pistachio butter basted Australian lobster tail.

International. Dinner. $16-35

★★★PIATTI RISTORANTE
2182 Avenida de la Playa, La Jolla, 858-454-1589; www.piatti.com
With its open kitchen and stone pizza hearth, this warm restaurant resembles an Italian trattoria. Sit in the terra-cotta dining room or out on the fountain patio while enjoying the lush salads, rustic pizzas and flavorful pastas.

Italian. Lunch, dinner. $16-35

★★★ROPPONGI
875 Prospect St., La Jolla, 858-551-5252; www.roppongiusa.com
Restaurateur Sami Ladeki has hit the jackpot with this popular dining spot. The tapas—Polynesian crab stack, crispy buttermilk onion rings and local halibut carpaccio, to name a few—are irresistible. There's also a sushi and regular dinner and lunch menus.

Asian fusion. Lunch, dinner. $36-85

★★★SANTE RISTORANTE
7811 Herschel Ave., La Jolla, 858-454-1315; www.santeristorante.com
After a popular run in New York at La Fenice, Tony Buonsante brought his authentic Northern Italian cooking to La Jolla in this intimate, elegant space. Dishes include eggless ricotta dumplings with Gruyère cheese and hearty lasagna Bolognese. Dine on the sidewalk terraces, in the elegant dining room with white tablecloths or at the cozy bar where you can browse the celebrity photographs.

Italian. Lunch, dinner. $16-35

★★★TAPENADE
7612 Fay Ave., La Jolla, 858-551-7500; www.tapenaderestaurant.com
The first item to arrive at your table when you dine at this restaurant is, of course, tapenade. What follows is expertly prepared Southern French food meant to evoke a summer day in Provence. Dishes include aged sirloin with black peppercorn sauce made with cognac and pommes frites and roasted duck breast with Yukon gold garlic mashed potatoes. Be sure to save room for the cheese plate or coconut crème brûlée.

French. Lunch (Monday-Friday), dinner. $36-85

SPA
★★★★THE SPA AT TORREY PINES
The Lodge at Torrey Pines, 11480 N. Torrey Pines Road, La Jolla, 858-453-4420,
800-656-0087; www.spatorreypines.com

This spa at the Lodge at Torrey Pines has an oceanfront setting and a surrounding forest that influence many of the treatments. There are numerous water treatments, including balneotherapy, a seawater bath in a hydrotherapy tub. Body scrubs use coastal sage and pine for exfoliation. Several facials combat aging, including a champagne facial that uses yeast extracts and bubbly. The spa also has a list of rituals on the menu, which blend body treatments with massage. The Aromasoul Ritual, for instance, uses Chinese massage techniques to increase the flow of energy and replenish vitality.

SAN JUAN CAPISTRANO
San Juan Capistrano developed around the Catholic mission for which it was named. Many of the buildings in town resemble the Spanish architecture of the church.

WHAT TO SEE
MISSION SAN JUAN CAPISTRANO
26801 Ortega Highway, San Juan Capistrano, 949-234-1300; www.missionsjc.com

Founded by Fray Junipero Serra in 1776 and named for the crusader St. John of Capistrano, the church was built in the form of a cross and was one of the most beautiful of all California missions. A self-guided tour includes the Serra Chapel, which is one of the oldest buildings in California, the padres' living quarters and three museum rooms exhibiting artifacts from Native American and early Spanish cultures. The mission is also famous for its swallows, which depart each year on St. John's Day (in October) and return on St. Joseph's Day (in March).

Admission: adults $9, seniors $8, children 4-11 $5, children 3 and under free. Daily 8:30 a.m.-5 p.m.

WHERE TO EAT
★★L'HIRONDELLE
31631 Camino Capistrano, San Juan Capistrano, 949-661-0425;
www.lhirondellesjc.com

This charming restaurant located across from San Juan Capistrano Mission features a variety of salads and sandwiches for lunch, but you'll also find tasty alternatives such as fresh salmon scramble and the picnic plate, with fresh fruit, pate, chicken and cheese. Dinner offers roasted duck, herb crusted rack of lamb and fresh fish.

French. Lunch, dinner, Sunday brunch. $16-35

SAN LUIS OBISPO
See also Morro Bay, Pismo Beach

San Luis Obispo (Spanish for St. Louis, the Bishop) is about halfway between San Francisco and Los Angeles on the Central Coast. The city, referred to locally as SLO or "San Luis," is one of California's oldest communities. It was built around the Mission San Luis Obispo de Tolosa, which was founded by Father Fray Junipero Serra in 1772. After the thatched mission roofs burned several times, a tile-making technique was developed that soon set the style for all California missions. The bustling downtown is full of shops, restaurants and students from California Polytechnic University, making it a pleasant stopover; it's also a good place to stop while touring the Edna Valley wine country.

WHAT TO SEE
MISSION SAN LUIS OBISPO DE TOLOSA
751 Palm St., San Luis Obispo, 805-781-8214; www.missionsanluisobispo.org
The fifth of the California missions founded in 1772 still serves as the parish church. An eight-room museum also contains an extensive Chumash collection and artifacts from early settlers. The first olive orchard in California was planted here, and two original trees still stand.
Daily 9 a.m.-5 p.m.

SAN LUIS OBISPO COUNTY MUSEUM AND HISTORY CENTER
696 Monterey St., San Luis Obispo, 805-543-0638; www.slochs.org
Across the street from the mission, this museum showcases local history exhibits and decorative arts reflecting Native American life and farm life.
Wednesday-Sunday 10 a.m.-4 p.m.

SPECIAL EVENTS
MADONNARI ITALIAN STREET PAINTING FESTIVAL
Mission Plaza, Monterey and 1039 Chorro streets, San Luis Obispo, 805-781-2777; www.slochamber.org
Local artists decorate the streets around the mission with chalk drawings. Music, Italian cuisine and an open-air market also set a festive mood.
Mid-September.

MOZART FESTIVAL
3165 Broad St., San Luis Obispo, 805-781-3008; www.mozartfestival.com
For this festival, recitals, chamber music, orchestra concerts and choral music held at various locations throughout the county, including Mission San Luis Obispo de Tolosa and California Polytechnic State University campus.
Mid-July-early August.

RENAISSANCE FESTIVAL
1087 Santa Rosa St., San Luis Obispo
Celebrate the Renaissance with period costumes, food booths, entertainment, arts and crafts.
July.

SLO INTERNATIONAL FILM FESTIVAL
San Luis Obispo, 805-546-3456; www.slofilmfest.org
This festival showcases the history and art of filmmaking with screenings of new releases, classics, short films and documentaries. Additional events include seminars, a film competition and the annual sing-along, where moviegoers dress as characters from the featured musical and channel their inner

Julie Andrews.
Early-mid-March.

WHERE TO STAY
★★★APPLE FARM TRELLIS COURT
2015 Monterey St., San Luis Obispo, 805-544-2040, 800-255-2040; www.applefarm.com
This quaint hotel combines the charm of a Victorian inn with the conveniences of a luxury hotel. Rooms feature four-poster beds, fireplaces and high-speed Internet access. There are free treats, including an evening wine reception and a welcome basket.
104 rooms. Restaurant. Pool. $151-250

WHERE TO EAT
★APPLE FARM
2015 Monterey St., San Luis Obispo, 805-544-2040, 800-255-2040;
www.applefarm.com
American. Breakfast, lunch, dinner. $16-35

★★CAFE ROMA
1020 Railroad Way, San Luis Obispo, 805-541-6800; www.caferomaslo.com
Italian. Lunch (Monday-Friday), dinner. Closed Sunday. $16-35

★CISCO'S
778 Higuera St., San Luis Obispo, 805-543-5555; www.cisco-slo.com
American. Lunch, dinner. $15 and under

SAN SIMEON
See also Morro Bay, Paso Robles
San Simeon is the home of one of California's most popular (and best) attractions: Heart Castle.

WHAT TO SEE
HEARST CASTLE
Highway 1, San Simeon, 800-444-4445; www.hearstcastle.com
If you want to see something awesome, take a tour of Hearst Castle. William Randolph Hearst, the media entrepreneur who built a publishing empire on newspapers and magazines, grew up camping on his father's ranch in Big Sur. With Hearst Castle, he attempted to build the most opulent castle and grounds in the coastal U.S. Construction began in 1919 under the direction of noted architect Julia Morgan and took 28 years to finish. Hearst spared no expense, hauling parts of ancient European buildings and the treasures within to adorn his compound. is the former home of William Randolph Hearst.

The estate includes 115 rooms and three guest houses. Features of the castle include the Refectory, a long room with a hand-carved ceiling and life-size statues of saints, silk banners from Siena and 15th-century choir stalls from a Spanish cathedral; the Assembly Room, with priceless tapestries; and the lavish theater where the latest motion pictures were shown. The grounds include the Neptune Pool, with a colonnade leading to an ancient Roman temple façade and an array of marble statuary, an indoor pool resembling a night sky and magnificent gardens with fountains and walkways. Hearst entertained some of the great figures of his time here, including Winston Churchill, Charlie Chaplin and Cary Grant. The place is completely over-the-top but yet down to earth (witness the ketchup bottles on the dining room table).

After Hearst's death in 1951, the estate was given to California as a memorial to the late publisher's mother, Phoebe Anderson Hearst. This landmark is so expansive, and its history so rich, there are five separate tours to guide you through it all. But if you want to marvel in this one-of-a-kind castle, reserve tickets well in advance. Day tours take approximately one hour and 45 minutes; evening tours take approximately 2 hours and 15 minutes. Reservations are recommended and are available up to eight weeks in advance by calling 800-444-4445. Tickets are also available at the ticket office in the visitor center.

Daily.

WHERE TO STAY
★★BEST WESTERN CAVALIER OCEANFRONT RESORT
9415 Hearst Drive, San Simeon, 805-927-4688, 800-826-8168; www.cavalierresort.com
This family-run Best Western is located just three miles from Hearst Castle. The hotel is, as it says, right on the ocean, and offers two restaurants, large, clean rooms and an outdoor pool.
90 rooms. Restaurant, bar. Pool. Pets accepted. $66-150

SANTA BARBARA
See also Ojai, Ventura
Spanish charm hangs over this city, with its colorful street names, adobe buildings and beautiful homes and gardens on the slopes of the Santa Ynez Mountains. It faces east and west on the Pacific Ocean along the calmest stretch of the California coast. Many wealthy people call this home—including Oprah. The large harbor can accommodate many boats (boat rentals and excursions are available).

WHAT TO SEE
EAST BEACH
Sun worshippers will love this picturesque stretch of sand located on East Cabrillo Boulevard. Amenities include a full beach house, snack bar, volleyball courts, play area for children and bike/rollerblading paths. It also hosts the Santa Barbara Art Show on Sundays.

EL PASEO
900 State St., Santa Barbara
Pick up a few stylin' souvenirs while you're away. Built between 1921 and 1924, this block of galleries, restaurants, and clothing and gift shops is considered the oldest shopping center in California, and a Santa Barbara landmark.

MISSION SANTA BARBARA
2201 Laguna St., Santa Barbara, 805-682-4713; www.sbmission.org

---

DAY TRIP: SOLVANG AND THE SANTA BARBARA WINE COUNTRY

While Santa Barbara offers plenty to do, a half-day or all-day road trip to the village of Solvang—the Danish Capital of America—and the Santa Ynez Valley's thousands of acres of award-winning vineyards (which were highlighted in the Oscar-nominated movie Sideways) is a must. Hop in the car and drive northwest on the 101 for about 32 miles until you reach Highway 246, which will bring you east to Solvang. This authentic Danish community offers quaint inns, Scandinavian restaurants that serve delicacies like aebleskiver and smorgaasbord, The Hans Christian Anderson museum and dozens of shops that sell everything from Old World antiques to home-made candy.

After you've had your fill of Danish delicacies, take Highway 246 to Alamo-Pintado Road, which will lead you north to Los Olivos and the Santa Ynez Wine Loop. This three-mile triangle features about 10 vineyards, including the charming Buttonwood Farm and Blackjack Ranch. In between tastings, you'll pass roadside stands selling apples, avocados, peaches, flowers, lavender—even whole pigs. Midway through the Wine Loop, you'll pass through the delightful town of Los Olivos, where you can stop for a bite to eat at a outdoor bistro, like the Los Olivos Café, Panino or Patrick's Side Street Café, peruse the local art galleries or visit more tasting rooms. And be sure to check out Jedlicka's Saddlery (2883 Grand Avenue, Los Olivos, 805-688-2626; www.jedlicka.com), an authentic Western store that has catered to ranchers and trail riders—reportedly including President Reagan—for more than 70 years.

This unofficial city landmark was built in 1786 as the tenth of the California missions to be founded by the Spanish Franciscans. A climb to the top of the mission's two towers provides a breathtaking view of Santa Barbara. Secular and non-secular activities take place in the mission daily.

Self-guided tours: Daily 9 a.m.-4:30 p.m.

SANTA BARBARA BOTANIC GARDEN

1212 Mission Canyon Road, Santa Barbara, 805-682-4726; www.sbbg.org

Set on 40 acres in Santa Barbara, this decades-old botanic garden allows visitors to traverse its 5.5 miles of walking paths through its 1,000-plus plant types as well as its vast herbarium including roughly 143,000 preserved species. While the botanic garden is best visited in warmer months, it is open year round and demonstrates the variety of plant life in southern California during all months.

Admission: adults $8, seniors and children 13-17 $6, children 2-12 $4, children under 1 and under free. March-October, daily 9 a.m.-6 p.m.; November-February, daily 9 a.m.-5 p.m.

SANTA BARBARA CERTIFIED FARMERS MARKET

805-962-5354; www.sbfarmersmarket.org

Each Saturday, local farmers head to the main marketplace in Santa Barbara's downtown to display a colorful bounty of agricultural products grown right in the city's backyard. (The market moves to different locations in the area during the week.) You'll find seasonal diversity year-round, rain or shine. Music and entertainment enliven the markets and enriches the ambiance. Closed Monday. Check the Web site for daily locations.

SANTA BARBARA MUSEUM OF ART

1130 State St., Santa Barbara, 805-963-4364; www.sbmuseart.org

The Santa Barbara Museum of Art is a privately funded, not-for-profit institution. Here you'll find cultural and educational activities as well as internationally recognized collections and exhibitions ranging from antique ties to contemporary art and spanning the globe. Don't miss the works on paper collection, the largest collection within the museum.

Tuesday-Sunday 11 a.m.-5 p.m. Closed Monday. Free Sunday.

SANTA BARBARA ROYAL PRESIDIO

123 E. Canon Perdido St., Santa Barbara, 805-965-0093; www.sbthp.org/presidio.htm

A former military headquarters and government center, this fortress was founded on April 21, 1782. It was the Spanish's center for defense against Native American inhabitants of the area, and two corners of the Presidio's main quadrangle remain. Today they stand as part of a state park and visitors can see what the living structures for soldiers based here were like. The location was carefully chosen as a place of outlook and defense.

Admission: adults $5, seniors $4, children under 17 free. Daily 10:30 a.m.- 4:30 p.m.

STEARNS WHARF AND TY WARNER SEA CENTER

State Street and the Pacific Ocean, 805-962-2526; www.sbnature.org

Once a major shipping hub for all of southern California, this pier, built in 1872, has dramatic views of Santa Barbara, and is now home to several fresh seafood restaurants, including the delicious Santa Barbara Shellfish Company and gift shops. The Ty Warner Sea Center, part of the Santa Barbara Museum of Natural History, is an interactive marine education facility where visitors have the opportunity to work like scientists, sample and test ocean water, study animal behavior and examine microscopic marine life. Daily 10 a.m.-5 p.m.

SPECIAL EVENTS
SANTA BARBARA INTERNATIONAL ORCHID SHOW

Earl Warren Fairgrounds, 3400 Calle Real, Santa Barbara; www.sborchidshow.com

Growers from around the world display their orchids at this show. March.

SANTA BARBARA NATIONAL HORSE SHOW

Earl Warren Fairgrounds, 3400 Calle Real, Santa Barbara, 805-687-0766;
www.earlwarren.com

One of the most impressive and well-known horse shows in the United States, it features champion jumpers, American saddlebreds, Tennessee walking horses and Welsh ponies.

Mid-July.

WHERE TO STAY
★★★★BACARA RESORT & SPA

8301 Hollister Ave., Santa Barbara, 805-968-0100, 877-422-4245;
www.bacararesort.com

THE CENTRAL COAST'S WINERIES

Alma Rosa Winery
7250 Santa Rosa Road, Buellton, 805-688-9090;
www.almarosawinery.com
Owner Richard Sanford, formerly a geography major at University of California at Berkeley, is a real maverick, having planted the first pinot noir vines here in 1970. In 2005, he started Alma Rosa with his wife, Thekla. Located on the Rancho Santa Rosa, the vineyards are certified organic and produce chardonnay and pinot noir, as well as pinot gris, pinot blanc and dry pinot noir rosé.
Daily 11 a.m.-4:30 p.m.

Babcock Winery
5175 E. Highway 246, Lompoc, 805-736-1455;
www.babcockwinery.com
Brian Babcock is a wine rock star, anointed one of the top ten small production wine makers in the world—the only one in the U.S.—by the James Beard Foundation. The winery produces chardonnay, pinot noir, pinot grigio, sauvignon blanc, syrah and a very good cabernet sauvignon. Babcock also has been experimenting with Italian and Spanish varietals, which he believes will be the next big thing in California winemaking.
Daily 10:30 a.m.-4 p.m.

Firestone Vineyard
5000 Zaca Station Road, Los Olivos, 805-688-3940;
www.firestonewine.com
Firestone has been around since 1972, making it one of the original wineries in Santa Barbara. It sits on a hilltop like the grande dame it is and merits a visit just to admire the pretty location and tasting room. It's also the place to take a tour if you'd like to see the workings of at least one area vineyard (you also learn how the Firestone family went from tires to grapes, which you're almost certainly dying to know). The winery, now owned by Bill Foley, produces chardonnay, cabernet sauvignon, merlot, sauvignon blanc and syrah.
Daily 10 a.m.-5 p.m. Tours start at 11:15 a.m., 1:15 p.m. and 3:15 p.m.

Foley Estates Vineyard & Winery
6121 E. Highway 246, Lompoc, 805-737-6222; foleywines.com
In 1998, Bill Foley purchased land on the Rancho Santa Rosa because of its south-facing hillside and limestone soil, key for producing pinot. Since then, he's built something of a wine empire, acquiring Las Hermanas Vineyard (formerly Ashley's Vineyard) and Firestone, and starting Merus in the Napa Valley to make cabernets. (In his other life, Foley is the chairman of the board of Fidelity.) The large tasting room is located next to the winery building.
Daily 10 a.m.-5 p.m.

With the Pacific Ocean on one side and the Santa Ynez Mountains on the other, Bacara is all about location. A fitness center, a saline-filled pool and secluded nooks for sunbathing flank more than 30 treatment rooms and indoor and outdoor massage stations. The spa offers an intriguing selection of global healing regimens, and an Eastern Origin menu, which features options such as reiki and shiatsu massages. The rugged terrain of the Santa Ynez Mountains is the perfect place for a rigorous walk, run or hike. Clay tennis courts, pools almost too pretty to swim in and yoga on the beach are just a few of the other fitness options.

360 rooms. Restaurant, bar. Business center. Pool. Spa. Pets accepted. $351 and up

★★★CANARY HOTEL
31 W. Carrllio St., Santa Barbara, 805-884-0300; www.andaluciasb.com

This delightful hotel is what you might imagine your perfect seaside cottage to look like: tall, four-poster beds with crisp, white sheets in front of a huge plasma TV, dark-stained wood floors, beautiful Spanish tile in the bath, and lots of homey touches strewn about—a pair of binoculars casually resting on a stack of books, pretty silver dishes, white candles in large glass hurricanes, a yoga mat in the closet, an iPod dock alarm clock. You may return home and decorate your own bedroom the same way. Restaurants and shopping are within walking distance, and the rooftop deck is the place to catch a cocktail before you crash in your relaxing digs.

97 rooms. Restaurant, bar. Fitness center. Pool. $251-350

★★★FESS PARKER'S DOUBLETREE RESORT
633 E. Cabrillo Blvd., Santa Barbara, 805-564-4333, 800879-2929; www.fpdtr.com

This grand oceanfront resort surrounded by gardens offers friendly service, from the complimentary airport transportation to the fresh baked cookies offered upon arrival. The guest rooms are elegant, and the sprawling white-washed property, with red-tile roofs and arched walkways, offers plenty of recreation.

338 rooms. Restaurant, bar. $251-350

★★★★FOUR SEASONS RESORT THE BILTMORE SANTA BARBARA
1260 Channel Drive, Santa Barbara, 805-969-2261; www.fourseasons.com

Recently renovated by Beanie Babies owner Ty Warner, this super-luxurious property on 20 lush acres on the Pacific Ocean pays tribute to the region's Spanish colonial history with its red-tiled roof, arches and hacienda-style main building. The guest rooms, located both in the main building and in separate cottages, feature a relaxed Spanish-colonial décor and include down pillows and plush bathrobes. Crisp, white cabanas line the sparkling pool. Besides offering a full menu of massages, facials and body wraps, the spa incorporates botanicals from the gardens into its treatments. After a day on back roads squinting to find wineries, an evening at the oceanfront Bella Vista restaurant is just the ticket, particularly if you get a table close to one of the outdoor firepits.

219 rooms. Restaurant, bar. Business center. Spa. Pets accepted. $351 and up

★★HARBOR VIEW INN

28 W. Cabrillo Blvd., Santa Barbara, 800-755-0222; www.harborviewinnsb.com

It would be hard to beat the location of this upscale motor inn—it's right where the city meets the shore near Stearn's Wharf, and it's just steps from the ocean. The comfortable rooms have private patios, and the complex includes a pool, an adults-only fitness center and beautiful gardens.

115 rooms. Restaurant, bar. Fitness center. Pool. $251-350

★★HOTEL OCEANA

202 W. Cabrillo Blvd., Santa Barbara, 805-965-4577, 800-965-9776;
www.hoteloceanasantabarbara.com

Rising up from Santa Barbara's popular West Beach, this beach-chic resort is modern and crisp, mere steps to the water and touristy Stearn's Wharf. Sun-dappled patios sporting bright yellow umbrellas provide perfect Pacific vistas. The grounds include landscaped parks, two swimming pools, a fitness center, and whirlpools, while the staff provides the excellent service one could expect from a high-end resort. Rooms reflect casual coastal elegance, with sleek canopied beds sporting Frette linens.

122 rooms. Complimentary breakfast. Pool. Spa. $151-250

★★★★SAN YSIDRO RANCH, A ROSEWOOD HOTEL

900 San Ysidro Lane, Montecito, 805-565-1700; www.sanysidroranch.com

Settle in at this 550-acre paradise and you'll see why John and Jackie Kennedy spent part of their honeymoon here, at this resort tucked away in the foothills of Montecito. Lushly planted acres are filled with fragrant flowers and plants, and stunning vistas of the Pacific Ocean and the Channel Islands can be seen in the distance. The bungalows, with their cozy blend of overstuffed chintz armchairs, oriental rugs and vaulted, wood-clad ceilings, provide luxuries like wood-burning fireplaces and specialty linens. Exceptional cuisine is a hallmark of the property, and the two restaurants here provide charming settings for the imaginative food.

41 rooms. Restaurant, bar. Fitness center. Pool. Pets accepted. $351 and up

★★★SANTA YNEZ VALLEY MARRIOTT

555 McMurray Road, Buellton, 805-688-1000, 800-638-8882;
www.santaynezhotels.com

This Spanish-style hotel, located in the Santa Ynez Valley at the gateway to the Santa Barbara Wine Country, is near more than 60 vineyards and wineries. The spacious guest rooms are stocked with Starbucks coffee and other amenities. Enjoy the heated outdoor pool or lap pool or hit the spa or steam room. The casual buffet breakfast in the hotel's restaurant is the perfect beginning to a busy day, and a friendly game of billiards in the Winner's Circle Pub is the perfect ending.

149 rooms. Restaurant, bar. Business center. Fitness center. Pool. Spa. Pets accepted. $151-250

WHERE TO EAT
★★★BELLA VISTA

Four Seasons Santa Barbara,1260 Channel Drive, Santa Barbara, 805-969-2261;

Besides incredible views of the Pacific from the open-air patio or the window-lined dining room, this restaurant inside the Four Seasons Santa Barbara offers expertly prepared, locally sourced fresh and organic food. Chef Martin Frost's specialties include free-range chicken breast filled with goat cheese, truffles, potato, eggplant and red pepper, or honey-cilantro glazed sea bass. The outdoor patio has several open-air fireplaces, perfect for cozying up to for dessert and after-dinner drinks.

American. Breakfast, lunch, dinner. $86 and up

★★★BOUCHON
9 W. Victoria St., Santa Barbara, 805-730-1160; www.bouchonsantabarbara.com

This French-Californian restaurant prides itself on using the freshest local ingredients available, including fish from the Santa Barbara Channel, produce from the surrounding countryside, meats and poultry from local microranches and wine from the Santa Ynez Valley. Order the pan-seared scallops with herb risotto, or try bourbon and maple-glazed duck. The "Molten Lava" chocolate cake is a sweet ending to any meal.

American, French. Dinner. $36-85

★★★DOWNEY'S
1305 State St., Santa Barbara, 805-966-5006; www.downeyssb.com

The menu at Downey's, which changes constantly, offers appetizers such as the Santa Barbara mussels with sweet corn and a chili vinaigrette, or homemade duck sausage with lentils. Signature entrées include grilled lamb loin or local sea bass with a ragout of prawns and spring vegetables. The relaxed setting combines to make the place a local favorite.

American. Dinner. Closed Monday. Reservations recommended. $36-85

★★★★MIRÓ AT BACARA RESORT
Bacara Resort & Spa, 8301 Hollister Ave., Santa Barbara, 805-9681800, 877-422-4245; www.bacararesort.com

Santa Barbara's luxurious Bacara Resort is home to the swank Miró Restaurant. Joan Miró-style artwork, deep red dining chairs, a contemporary carpet and fantastic views of the Pacific Ocean set the scene, while the chef creates masterful renditions of traditional Spanish cooking such as oak-grilled lamb chops with aged sherry and pan roasted lobster with oven-roasted tomatoes. The 12,000-bottle wine cellar has something to match every meal. For a more casual alternative, the Miró Bar and Lounge features homemade sangria and tasty tapas.

Basque, Catalonian. Dinner. Closed Monday. Outdoor seating. Bar. $86 and up

SPAS
★★★★BACARA SPA
Bacara Resort & Spa, 8301 Hollister Ave., Santa Barbara, 805-968-1800, 877-422-4245; www.bacararesort.com

A saline-filled pool and secluded nooks for sunbathing flank more than 30 treatment rooms and indoor and outdoor massage stations at this heavenly spa. You'll find a variety of traditional treatments here, as well as an Eastern menu that offers Thai massage, reflexology and shiatsu. Ayurvedic treatments include the Shirodhara with Tibetan foot treatment, in which a technician pours warm oil on your forehead (or "third eye"), gives you a scalp massage and applies a warm thermal foot wrap. You'll feel more Zen from head to toe. The rugged terrain of the Santa Ynez Mountains is the perfect place for a rigorous walk, run or hike. Clay tennis courts, pools almost too pretty to swim in and yoga on the beach are just a few of the other fitness options.

★★★★SPA AT FOUR SEASONS RESORT SANTA BARBARA
1260 Channel Drive, Santa Barbara, 805-969-2261, 800-819-5053; www.fourseasons.com

Pure luxury sums up the look and feel of this oceanfront spa, whose design echoes the Spanish colonial style of the Four Seasons Resort in which it's located. Treatment rooms are more residential than spa-like, with kiva fireplaces, plush treatment tables and mission-style furniture. Since you're in wine country, you must try one of the vino-centric treatments. The Vineyard Harvest has you soaking in grapeseed, jasmine, rose and red wine—all of which are full of antioxidants that supposedly help your skin (it can't hurt). A chardonnay clay wrap is then used to remove toxins, followed by a massage. And why not drink the stuff at the same time? A cheese plate and a glass of local wine come along with the treatment. Now that's what we call super-relaxing.

TEMECULA
See also Fallbrook

Most people associate winemaking in California with Napa and Sonoma valleys. But there's serious Southern California wine tasting in the Temecula Valley, about two hours away. The Temecula Valley, bordered on the west by Camp Pendleton Marine Corps Base and the Cleveland National Forest, is also home to five championship golf courses and casino gambling at the local resorts.

WHAT TO SEE
CALIFORNIA DREAMIN'
33133 Vista Del Monte Road, Temecula, 800-373-3359; www.californiadreamin.com

This company offers sunrise balloon rides over Temecula wine country, as well as spectacular daytime forays over the Pacific and the Del Mar bluffs. The baskets accommodate six, nine or 12 people, making it perfect for families. Adrenaline junkies may prefer to schedule a ride in a World War I-style biplane. Daily.

CALLAWAY VINEYARD AND WINERY
32720 Rancho California Road, Temecula, 800-472-2377; www.callawaywinery.com

If the name sounds familiar, that's because founder Ely Reeves Callaway Jr. was a leader in the golf industry, especially after the success of the Big Bertha golf club. He began Callaway Vineyard and Winery in 1969, the first in the area. The wines are in limited production, so it's worth a stop here to taste, and to stock up if you so desire. The onsite restaurant boasts vineyard views and Mediterranean tapas.
Daily 10 a.m.-5 p.m.

FILSINGER WINERY

39050 De Portola Road, Temecula, 951-302-6363; www.filsingerwinery.com

This family-owned and operated winery has been around since 1978 and produces about 3,000 cases of wine a year. The winery has won many awards for their Gewurztraminer.

Friday 11 a.m.-4 p.m., Saturday-Sunday 10 a.m.-5 p.m.

STUART CELLARS

33515 Rancho California Road, Temecula, 888-260-0870; www.stuartcellars.com

This family-run winery is a wonderful retreat. Bring a picnic lunch and enjoy it on the winery grounds with views of the Temecula Valley.

Daily 10 a.m.-5 p.m.

SPECIAL EVENT
BALLOON AND WINE FESTIVAL

Lake Skinner, 37701 Warren Road, Temecula, 951-676-6713; www.tvbwf.com

This fest offers wine tastings, a hot-air balloon race, musical entertainment and children's activities.

Early June.

WHERE TO STAY
★★★PECHANGA RESORT & CASINO

45000 Pechanga Parkway, Temecula, 951-643-1819, 888-732-4264;
www.pechanga.com

Designed in the Prairie School style, this resort has spacious rooms with floor-to-ceiling windows and large bathrooms. One-bedroom suites include a wet bar, separate sleeping quarters and one and a half baths. The 188,000-square-foot gaming floor makes this the biggest casino in California. Dining options abound.

517 rooms. Restaurant, bar. Pool. Spa. $151-250

★★★TEMECULA CREEK INN

44501 Rainbow Canyon Road, Temecula, 951-694-1000, 877-517-1823;
www.temeculacreekinn.com

This hotel offers the perfect combination of work and play, with ample meeting space and a 27-hole golf course. Comfortable guest rooms overlook the golf course or mountains. The hotel's Temet Grill offers cuisine to complement wine from the area's many vineyards.

130 rooms. Restaurant, bar. Tennis. Golf. $151-250

WHERE TO EAT
★★BAILY'S

28699 Old Town Front St., Temecula, 951-676-9567; www.baily.com

This fine dining local favorite on top of Front Street Bar & Grill focuses on seasonal ingredients and offers an extensive wine list. The menu is centered around a variety of seafood items, including a fresh fish of the day, as well as several steak selections. Every Tuesday features a four-course prix fixe menu that changes every week and is only $20. Friday and Saturday nights bring a sinful Death by Chocolate buffet.

American. Dinner. $16-35

★★CAFE CHAMPAGNE
32575 Rancho California Road, Temecula, 951-699-0099; www.thorntonwine.com
Dine inside the warm and cozy French country space or out on the patio overlooking Thorton Winery on a sunny day. The fusion menu includes suggested wine pairings. For example, the crispy roast duck would be lovely with the Thorton 2005 OVOC Zinfandel. A nice selection of appetizers includes warm brie, a vineyard tapas plate with salami, roasted peppers, herbed goat cheese and more, and calamari finished in a Thorton Brut-Dill Beurre Blanc. Lunch includes a vareity of sandwiches such as a lamb pita and grilled ham and gouda.
French. Lunch, dinner, Sunday brunch. $36-85

VENTURA
See also Ojai, Santa Barbara
What was once a mission surrounded by huge stretches of sagebrush and mustard plants is now the busy city of Ventura. Today, uncrowded beaches, harbor cruises and whale-watching lure visitors here. Ventura is also the main point to reach Channel Islands National Park.

WHAT TO SEE
ALBINGER ARCHAEOLOGICAL MUSEUM
113 E. Main St., Ventura, 805-648-5823
This preserved archaeological exploration site and visitors' center downtown showcases evidence of Native American culture that's 3,500 years old. Audiovisual programs are available.
Wednesday-Sunday 10 a.m.-4 p.m.

ISLAND PACKER CRUISES
1691 Spinnaker Drive, Ventura, 805-642-1393; www.islandpackers.com
Island Packers offers travels to all five islands that make up Channel Islands National Park. Reservations are required.
Memorial Day-Labor Day, five islands; Labor Day-Memorial Day, two islands.

MISSION SAN BUENAVENTURA
211 E. Main St., Ventura, 805-643-4318; www.sanbuenaventuramission.org
This is the ninth California mission and the last founded by Father Junipero Serra in 1782. The museum (enter through the gift shop at 225 E. Main St.) features the original wooden bell in the tower.
Museum: Monday-Friday 10 a.m.-5 p.m., Saturday 9 a.m.-5 p.m., Sunday 10 a.m.-4 p.m. Church and gardens: Daily sunrise-sunset.

SAN BUENAVENTURA STATE BEACH
Harbor Blvd. and San Pedro St., Ventura, 805-968-1033; www.parks.ca.gov
Approximately 115 acres on a sheltered sweep of coast, this state beach offers swimming, lifeguards in the summer, surfing, a coastal bicycle trail access point, picnicking and concessions.
Daily sunrise-sunset.

VENTURA HARBOR

1583 Spinnaker Drive, Ventura, 805-642-8538, 877-894-2726; www.venturaharbor.com

The harbor accommodates more than 1,500 boats, including sport fishing and island boats, sailboat rentals and cruises. Swimming and fishing are also permitted. Hotels, shops and restaurants surround the harbor. Channel Islands National Park's headquarters is here.

SPECIAL EVENTS
WHALE-WATCHING

1691 Spinnaker Drive, Ventura, 805-642-1393; www.islandpackers.com

Gray whales can be spotted December to March; blue whales can be seen July to September.

WHERE TO STAY
★★★MARRIOTT VENTURA BEACH

2055 E. Harbor Blvd., Ventura, 805-643-6000; www.marriott.com

The Marriott is a good choice for business travelers or families taking in Ventura. The comfortable rooms feature the new Revive bedding. The pool, with tropical landscaping, is a nice spot to relax. The restaurant serves flavorful Baja coastal cuisine.

285 rooms. Restaurant, bar. Pool. $61-150

INDEX

NUMBERS

A

B

K

L

S

★
★
★★ **INDEX**
★★
★

201

INDEX ★★★★★

LOS ANGELES

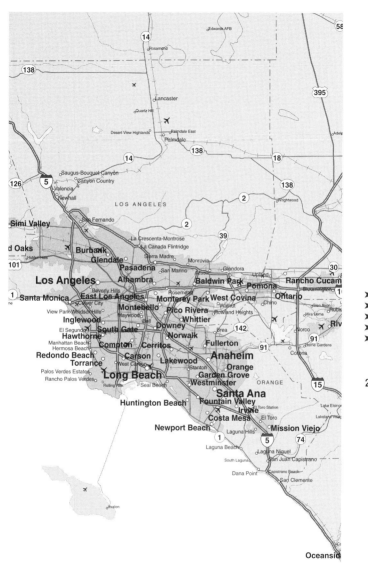

SOUTHERN CALIFORNIA

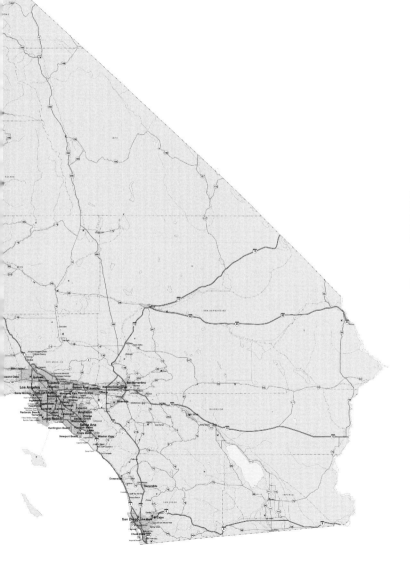

NOTES

NOTES

NOTES

NOTES

NOTES

NOTES

NOTES

NOTES

NOTES

NOTES

NOTES

NOTES

NOTES

NOTES

NOTES

NOTES

NOTES